J. J. Wall, 1967
Orland, Calif.

HANDICAP RACE

DOROTHY CLARKE WILSON

The Inspiring Story of Roger Arnett

HANDICAP RACE

McGraw-Hill Book Company ·
New York · Toronto · London · Sydney

ACKNOWLEDGMENTS

The author wishes to make grateful acknowledgment:

To Reverend Roger P. Arnett and his wife LaVerna for generously sharing the intimate details of their life experience through tape recordings, interviews, family papers, pictures, and much lengthy correspondence;

To other members of the family for their invaluable cooperation, including Vivian and Adolph Beyer, Vivian and Eldred Waters, Richard and Val Arnett, Ronald and Bertha Arnett, and Faye Arnett Cloer;

For professional and personal details to Dr. A. L. Arnold, Dr. Robert Berry, and Dr. Leonard Himler;

To the many friends of the Arnetts who contributed encouragement and information, including: Mr. and Mrs. Norman Hagan, Mrs. Treva Scheifele, the former Elizabeth Willman, Mrs. Doris Ritter, Reverend and Mrs. Harold Dakin, Reverend and Mrs. Al Hartoog, Mr. James Alward, Mr. and Mrs. Ralph Ridenour, Mr. and Mrs. Victor Hopeman, Mr. and Mrs. Charles Dynes, Miss Letah Stewart, Mr. and Mrs. Clarence Mente, Mr. Harvey Dicks, Mrs. Addie Chilson, Mrs. Barbara Hass, Mrs. Rachel Wilson, Mr. and Mrs. Roy Miles, Reverend Allen Rice II;

For generously permitting the use of intimate details of their own life stories, to Frank Aymer, Stefan and Carolyn Florescu, Faye Sloan, Gabriel and Vivian Wellett;

To the library of Eastern Michigan University for its cooperation in opening the files of the *Normal College News*.

Foreword

Reading the story of a paraplegic doctor in India, a book called *Take My Hands*, Roger Arnett felt a peculiar identity with this Christian woman of another race and culture whose experience and purpose so paralleled his own. He wrote to the author of the book asking for the address of Dr. Mary Verghese.

"You sound as if you might have an interesting story yourself," the author wrote back.

"If there's a story," replied Roger, "it's my wife LaVerna who has it. It's she who has shown the courage, the patience, the steadfast devotion which have made everything else possible."

But the author did not think so. She found it difficult to persuade Roger to let a story be written about himself. He agreed only when convinced that such a story might possibly encourage others with similar handicaps and that it might instill in some persons a concern for the ministry to special human needs which had become the major purpose of his life.

HANDICAP RACE

1

Five . . . six . . . seven . . .

Coach Lloyd Olds stood watching his star distance runner click off lap after lap of the small indoor track, twenty-two of them to the mile. Although some eight or ten other runners were pounding the boards of the old gym, his trained eye focused on only one.

Eight . . . nine . . . ten . . .

Checking his stop watch at the end of each lap, Olds nodded approvingly. Potter was close to his record mark. He might be running in actual field competition instead of in routine practice.

Thirteen . . . fourteen . . .

The coach's vision suddenly sharpened, widened to include two figures, one perfectly coordinated and rhythmic, the other lanky, awkward, unskilled, but clinging to it like a shadow. Olds strode over to the freshman coach.

"I say, Marshall, who's that greenhorn trailing Potter?"

Marshall grinned. "Yeah. I've been watching him, too. One of the fellows in Phys. Ed. 105. I can't tell his name offhand."

Twenty . . . twenty-one . . . twenty-two.

The lanky runner was hurrying toward the locker room when Coach Olds intercepted him. "Hey, you, come here!"

The young man reluctantly obeyed. It was five o'clock and, the hour of his physical education class finished, he was obviously in a hurry to get away. "Yes, sir?"

The coach looked him up and down, the whole six feet of him, noting but idly the bush of waving brown hair, the candid blue eyes and strong-boned features; concentrating on the long, bony legs and oversized feet, the breadth of chest, surprising in such an angular frame. The fellow had just run a mile in excellent time even for a veteran and he wasn't even breathing hard!

"What's your name, son?"

"Arnett, sir. Roger."

"Do you know who that is you were tailing?"

"No, sir."

"That's LeRoy Potter." The blue eyes were politely blank. "Good heavens, boy, doesn't the name mean anything to you?"

"I'm sorry, sir. Should it?"

"My dear Arnett, Potter is just our star distance runner here at Michigan State Normal. He's set many state records and been a close runner-up in National." The coach smiled wryly. "Probably you don't know who I am, either. Well, I'm Olds, track coach of the varsity team."

"Oh! Sorry to be so ignorant, sir, but—well, I just haven't had time for athletics."

"Well, you're finding time from now on." The coach jabbed a firm finger into the broad chest. "See here, Arnett, I want you to come here every night and run. Marshall will tell you how many laps and give you some training in technique. You're going out for track. Understand?"

"Y-yes, sir. But—I'm carrying a pretty heavy schedule. I'm not sure—"

"Listen, boy." The coach was used to giving precise orders and having them obeyed. "You're as raw and awkward as they come. You're taller than the average runner, and heaven knows your feet are too big. But you've got something here." He jabbed his finger deeper into the broad rib cage. "Maybe it's extra good heart and muscles. Maybe it's just plain guts. I want to find out if you've got what else it takes, the *will* to *win*. Have you?"

"I—I don't know, sir."

"Tell me this, son." Olds' keen eyes drew the boy's uncertain gaze like magnets. "Wouldn't you get a kick out of beating somebody like LeRoy Potter?" As the blue eyes struck sparks, he nodded with satisfaction. "You'll find the time," he said confidently.

Young Roger Arnett bolted to the locker room, took a hasty shower, and changed into street clothes. Brief though the interview had been, it had played havoc with his tight schedule. It was five

2

fifteen when he emerged from the old gym on that day in late February, 1929. A quarter hour already lopped from his allotted four hours of sleep! But the brisk winter air was even more invigorating than the steam and chill of the shower. Filling his lungs full, he jogged past the big round water tower, Ypsilanti's ancient stone landmark, and kept running all the way to McDougall's, the eating house on Normal Street, where for forty cents he wolfed down a plain but hearty meal of roast beef, potato, vegetable, and pudding, the major third of his dollar-a-day diet.

In spite of his haste it was five fifty before he reached his lodging-house on Pearl Street and bounded up the stairs. The two rooms shared by himself and three other students were empty, his house-mates having gone to dinner. Setting his alarm for nine forty-five he tumbled into bed. Returning from supper, his roommate Dick Schoenbaum tried painfully to be quiet and, settling himself for study, carefully focused his desk lamp so it would not shine on the sleeper. The other students, Norman Hagen and August Peters, were equally considerate, closing the door of their room across the hall. But they need not have worried. Once asleep, a healthy youth who had spent twenty hours in constant activity, one of them on an indoor track, was immune to most disturbances.

But at the jangling of the alarm he was up like a shot, had to be, for he had given himself a minimum of leeway.

"How can you!" yawned Dick. "A good eight hours' sleep last night, and already I'm bushed."

"Necessity," retorted Roger cheerfully, pulling on his khaki jeans, "is mother to lots of offspring beside invention."

He had left himself only ten minutes to cover the mile to the Standard Gas station where, from ten in the evening to seven in the morning, at forty cents an hour, he was on duty for seven nights a week, with an occasional weekend off for visits home. Until midnight he was fairly busy, but the next seven hours were ideal for study, sallies to the gas pumps through the nipping February night and dawn coming just often enough to blow his mind clear. The application had paid off during the fall term with two A's and three B's, a record which he intended to improve during this winter term. He was determined also to graduate in three years. Even with the eleven semester hours credited from his previous year at Northwestern, this meant carrying at least five subjects most terms instead of four, plus certain designated hours of Physical Training. He had

3

signed up for the latter early in his course merely to get the requirement out of the way, not because he had the slightest interest in athletics. The class in indoor track had seemed as least demanding as any. He had simply gone up to the gym, been issued indoor track shoes without spikes, as well as a gym suit with sweat shirt and pants, and been told to run. And now this fellow Olds was practically ordering him to spend five or six hours running each week instead of two and a half! A determined character if he had ever seen one!

But Roger was determined, too. He was here at Michigan State Normal College for one purpose, to prepare himself for the teaching profession as quickly and creditably as possible and *without going into debt*. He was not going to make the same mistakes which a year ago had brought his college career abruptly to an end.

In September, 1927, he had left his home in Owosso, Michigan, for Northwestern University with total assets of a summer's earnings in an iron foundry, the loan of two hundred dollars from an Elks' Fund scholarship, a cheap violin, and the name of a sorority where his high-school music teacher, Mr. Champion, had earned his meals by doing dishes. It was Mr. Champion also who had inspired him with the confidence that he could become a professional musician. His liabilities had been even more impressive: uncouth manners, profound ignorance of the world of culture, hayseeds that really showed. Only the sorority had proved a reliable asset. The same landlady had given him the same job washing dishes. But with violin and piano lessons twice a week and the cost of lodging in Chicago, the money had dwindled at an astonishing rate. And thrust into the competition of genuine musicians, the country boy from Michigan had soon found his mediocre talent hopelessly outclassed.

"Come home any time," his parents had written when he confessed to discouragement and homesickness. "As long as you're working for an education, you can be sure of your board and room with us. It's all we can do for you."

By dint of sheer persistence he had managed to finish one semester, returning home minus money, a little of the ignorance, and many of the hayseeds. For the improvements he had his roommate Gunnar Malmin to thank, a much older, serious graduate student from St. Paul, from whom he learned far more than from his teachers. Although Gunnar must often have despaired of Roger's potentials in music, he had never discouraged him. Gently he had tutored his

4

gauche roommate in the niceties of etiquette, inspired him to change direction without losing sight of his educational goals. Back in Owosso with appetite whetted for college, Roger had gotten himself two jobs in the foundry and, thanks to his parents' contribution of room and board, had earned enough to see his way through a full year if he could find part-time work and be saving in expenditures. So here he was at Michigan State Normal, sights set on a career of teaching math and science, determined that this time there should be no interruption. This job in the gas station was his insurance.

Leaving the station at seven in the morning, Roger had just time to pick up a hasty breakfast at a corner restaurant, return to his room, and get ready for the day's classes which began at eight. His three housemates, late up as usual, were just leaving for breakfast. So irregular were his hours that Roger felt himself an outsider among them. He scarcely ever saw Dick, his roommate. But Norman Hagen, handsome, friendly, good-natured features topped by crisply curling blond hair, was in Roger's French class, and he wished they had more time to get acquainted. Passing him on the stairs, Norm clapped Roger on the shoulder.

"Bon jour, pal. Il fait froid, n'est-ce pas? Mon Dieu, how can you look so wide-awake!"

Roger sloughed the grime of his night's work down the washbowl, carefully wiping the oily ring from the porcelain. He smiled grimly as he did so, remembering his uncouthness at Northwestern. At home there was no running water, only a pump and washbasin. A young senior monitor had had to instruct him in the proper use of a lavatory, washing it of grimy sediment after each use. At least he would never make *that* mistake again.

But what about others? Would he jeopardize his single purpose in college by following Coach Olds' suggestion? His time and money were already budgeted to the minute and penny. What would track practice do to his meager allotment of sleep? And suppose he got involved in meets. Would his earnings be curtailed? The doubt nagged him all day, bringing an unusual sense of fatigue, and even when he came out of his last class at four in the afternoon he had not made up his mind. Glad to postpone decision, he turned gratefully toward his lodginghouse and a generous five hours of sleep.

A brisk wind was blowing. It struck him head on, banishing all fatigue. Instead of bending to it, he braced his shoulders, lifted his face. Above the yellowed stones of the water tower light clouds

5

were scudding, tumbling, racing. His blood tingled. Muscles flexed. Almost without his volition he turned again and ran toward the gym.

He had been running each night for perhaps two weeks with no more obvious results than loss of sleep and sore muscles. Apparently Coach Olds had forgotten his existence. Except for a few elementary pointers Marshall's instructions had been confined to a terse "Keep on running, boy."

Athletics, Roger had always assumed, were a luxury indulged in solely for the fun of it. What an error! True, it had been fun chasing LeRoy Potter around the track that day. But practice during these two weeks had involved little competition. It had been work, heavy, monotonous, grueling. Lap after lap he ran, without accomplishing anything or getting anywhere, like a farm horse threshing grain on a treadmill. He felt less than a man, a robot, but a conscious one that ached and groaned in every joint. Yet once he had started it did not occur to him to stop. He was not that kind of person. Besides, he was used to work that was heavy and monotonous and grueling. Certainly this was easier than shaking hot castings out of the sand in a stove foundry.

Roger suspected that Marshall was dubious about his chances. "You run flat-footed," the coach commented once disparagingly. But another time he regarded the raw young freshman with respect, almost admiration. "I've been looking up the record on your physical, Arnett. The examiner notes that you have one of the biggest lung capacities of all the students in the college."

Thanks to those iron castings, Roger thought wryly, both for the lungs and the flat feet!

His first test came at the end of the two weeks in a track meet between the classes. All men of the college were eligible as well as those on the track squad. Since the facilities at Ypsilanti were too small, the meet was held in the gymnasium of the University of Michigan at Ann Arbor.

"We're putting you in the two-mile." Roger was given his assignment.

Without further instruction or preparation he was herded into a car with a crowd of other freshmen and driven to the Waterman Gymnasium eight miles away. It was a ten-lap track, seeming huge beside the one where he had been practicing. As far as he knew, he

6

had never run two miles at a stretch. But when his turn came he was not at all excited. After all, it was just a matter of running, and he had been doing plenty of that.

The group against whom he was pitted were all strangers. He had no idea that one of them was Merlin Wolfe, Normal's star two-miler. He only knew that after the first couple of laps one runner was pulling away from the others, and he seemed a good one to follow. So he clung doggedly to his heels. After the first ten laps, which made a mile, his lungs seemed full to bursting. His feet felt weighted with lead, and his leg muscles throbbed, but somehow he kept them pumping. And after two or three more laps he found himself relaxing. Breath came more easily. He found it easier to adjust to the pace of the man in front, perhaps because his competitor was slowing down. Oddly enough, it never occurred to him to try to pass. It was doubtful if he could have done so, anyway, for the two-mile star was out to win. But when Wolfe crossed the finish line, Roger was not far behind.

Not until he was on his way back to Ypsilanti did he discover that he had done something unusual in coming in second. Wedged into the back seat of a car, he listened to his companions discussing the strange new comet which had flashed into the orbit of the star two-miler. Did anybody know who he was? Freshman, maybe? Certainly not one of the track squad, or they would have recognized him!

"He sure gave Wolfe a chase," commented one with a chuckle. "I'd like to have seen old Merl's face if he'd won!"

"I thought he was going to," threw in another. "Awkward-looking guy, reminds you of a daddy longlegs, but he sure could run. Who do you suppose he was?"

Roger did not enlighten them, merely grinned to himself in the dark.

After that night his track training began in earnest. He continued to go to the gym each night after classes, but no longer with the simple directive just to run. Marshall spent many hours supervising his practice. Occasionally, while endlessly circling the track, Roger would see Olds watching him, keen eyes narrowed, and presently he would be called over to receive curt criticisms tempered by an encouraging clap on the shoulder.

Not excepting the hot, heavy job of shaker-out in the foundry, it was the hardest work Roger had ever done. Muscles seldom used before screamed in violent protest. Every step became agony. He almost had to crawl on all fours to go up the stairs to his lodging and classes, and it was equally painful to go down them. After his four hours of sleep in the early evening, merely getting out of bed was a major achievement. The first few steps were like walking on hot plowshares.

"Give me tennis," commented Norm Hagen, who was nursing sore biceps from his own spring practice. "I'd rather have crippled arms than legs."

"Yeah?" jibed Roger. "Even with that weekend date with Jo coming up?"

Practicing one afternoon in late March, Roger saw both Marshall and Olds watching. When he had run his twenty-two laps they called him over.

"We're sending you to Detroit next week," announced Marshall, "for the AAU."

"AAU?"

They smiled pityingly at his ignorance. "Amateur Athletic Union. Special Handicap Trials. There'll be runners from all over the nation, some from foreign countries. We've decided to put you in the two-mile handicap race."

"Handicap race?" echoed Roger vaguely.

This time Marshall did not smile. He exploded. "Good heavens, boy, don't you know *anything?* What good do you think you can do on a track squad if you don't even know the simplest—"

"He can run," threw in Olds drily.

The AAU meet was held in the Detroit Olympia Stadium, a huge barnlike building so cold on that Thursday evening that the chill seemed to penetrate one's bones. But Roger's sense of coldness was as much emotional as physical. Herded with his teammates into a side room to await directions, he stood apart from the others, painfully self-conscious. This was his first appearance as a member of the track squad, and he sensed their curious, speculative glances. Not for years had he felt so much alone, an outsider. They looked all alike, trim, well knit, evenly proportioned, slim-footed; and as they flexed knees and elbows, limbered muscles, their motions were smooth as silk. Only *he* was different, a scarecrow among Greek statues, overtopping most of them by a half a head, reed thin, gangling, his size eleven track shoes sticking out like a skin-diver's fins.

8

Coach Olds came striding in, a powerhouse of voltage, barking precise orders, making minute inspections, charging each member of the squad with that electric energy which for eight successive years had kept his indoor track team undefeated in dual competition. Suddenly he spied Roger.

"Oh, there you are, Arnett! Know all the rest of the gang, do you? Look, fellows, meet our newest recruit. Marshall's already found a good name for him. Honest Abe!"

One of the team guffawed, and soon the rest were chortling appreciation. "Not bad, Coach!" "Sure looks like it, doesn't he!" "Hi, Abe, welcome to our midst!"

The laughter was friendly, the comparison certainly not unkind. But he found himself flushing. Coach Olds' orders for Roger were more specific because of his ignorance. He was told when to start to warm up, how many laps of the track to make, still clad in his sweat suit, by way of practice. His muscles were so sore that each jolting step was sheer agony. But Olds knew his business. After the prescribed laps his nerve ends were no longer screaming protest.

In a handicap race, he learned, many runners of varying qualifications were entered. Two of these men at one time or another had held world records. To make the contest fairer for all and give the most skilled greater competition, the runners would be placed over a distance of one hundred yards rather than standing side by side as usual for the start.

"And remember this time you're out to win," snapped Olds. "It's no game of 'follow the leader.' Pass all the men in front of you, and don't you dare let the ones behind pass *you!*"

Thrust into this huge theater in the round, Roger had an actue case of stage fright. The rows of spectators tightened about him in suffocating coils. He felt like the victim in a Roman arena. Even the lions were present, his competitors, five of them lined up at varying distances in front of him, two behind him, one at ten yards, the other at twenty-five. The one farthest behind was a renowned runner from Scandinavia, who at one time had held the world's two-mile record.

He saw the other runners peel off their sweat suits, and belatedly he did the same, his fingers all thumbs. The room was like an icebox, but sweat beaded his body. His throat felt full of sand, his stomach compressed into a tight ball. Standing in sleeveless undershirt and shorts, he felt grotesquely naked, sure that all those hundreds of eyes were focused in derision on his stringy figure, his overly large feet. The other contestants were arching knees, jiggling up and down like divers ready to plunge, but he stayed glued to the floor.

"Get ready!" Coach Olds called from the side lines.

How! thought Roger in a panic. A little man appeared, yelling, "On your mark . . . get set . . ." A shot rang out. "Run!" barked Olds.

Roger ran. He passed one of the men in front of him, then another. It was easy. He was conscious of little or no exertion. A heady elation possessed him. He could win this race without half trying. Then someone passed him. With a burst of speed Roger shot off after him. Presently the two of them passed another runner. Roger tried to count the laps, the number of times his feet crossed the starting line and the referees' stand. One . . . two . . . three . . . Sixteen of them there were to the two miles. During the fifth lap he and the other man passed still another runner. After that Roger lost count. The tight coils of spectators dissolved into a blur. Shouts and cheers, pounding feet, clapping hands, all were drowned in the fierce beating against his eardrums. There was only one reality, the flying figure in front of him.

Easy? Arms and shoulders became leaden weights, his legs red-hot piston rods. The scant breath he was able to suck in stuck in his throat and almost choked him. His lungs screamed for more oxygen. But somehow he kept going. He was vaguely conscious that he and the man he was following had passed another . . . and another, but he saw them through a reddened blur. Would it never end? Another lap, and he was sure his veins would burst. It was neither strength nor will now that kept him going, just automation.

Finally the signal came. They were on the last lap. He felt rather than saw someone close behind him, and soon another runner whizzed past both him and the man he was following. Then he saw the two of them pulling away. He made one last superhuman effort, but it was too late. When he crossed the line, the second runner was just ahead of him. Exhausted almost to unconsciousness, Roger stumbled off the track, wanting nothing except to lie down and black out. But a pair of iron arms kept him upright.

"Keep walking," snapped Olds. "Don't stop, keep walking!"

Even when Roger had partially gotten his breath and was able to move without stumbling, the coach kept his arm about him. "You did fine, boy. I'm proud of you. That man who came in first was the world champion, and the runner-up has a national reputation. You didn't break any records. Your time was just fifteen seconds behind Potter's mark. But you made a brilliant attempt. I'm expecting great things from you."

With nerveless fingers Roger pulled on his sweat suit and staggered lightheadedly toward the dressing room. So this was a handicap race, was it! You just ran and ran until you couldn't possibly go any farther, and then you kept on running some more!

Roger made no sensational records in outdoor track that spring term, although he helped bring the freshman team to victory in at least three dual meets. But all these achievements, including the award of his track jersey in his freshman year, were unimportant beside the ten A's and eight B's on his year's report. The record was sullied by a lone "C" in rhetoric. The night hours at the filling station had paid off, if not in sleep.

They had paid off in cash, too, for he had a small amount of money left over. A car would be a good investment, he decided. He could use it for traveling the seventy miles home on weekends, and it would also save time going to and from work, the two miles between home and foundry in Owosso, two miles between lodging and gas station here at College. He went to Detroit and for $75 bought a 1926 Ford roadster with a rumble seat. Few college men owned cars, and as he started home to Owosso late at night, he felt a glowing pride.

Summer brought no holiday. As in previous vacations he got a job, two, in fact, in the stove foundry where his father had been employed for years. Getting up at four thirty, Roger would do what is known as "cutting the sand" for the molders. From there he would go to the pattern shop, scraping patterns until about two in the afternoon, when the furnace was fired and the molders poured the hot iron into their castings. Back in the foundry he would shake the hot castings out of the sand, let them cool, then carry them to the fore part of the foundry floor. He returned home at eight or eight thirty, usually too tired for recreation. But Roger was not afraid of hard work. His father had seen to that, less by precept than by example.

For, although unskilled and with meager education, James Arnett had been willing to work hard at any job paying an honest dollar, and had somehow managed to support his growing family.

Roger knew nothing about his birthplace except that it was somewhere "a little west of Ithaca." His first memory was of a small two-room house somewhere in the country. It was the winter of 1912, some months after his sister Vivian was born. The house must have been hard to heat, because Mother had placed the baby in her high chair close to the stove to keep her warm. Somehow Vivian teetered the high chair and fell forward on the hot stove. Her screams brought Mother running, her grief and pain far more inconsolable than the baby's.

Fire seemed as fierce an adversary in those days as poverty. In the basement of the house a neighboring farmer had stored his potatoes for the winter. An oil burner had been placed there to keep them from freezing. One day the house filled with smoke. Dad rushed to the basement to find the kerosene heater ablaze, shooting flames to the ceiling. Somehow he managed to carry it up the stairs and out the door. Of course he was badly burned, but his home was saved. Later that same winter Roger and his brother Irving were experimenting with matches. Behind the house was a huge pile of pine stumps being dried for firewood. To the boys' horror the pile caught fire and was soon a roaring blaze. Dad was working that day on a neighbor's roof in sight of the house. Warned by the smoke, he dashed home and with his own hands pulled every one of the blazing stumps away from the house. It was not lack of courage or of hard work which kept his family's fortunes at bare subsistence level.

The next house was a little less humble, although one of Roger's poignant memories was of his mother's tying streamers of newspapers to a broomstick and shooing the swarms of flies out the front door. Instead of a day laborer Dad now became a sharecropper, tilling an eighty-acre farm for a Sumner doctor, who supplied the horses and tools. Here, given the chance to plant a garden, raise chickens, and keep a cow, the family fared better, and Dad's hard labor bore more substantial fruits, among them a crop of watermelons so big and luscious that people came from miles around to buy them.

There was an orchard on the farm, and in the fall Dad had some apples made into cider, a barrel of which was allowed to ferment. Neighbors who came in for the evening to enjoy music and a bit of dancing began to make frequent visits to the cellar. When one of them had to be assisted bodily up the stairs, Mother took the situation firmly in hand. Saying nothing, she waited until Dad went to town the next day, descended to the cellar, and poured a generous quantity of rain water into the barrel. The matter was settled once for all, and without argument. Dad understood.

He understood also when she sternly insisted that her two sons must not ape their father's habit of profanity, acquired during his boyhood years as a sailor, yet in spite of her pain and disapproval tolerated it in himself. No doubt she recognized, as Roger did later, that it was inspired by a deep sense of insecurity and inferiority. Limited by meager education, naturally inarticulate, he knew no other way to express himself.

James Arnett was not content with being a sharecropper. He wanted land of his own. After two years on the farm he had accumulated a cow and calf and a hundred chickens. Hearing of land up in Clare County, a hundred miles away, available for homesteading, he went up during the second summer and staked out eighty acres. It was fertile land, abounding in grasshoppers.

"Fine!" he exulted. "I can bring my chickens up here, and they can live on these grasshoppers. It will cost nothing to feed them."

That September he moved his family and possessions: animals, chickens and coops, wife, three children, and a few sticks of furniture. It took all his savings. There were no buildings on the eighty acres, but a mile away there was an empty log house which became their temporary shelter. Hopeful, enthusiastic, Dad set up his chicken coops on his own land and, eying the grasshoppers with anticipation, let out his chickens. All day they feasted. But the next day there wasn't a grasshopper to be found in the whole area. His dream had burst like a bubble. But after three days hope rose again. He had a whole case of eggs. He took them to Lake George, the nearest town, four miles away. The proprietor of the one store was happy to buy the eggs at the fabulous price of fifty cents a dozen. Dad was jubilant—until he went back with the next case. Weeks and months later the eggs were still there in the store, unsold.

It was the hardest winter they had ever spent. The cracks in the walls of the log house were wide enough to see through, and soon every chair had lost at least one leg because of the knotholes in the floor. Dad earned their living by trapping muskrat, mink, and raccoon, but it was hard work yielding little income. The chickens had to be sold. Not long before Christmas Dad sold the cow and the calf. Christmas promised to be bleak, but at least there was a little money to buy presents. Mother sent to a mail-order house for some peanuts and candy. They waited and waited for the package to come. Finally just two days before Christmas they went to the station to inquire about it. The stationmaster gave it to them. It had been broken open and all the food taken. Never would Roger forget the disappointment of that moment.

If Mother rebelled at this life of rigor and deprivation, her children never knew it. The nearest neighbor, an old lady, was a mile away, the mailbox a mile and a half along an Indian trail. Mother had her own brand of quiet courage. One day when she was returning home with the mail a big muskrat appeared on the trail in front of her, refusing to let her pass. She picked up a stone, killed it, and brought it home to add to Dad's trapping stores. Another time, when Dad was away on his trap route, a group of men came clattering down the road in a wagon, singing and shouting. Hastily Mother herded the children inside and shut and bolted the door. When the men pounded on it so hard it seemed they would break it down, she put Vivian in the second room, placed the two boys behind her, and opened it.

"Yes, gentlemen, what can I do for you?"

The strangers eyed the pretty young woman with unmistakable relish.

"Ha, hear that, fellers? She wants to know what she can do for us. What shall I tell her?"

The others laughed uproariously. "O.K., sister. Suppose you give us a little food—first."

"Certainly," replied Mother calmly. "I'm sorry my husband isn't here to welcome you, but I expect him soon. Do come in, gentlemen."

Something in her quiet and aloof dignity penetrated their tough armor, and as they sat gingerly on the three-legged chairs waiting for the food, they became more and more subdued. Sensing her need, the boys kept close to Mother as she worked over the wood stove. After she had fed the men a good hot meal, they stood around awkwardly for a while, then thanked her and went away.

It was in this house that Roger had a narrow escape. In the floor of the large kitchen-living-dining room was a trap door leading to the cellar. One day Mother sent him down to get some fruit which she had canned the previous summer. It was the winter of 1914, and she was reading from a newspaper about the war just started in Europe. Roger was so interested in the story that when he came up he forgot to close the trap door. Listening, he stood on the edge by the table, leaning on his elbows. Stepping back later, he fell down through the opening, striking his back against the opposite edge. He was knocked unconscious, but luckily no bones were broken. Mother was sure that he was being spared for some great purpose in life.

That winter she became very ill, but with no neighbors, no doctors within miles, she simply had to keep going. Even though they were able to move to another log house two miles away, with a tight floor and no cracks in the walls, the racking cough and alternate fever and chills persisted. When they were finally able to make a trip to Mt. Pleasant and see a doctor, he exclaimed, "My goodness, woman, you're lucky to be alive! You've had pneumonia!"

By spring Dad had made up his mind. "This is no place for women and children. We're going back home."

They left with nothing but the clothes on their backs, traveling by train and stagecoach, roads impeded by flooded fields and rivers. Finally Dad got a job in a brickyard in Corunna, three miles from Owosso, the biggest town the children had ever seen. The house they rented, tiny and shabby, seemed like a palace. Dad's earnings were small, and there was furniture to buy. But he was frugal, even putting mustard on the sandwiches he took to work because he begrudged himself butter. And although he became ill on the meager diet he always managed to keep working. After a year he got another job as night watchman in a factory in Owosso, and the family moved there.

Back in Owosso this summer after his first year at Michigan State Normal College, Roger felt like the chambered nautilus, dragging behind him all the outgrown shells of his childhood and youth. He had only to walk through town to relive the family's long struggle to emerge from poverty.

There was the little house on Cedar Street where they lived first, close to the factory because Dad had no means of transportation, not even a bicycle. After a year they managed to accumulate a bit of cash and made a down payment on a bigger house, made of cement blocks, a short distance away. They were living here when the end of World War I came, with its wild celebrations.

Then work became slack, and Dad lost his job. They could not keep up payments on the house. A neighbor offered to buy it for the price they had paid, $1,600. Dad wanted to sell. Mother insisted it was worth $200 more. For the first time the children heard their parents quarreling. But Mother won. The buyer came up on his price. It was the extra money which made possible the purchase of the house at 622 Queen Street, where they had lived ever since.

It was an old house, foundation gone, roof sagging, no basement but a "Michigan cellar," a mere hole in the ground. The neighborhood was poor, but it was a home. Dad put a foundation under it, dug out the basement and cemented its walls. Soon an opening came in the foundry in the department known as the cleaning room. When the iron castings came out of the mold, they were covered with sand, which had to be removed. It was extemely hard work, noisy and precise, and few people would undertake it, but Dad jumped at the opportunity. He studied the job, learned how to pack the castings into the mill so they would not break yet come out clean where the jacks had rubbed against them. Although it was piecework and dependent on the demand for stoves, it meant reasonable security.

There was the grade school where for a half-dozen years a shy, self-conscious child in made-over suits and shoes resoled with cardboard, Roger endured torments. The teachers seemed bent on exposing his awkwardness and ignorance. He was poor in penmanship, in spelling, reading, art—in fact, in everything except arithmetic, and even in that he found it impossible to do problems at the blackboard. It took him three years to get through the fifth and sixth grades.

"Tomorrow," one teacher gave as an assignment in English, "be prepared to tell the class some odd thing you have done." When Roger's turn came, he stammered, "I—I don't know of anything." The teacher laughed with the class. "You mean to say you don't do anything queer?"

He would have had little time for friends, even if he had not been too shy and withdrawn to make them. He was carrying a paper route at ten, working in the foundry in his early teens. Dad took over the extra job of cleaning the mill room, and Roger went over after school each afternoon and helped him. He earned eighty cents a day.

But he did not miss having close friends. The family was a well-knit unit and made its own recreation. On Sunday, Dad's day off, they took hikes into the country, where Mother displayed an uncanny knowledge of herbs and flowers. In the fall they would go

16

nutting, so that on winter evenings there were hickory nuts, walnuts, butternuts to crack. When there was enough money Mother would make candy for riotous taffy pulls. They would bring out the carom board or play "railroad pedro," a game ideal for five people. And as soon as the boys were old enough Dad taught them to hunt and fish. They acquired a dog, a blue-tick, black and tan, and enriched the family diet with squirrels and rabbits.

When Roger was twelve, Irving eleven, and Vivian eight, Dad managed the purchase of three bicycles, and their weekend hikes turned into camping expeditions. Mother and Vivian would bake all the week getting ready for the outing, and on Saturday Dad would take Mother on his bicycle, Roger would take Vivian, and on the third Irving would pile the fishing tackle, pup tents, and food supplies. Then off they would go into the country to a camping spot on the Shiawassee River.

The acquisition of a secondhand Ford touring car when Roger was fourteen widened their horizons to inexhaustible limits. Now they could go hunting, fishing, berrying, camping a hundred miles away and even farther. Trout caught in a brook near Lake Leelanau and fried outdoors were ample compensation for the steaks and chops they were never able to afford. For the children discomforts only made the jaunts more memorable: the all-night attack of pismires when they insisted on sleeping out of the tent and woke up looking like measles victims; the rough, rattling ride to Niagara Falls over roads that set their teeth chattering and their heads bumping the car top. Often, with Mother leading, they would sing as they traveled, the popular songs of the day such as "Long, Long Trail" and "K-k-k-katy." If Mother took less enjoyment in these rigorous expeditions, she gave no sign. Always she would accompany them and go singing through the countryside.

But it was the violin, not the car, which did most to widen Roger's horizons. He started taking lessons when he was in the seventh grade and practiced faithfully. Late in the year the seventh grade of Emerson School visited the seventh grade of another school, and several pupils were asked to perform. Miss Tripp, his teacher, helped him prepare a simple number. It was the first time he had ever stood before a group with confidence and without competition. He was applauded. His ego blossomed. He had acquired identity. He was a *person.*

School became less of a torment. Entering high school, he daringly chose the college course, although the two years of Latin nearly proved his downfall. Math was his first love. To express his appreciation to Miss Tubbs, his math teacher in sophomore year, he took her a gift of two carefully cleaned rabbits. By his junior year, Latin conquered, he was getting creditable marks in all subjects in spite of the work in the foundry morning and night. He would get up with Father and Irving at four, go to the foundry, load a wheelbarrow with three or four hundred pounds of iron castings, wheel it down the alley, through a swinging door, and down a ramp into the mill room, once, twice, many times. Then in the evening he would go again and do his cleaning job.

But he still found time for music. For many years he played in a small orchestra which Miss Tripp conducted at the Methodist Church. Then in his senior year came Mr. Champion, Owosso's first full-time music director, young, serious, music his first and only love. He believed Roger had the capacity to become a public-school music teacher. He put him in the first chair of the violin section. He gave him instruction in clarinet so he could play in the high-school band. When Miss Tripp left, Mr. Champion encouraged Roger to assume direction of the Methodist orchestra. The departure of Miss Tripp left the town without a violin teacher.

"Roger, why don't you take some pupils?" suggested Mr. Champion.

Roger gasped. But the man's confidence was contagious. By the middle of the year the boy had twenty pupils, nineteen violin, one clarinet. By springtime his orchestra gave a concert in conjunction with a recital by his twenty pupils.

That year he even found time for a few dates with Elizabeth Willman, daughter of the superintendent of schools. Three weeks before the spring prom Elizabeth, a junior, decided that Roger must escort her to it. He had never danced a step.

"I'll teach you," she promised comfortably. "It's easy, like marching."

Not exactly, he discovered to his chagrin. But she was a patient teacher. He did not own a suit. Mr. Trythall, his physics instructor, saw his plight. He knew one of the clothiers in town who had a suit much too long in stock, and bought it for Roger. It was the nineteen-year-old youth's debut into society. Now, at twenty-one, he still felt almost as gauche and tongue-tied in the presence of girls as on that night. He was far more at home with the rough, ill-mannered, jocularly profane workmen with whom he spent his summer days in the foundry.

2

He returned to his academic field in the fall, expecting to work the same tough furrows in the same eighteen-hour daily rounds, never dreaming that in the arid soil there were already planted the seeds both of triumph and of tragedy.

During October, 1929, the exploits of the new track star flashed headlines across Michigan news media.

"ROGER ARNETT CROSS-COUNTRY FLASH OF STATE NORMAL TEAM..."

"ARNETT SETS NEW FOUR-MILE MARK ON LOCAL COURSE. Local Star Betters His Own Record Set Last Week against Detroit ..."

"ARNETT LEADS TEAMMATES TO THIRD CHAMPION-SHIP ... Arnett, running a beautiful race for the Hurons, set a new conference record of 23 minutes 50 seconds for the 4½ mile grind. His performance broke by more than a full minute the old conference record of 25:03. . . . A team trophy, a gold statue, and six medals were awarded. . . . Arnett, winner of the meet, received the gold statue and a gold medal."

After he had copped first place in a dual meet with Ohio Wesleyan, running the four-mile in 21:18, the *Normal College News* exulted, "Great things are expected from this lanky Owosso boy, the greatest 'find' Coach Olds has uncovered in years." And the Owosso *Argus-Press* expressed its pride in a glowing headline: "FORMER OWOSSO HIGH STUDENT SURPRISES WITH TRACK SKILL."

No one was more surprised than Roger. Last year he had been a nonentity, conspicuous on campus if at all, because of his rustic appearance and awkwardness. Now suddenly, overnight, he was an "ace," a celebrity. Coeds turned to cast him adulatory glances. Upperclassmen clapped him on the shoulder and wished him luck. Even his professors seemed to regard him with an interest and respect which the mere earning of good grades had not elicited. So consistent had been Coach Olds' victories, his team having won the state intercollegiate cross-country meets for six consecutive years, that college spirit approached the religious fervor of the ancient Greeks for their Olympiads.

But Roger was too busy to let his head be turned by an invisible olive wreath. He was taking five subjects instead of the usual four, and with the hours of running practice, to say nothing of the actual meets, his four or five hours of sleep were cut almost to nonexistence. He gave up the night work in the filling station and got a job washing dishes from five to eight in the Graystone, a local restaurant, which earned him his supper and a small wage. Coach Olds also gave him a part-time job in the gymnasium, working in the locker room, handing out sweat suits, and attending to other small details, which paid him thirty dollars a month. Roger was determined, moreover, that none of these activities should interfere with his primary purpose in college.

"A quiet and studious lad," the *Normal College News* described him. "Eight months ago he had never had on a track shoe. Now he is the state and conference champion. But he takes the races as they come and slips away unnoticed, caring not for the spotlight. Individual glory means nothing to him. He sets the pace in every run and the other three members of the 'Four Horsemen' are close behind."

The "Four Horsemen"—Arnett, Morcombe, O'Connor, and Bauer—were on the six-man squad that Olds took to Cincinnati in November for the last and most important meet of the season, a national contest, the Amateur Athletic Union's Junior Cross Country Championships. Roger knew that fans all over Michigan were depending on him to win for the Hurons this nationwide victory. As he moved into position for the grueling six-mile race, his ears were full of cheers, applause, shrill pleadings, Coach Olds' stern injunctions.

"Yea, Ypsi! Yea, Arnett! Come on, Rajah! We're counting on you!"

"Get the lead, boy, and keep it. But don't force it. Save yourself for the final stretch. Then give it all your guts."

Roger listened with shy and incredulous embarrassment. His career as an athlete still seemed unreal. Preposterous to think that he, the lumbering oaf, could run against experts and win. It took all the proddings and pep talks of his new roommate, Norman Hagen, to make him even attempt each competition, so scant was his self-confidence. "Cripes, feller, what's your backbone made of, jelly? Get out there and *run*. Can't you get it through your thick skull that you're a *winner?*"

Norm did more than give pep talks. Although he hated track meets, he joined the cheering section of every one where his roommate was running. Roger felt him there now, a goad to his flagging confidence.

But once the gun blasted and the race was on, he needed no such stimulus. The lanky frame shot into motion. The long legs grown muscular from years of trucking iron castings began pumping. His nerves tingled. Energy charged through him as if triggered by an electric current. Much as he liked indoor and outdoor track, cross-country was his element. Here was no reek of musty boards, no stale dust to clog the nostrils or blur the vision. The November air was clear and sharp. It stung him into action like a goad. He lifted his face to it, exulting in its resistance as he swept through it. Nor was this a smooth, even course, like a gym floor or a race track. It went up hill and down, thrust obstacles in the way, challenged a man's endurance even beyond its limits.

After the first spurt of a mile or so he settled to a more even jog, realizing that he must conserve his energy, taking his cue from his teammates, Morcombe and Bauer, to whom the six-mile grind was a favorite distance. They were competing against such strong teams as the Detroit Y, Indiana University, Ohio State, Pittsburgh, and Penn State. Deliberately he resisted the impulse to forge faster when others passed him. Long before he reached the halfway mark the exultation was gone. He was an automaton, wound up long ago and running without human impetus. The movement of limbs was but another unconscious reflex of his body, along with pounding heart, sweating pores, running eyes, hammering temples, near-to-bursting lungs. At four miles the invigorating air turned into a furnace, the ground a bed of hot coals seen through a red haze of sweat and tears. He was aware neither of competitors nor of spectators, only of the fierce stolid pumping of his limbs; finally not even of that. The passing of the five-mile mark made no impression. Yet somehow he kept going.

Then suddenly it was over. The pounding in his ears became cheers. The red haze resolved itself into faces. Coach Olds was propping him up, prodding him to consciousness, sharply exhorting him to "Walk, man, walk! For heaven's sake, keep moving!" Hands were clapping him on the shoulders.

"You did it, Rajah, old boy! We knew you could, and you did. Bravo!"

The college annual summed it up: "Roger Arnett ran a beautiful race, covering the very difficult six-mile course in 31 minutes and 33 seconds to take first place in the team's scoring."

The event won the national championship for Ypsi. The team received a large silver plaque, and each of the men was given a medal. Roger had lost six pounds in the race, one pound for every mile, but he reckoned the winnings outweighed the losses. And by no means the least of the rewards of that cross-country season was the hearty confidence of his teammates which had changed the good-naturedly derisive "Abe" to "Rajah."

In fact, friendships, not fame and medals, were the most valued by-products of his second year in college. Two promised to be life enduring, one with a man, the other with a woman.

The man was his new roommate, Norman Hagen. The two had much in common. Norm also was working his way, spending his summers tutoring the two sons of a wealthy Detroit family. He was serious about his books yet full of fun and humor. Handsome, blond, curly-haired, a popular campus leader, star tennis player, and an extrovert to his fingertips, Norm possessed the confidence and ease of manner which Roger lacked, and these complementary traits contributed as much to their friendship as their similarities. Often they would sit up half the night confiding in each other, arguing, discussing jobs, world conditions, the depression which in this first year of the thirties threatened to shadow their futures, girls, marriage. They made a bet whereby the first one to get married would owe the other a box of candy.

Roger's Ford roadster became an economic as well as a recreational asset. During the years they were roommates they often traveled weekends to one of their homes, Norm's in East Detroit or Roger's in Owosso. Both were on a lean income and a skimpy diet.

Returning to college, they would bring all kinds of goodies cooked by their respective mothers, enough to supplement their diet for a week. Their pastimes were often as silly as their talks were serious. They cultivated the skill of talking in unison. Riding along in the open roadster, perhaps they would spy a farmer by the roadside. Then, working up to the proper rhythm as they approached— "One, two . . . One, two, three"—they would yell in concert, "Hi, John!" Or when they saw their landlord working in the yard, they would derive great glee from his puzzled expression as they chanted with one voice, "Hi, Mr. Squiers!"

It was with the help of Norm and his girl friend, Josephine Daisher, that Roger began dating Alice Barber. Occasionally his duties at the Graystone would involve leaving the kitchen and waiting on customers or clearing the tables. Early one evening in the fall, when his dishwashing relief had arrived, business was rushing, and he stayed to help clear the tables. Spying a familiar face in a corner of the room, he moved toward it.

"Well, well, if it isn't the beautiful and charming Josephine!" he quipped with a familiarity born of frequent meetings, born also of a new ease and self-confidence growing out of his athletic successes. "And where, may I ask, is the doughty Napoleon?"

"Studying, I hope," returned Jo, "though I wouldn't be surprised if he is still on the tennis court. You know I can't compete with his first love."

"Imagine!" Roger shook his head in mock amazement. "How any man could prefer that kind of courting—!" He stopped suddenly, conscious that a very pretty, very well-dressed and self-sufficient young woman was regarding him with quiet amusement.

"Norm's roommate, Roger Arnett." Jo introduced him to her companion. "This is Alice Barber, Roger. You must have heard of her."

Roger nodded. He felt suddenly gauche and tongue-tied, painfully conscious of his big white kitchen apron. "I—I'm pleased to meet you," he muttered.

"At least I've heard of you," said Alice composedly. "Ypsi's mighty harrier! You're the talk of the town back in Tecumseh, where Jo and I come from."

Roger flushed even more deeply. Was she making fun of him? He looked at her more intently to make sure, decided to his surprise that she wasn't, and kept on looking. To his further surprise he found himself dropping down into the vacant chair between them and awkwardly but persistently pursuing conversation. Wouldn't they like a Coke? No, thank you, they had just had one. Then maybe a hamburger? Even his belated glimpse of bread and mustard remnants on their two plates and the gleam of amusement in Jo's eyes failed to squelch him. Somehow he kept them talking, all the time vibrantly conscious of the girl beside him, of the proud set of her head, the sure, confident motion of her hands, the soft wings of hair neatly framing her face. When finally Jo pushed back her chair determinedly, he summoned all his courage and made the plunge.

"I say—I'm just about through here. How—how about getting Norm, and the four of us going out on a double date?"

Jo looked at Alice, and the two exchanged a mute but communicative parley. "Oh, I'm sorry." Jo sounded genuinely regretful. "Not tonight. We're tied up. Alice has sorority business, and I have to study."

"Then—later, maybe?" Roger was amazed at his persistence.

Another swift exchange. "Sure. Why not?" Jo's smile was frankly mischievous. "How about going to church together, the four of us, on Sunday?"

At Roger's quick assent both girls looked disconcerted. So did Norm when Roger came bursting in on him a few minutes later with an enthusiastic, "Hey! I've just arranged a double date for us!"

"So? Who's going?"

"You and I, and Jo and Alice Barber."

"Alice Bar—Look, feller, you're joking! Do you know who she is?"

"Sure. She's a friend of Jo's. I just met her in the Graystone."

"Yes, and she's also a senior, an all-'A' student, a brain, president of her sorority, and one of the biggest wheels on campus!"

"One of the prettiest, too." Roger looked defiant. "So what?"

"All that culture?" Norm groaned. "She's way out of our class. How in tarnation did you happen to pick her?"

"Because—" Roger felt himself flushing. "I—happen to like her, that's all."

"O.K." Norm sighed. "Where do we go, and when?"

"To church. On Sunday."

Norm's enthusiasm sank to new lows. But the agreement had been made.

24

On Sunday, the date was not too successful. The girls were not ready (probably having failed to take the commitment seriously), and the four had to sit in the last row in the balcony. But Roger was content. He had had his first date with Alice.

The next outing of the foursome was a trip into the country in Roger's roadster. Its most memorable by-product was a picture Norm took of Roger holding a handful of hay wisps toward an uninterested cow. Not being expert in photography, Norm posed Roger in the near foreground, the cow safely in the rear, the result showing an overly tall, lanky male feeding a midget bovine.

Fortunately the car was more amenable than on some occasions. Once, when Norm borrowed it to take Jo home to Tecumseh thirty miles away, he had three flat tires on the way there, four on the way back. For some time he would not speak to Roger. The gall of loaning him a seven-flat potential!

Roger's dates with Alice became more and more frequent. Gradually he lost his awe in her company, and, in addition to mutual attraction, they discovered that they had much in common. Both were good students, enthusiastic about the prospect of teaching. They enjoyed the same recreations. Being president of her sorority, Alice had passes to all the fraternity and sorority dances on campus, and they often attended them together. Thanks to Elizabeth Willman and her successors, Roger was by now a fair dancer. Many of the dances were formal, so he had to invest in a tuxedo and black tie. The latter almost proved his undoing. He could not learn to tie it. Norm was usually there to act as valet, getting the proper perspective by taking a rear stance. But one evening he had to leave earlier than his roommate.

"But—how am I going to tie my tie?" protested Roger in a panic.

"Oh—Mrs. Squiers is home. She'll do it."

However, just before leaving Josephine's house Norm got a frantic phone call. "Norm, you gotta come back here and tie my tie. Mrs. Squiers left!"

Taking Jo with him, Norm backtracked to the lodging.

Properly tied and tuxedoed, Roger felt himself a creditable escort and was almost completely at ease at these functions . . . except once. It was the second dance he attended, and never would he forget it. Earlier that Friday he had run in a track meet, hampered by a very sore foot. As he danced, it became more and more painful, but he said nothing and kept on dancing. By morning it was so bad that he had to consult the college physician.

"You've got to get over to the school hospital," he was told bluntly.

He had developed a bad abscess on the bottom of his foot, so infected that it had to be lanced. When Alice heard, she was deeply chagrined. Why hadn't he told her? Roger didn't know himself. Reluctance to pamper himself? Fear of upsetting another person's plans? Or just the simple pleasure of holding a certain girl in his arms, no matter what pain it involved? As yet he found it hard to analyze his emotions, especially where they concerned Alice Barber. But he was back running track again the following Friday.

The indoor season which began right after the Christmas vacation offered fully as great challenge as cross-country. One of the most important meets, with the University of Michigan and Michigan State, was held on a bitterly cold night in February. To Roger's surprise before he went out on the track he saw his father and mother, brother and sister coming toward him. Hearing and reading about his prowess, they had traveled all this distance to see him run. Perhaps their presence inspired him, for he ran one of the best races of his career. His chief opponent was Lauren Brown from Michigan State, an ace two-miler unbeaten during the previous season. By winning over Brown, Roger set a new field house record at the University of Michigan.

"Arnett, First to Defeat Brown of State," the Owosso *Argus-Press* headlined proudly, "is State Normal Ace." It continued, "Roger Arnett, sophomore at Michigan Normal, has proven one of the outstanding distance runners there of all time."

Even though the next month, March, Roger yielded first place to Brown at Notre Dame, his triumphs during the indoor and outdoor track seasons continued to mount. In April he copped the two-mile run at Oberlin, and at the Drake Relays for Big Ten Schools he ran the fastest two-mile race in his career, not many seconds behind Martin of Purdue, who came in first. In May he took first in the mile and two-mile in a meet with Detroit City College. A little later in the State Collegiate meet in East Lansing he was entered in both the mile and two-mile. In the mile, which came first, he ran among the leaders, and, though near the end he was nosed out by Ray Swartz from Western State in Kalamazoo, both of them had broken the state record. Then the two-mile came up. Lauren Brown, who was fresh, not having just run the mile, nosed him out again, but he pressed Brown to a new track record and came within six seconds of

26

the world record. Here he had broken two state records, yet had placed only second! A week later the coach took a few of his best runners to the National Collegiate meet at the University of Chicago, and here again Roger broke the national collegiate record, yet came in only sixth. Frustrating, to say the least!

In spite of his preoccupation with track and romance, his scholastic record remained high, for he never let himself forget his reason for being in college. That is, hardly ever. Only once did he make the almost irreparable mistake of cheating. He and Norm were facing the dismal prospect of a test in French, for which they were not too well prepared. They rationalized the possibilities.

"We haven't ever cheated. Plenty of other fellows have."

"We've been very busy representing the college in extracurricular activities. Therefore we should be justified in cheating a little."

"O.K. But if we're going to do it, let's do it up right!"

Figuring that the test would require a knowledge of vocabulary, they arranged all the anticipated words in alphabetical order on small cards. Tests were usually given to alternate rows from front to back. Norm was to hold half the cards, Roger the other half, but both must write down both sets of questions. Then each would fan out the required cards for the other. What a fiasco! It took so long to answer both sets of questions that they lost valuable time. Then words on one card would be required for both of them. Long before they finished time ran out, and the teacher, Miss Wolfe, called for the papers. Roger, on the aisle, rose from his seat, and—Oops! All his cards spilled to the floor. He stared at them transfixed.

"Pick them up!" hissed Norm, and helped him gather the glaring evidence.

The boys never found out whether Miss Wolfe guessed the truth, but neither of them received a good grade that term. The one "C" stood out like a sore thumb on Roger's report. He vowed fervently never to cheat again.

On another occasion, too, preoccupation with vocabulary got the boys into trouble. Inspired by an English course that demanded prolific use of the dictionary, they developed a passion for strange or multisyllabic words. Instead of approaching the girls with a "Could I have this dance?" they would babble, "Your talent in the terpsichorean art so consumes my emotions that I solicit your detention within my anterior limbs during the orchestration of this vulgar composition." But sometimes this game brought unexpected results, as when they came across the word "xanthochroid," meaning of blond complexion, and devised an interesting sequence whereby the knowledge might be exploited.

"What a pity," Roger told Alice in confidence, "that Norm and Jo are no longer friends!"

"Why not?" demanded Alice. "I didn't know they had quarreled."

"Well, it's because—" Here Roger resisted until Alice was driven nearly to distraction. Finally he whispered with dire solemnity, "Did you know Norm is a *xanthochroid?*"

Alice burst into tears. Hastily Roger explained, but she failed to regard the deception as a joke. She was cool to him for days.

As the year passed, however, the two were thrown together more and more. Roger's selection by Kappa Delta Pi, an international honorary and professional fraternity in education to which only about fifty of the fifteen hundred students were elected, was not only a gratifying honor but an opportunity to see more of Alice. But as their romantic interest heightened, such meetings in groups and frequent weekend dates were not enough. They sought other opportunities to be together.

Since the coeds were not permitted dates except on weekends, more informal meetings had to be devised. Some evenings they would meet in the library, then he would drive her home. On one such occasion they were sitting in the car outside the Tri Sig house when two women, one of them the dean of women, Miss Lydia Jones, walked by. After passing them, Miss Jones turned and with great deliberation appeared to be pointing at something in the sky. Both Roger and Alice got her message. She had seen them. As soon as she was out of sight Alice hastily entered the house.

Roger was taking a photography course in physics that year. It involved not only taking pictures but spending many hours in the laboratory developing them. Alice would sometimes go along and watch the process. The hours together undoubtedly contributed to the development of romance as well as pictures. One evening when they prepared to leave they found the door of the science building locked. It was a tense moment. Although well realizing the danger to their reputation and that of the school should their predicament be discovered, Roger hid his genuine consternation under a mask of flippancy.

"Oh, well, the janitor should come along before classes. I'll make you up a nice bed on one of the lab benches."

Alice was close to panic. "How you can joke—! Do you realize what this could do to me? Why, I—I might even get expelled, or at least be the laughingstock of the whole college! Please do something!"

"Don't worry," assured Roger. Evidence of dependence in the competent Alice gave him a sense of intense well-being. "I'll get you out."

He did. Finding a window near ground level in the rear of the building, he crawled out, and with some encouragement she slid down into his arms. Then, lifting himself to the sill, he closed the window. A simple solution, yet it gave him the warm feeling of a knight having rescued fair lady, a not unwelcome boost to his still depressed ego.

Near the end of the year Roger gave Alice the tiny gold track shoe which was awarded him along with his school letter, a poor replica of the size elevens which had taxed all the gym's ingenuity to find, but symbolic of his many triumphs. It was symbolic now of another victory even more prized, for while it did not signify an actual engagement, it was equivalent to an understanding. Roger could not plan on marriage yet. He still had at least a year and one summer to go to complete his education. But he saw Alice graduate, deliver a stirring valedictory address, and accept a teaching position in the fall, all with the satisfied confidence that she would share his future.

The summer of 1930 was much like the preceding one. Roger worked from four thirty in the morning until eight or eight thirty at night cutting sand, scraping patterns, shaking out hot castings, wheeling huge loads of iron, all with an even greater determination to get himself through college without debt.

There was one difference, however, about this summer. He was a celebrity in Owosso. Small boys stared, shining eyed, when he passed them. Girls regarded him with an alert new interest. High-school boys respectfully requested his autograph, obviously far more impressed by his achievements than by those of the town's chief celebrity, James Oliver Curwood, whose Norman "castle" at the corner of John and River streets dominated the landscape just across the Shiawassee River from the high school. Even Roger's mother displayed an unmistakable, if reluctant, pride.

"I just hope all this hero nonsense doesn't go and turn your head!"

But he noticed that she had carefully clipped every article about him from the *College News* and the local newspapers, even the smallest item that mentioned his name, and filed them away among her treasures.

That summer the family became sufficiently prosperous to exchange their 1922 Dodge touring car; an old but sturdy model with a high chassis and big, narrow-tired wheels, for a more modern 1927 model. Roger profited by the exchange, since they let him have the old car, even in its dotage a far better mechanism than his Ford roadster. It took him on several weekend trips that summer to see Alice in Tecumseh, and, well satisfied with his summer's assets, he set off in it for college in September, little guessing into what uncharted wildernesses it was destined to carry him.

The *Normal College News* had to keep its presses rolling to keep pace with Roger's victories that fall of 1930.

October 9. "Captain Arnett and mates ran away with all honors in second dual match with Ohio Northern University: 15 to 45."

October 23. "Arnett in great form as Normal upsets Miami University."

October 30. "Arnett Heads Pack at University of Michigan. Arnett won by a good five yards from Austin, Michigan ace."

November 6. "Ypsi won fourth straight Michigan Collegiate Conference cross-country championship at Kalamazoo. Arnett was far superior to Ray Swartz of the Hilltopper squad, a quarter mile ahead of the Western ace, breaking the old record by two minutes and avenging the defeat suffered last spring from Swartz in the mile race at East Lansing."

November 13. "Team swamps Oberlin. Again Arnett led the field."

November 20. "Varsity Harriers Cop Seventh State Crown. Captain Arnett set a terrific pace in the state intercollegiate run last Saturday to break the course and state record held by Lauren Brown of the Spartans by 1 minute, 13 seconds."

Coach Olds was jubilant. There were no limits, he asserted, to what the star might do. Already he was being spoken of as a certain candidate for the Olympics, to be held in Los Angeles in 1932.

"You're going to the Olympics," Norm told him firmly with the same persuasive confidence he would have used a year before to prod, "You're going to run this race and win it."

"Me? The Olympics! You're joking." Roger pretended to scoff at the idea, but his quick flush was revealing. "You—really think so?"

"Of course I do."

"Then you're nuts." Roger pushed his books aside, got up, and threw the window open. He was still flushed when he returned to the table where the two had been studying, and his blue eyes were bright. "What—makes you think so?"

"Because," Norm tipped back his chair, folded his hands behind his blond head, and studied his roommate, "you're Roger Arnett. Not the same Roger I knew first. Remember him—gawky, tumbling all over his big feet, scared to look a girl in the face, hayseeds sticking out all over him?"

Roger grinned. "Do I!"

"And not the Roger I knew last year either. Remember how I used to have to blow up your blasted ego before every race, you were so sure you couldn't win? Well, I haven't had to do it this year, have I?"

"No. Guess you haven't."

Norm continued to appraise him critically—the unwavering blue eyes deep set under heavy brows, the rugged cheekbones, firm mouth, and square chin, the upreared wave of hair which always managed to look a little ruffled by the wind. "That's why I say you'll go to the Olympics. Because I've watched you grow, seen you prove that you've got the guts to do any blamed thing you really want to do. And you want to go, don't you?"

Roger did not answer. But instinctively the muscles of his legs flexed, his pulses quickened, and every fiber of his body tensed to a silent "On the mark!" Yes, he wanted to go to the Olympics more than anything in the world. Except, of course, he assured himself hastily, to graduate with high marks and without debt, to become a teacher, and to marry Alice.

It was a miracle that he was able to maintain the high marks those fall and winter terms, he was so busy with other activities. Besides being captain of cross-country, he was secretary-treasurer of the Chemistry Club, secretary of the Men's Union, and, most responsible position of all, president of the Varsity Y Club, a much-coveted office. Organized to keep former Ypsi athletes in touch with athletic activities after they left college, it encouraged their return to athletic events on campus. That year, thanks in part to Roger's efforts, more than fifty graduates registered at the club headquarters.

The problem of financial independence was even more harassing. Roger became niggardly in his efforts to budget his meager funds so they would last through the summer session. Norm was also short of funds, and there came a time when the two had to limit themselves to one hearty meal a day. Necessity made conniving necessary. Their genial landlady, Mrs. Squiers, often invited them downstairs for a rubber of three-handed bridge, and they accepted joyfully, less for the bridge than for its generous accompaniment of sandwiches, cake, or cookies. Once, in Mrs. Squiers' absence, hunger became so dire that they even resorted to thievery. Descending to her kitchen, they appropriated two or three slices of bread apiece—no butter, or jam, they would not stoop so low as that—just *bread*.

Soon after her return Mrs. Squiers asked if they had seen Johnny, her twelve-year-old son. No, they responded innocently. Why? "My land," was her response, "I don't know what's going to happen. That boy! He ate almost half a loaf of bread!"

Realizing the jig was up if Johnny squealed, the boys hung around the front door until he returned, then ushered him upstairs and entertained him until they heard Mrs. Squiers close her bedroom door. The theft was not mentioned again—for twenty-one years.

"Who do you suppose I saw," wrote Norm long afterward to Roger, "when I was on shore leave in San Francisco? In an officers' club I spotted an ensign who looked strangely familiar. Little Johnny Squiers! I told him all about the theft, and he laughed and laughed. 'Why on earth didn't you tell Mom?' he asked. 'She thought you boys were tops. She'd have given you the whole loaf and welcome.' "

In late November came the Central Collegiate Cross-Country meet with all the best teams of the Midwest competing. Roger knew that his chief competitor would be Clark Chamberlain, Michigan State runner who had won in the NCAA meet the week before, in which Roger had not participated. The meet was held in East Lansing, which gave Chamberlain a slight advantage. But Roger was confident. He had never felt more fit, and he wore a brand-new pair of track shoes, their half-inch spikes as tingling sharp as his own nerve ends.

The course started and ended in the stadium. After the first quarter mile it lay "cross-country" through woods, fields, trails, up hills and down, a bewildering variety of terrain. About a half mile from the start it narrowed into a path perhaps four feet in width. Roger was in the lead by five yards. Suddenly, without warning, he saw a number of wooden shingles scattered on the path. Too surprised to swerve, he crashed into them, the sharp spikes of his right shoe sinking so deeply into one that he was unable to shake it free. He had to stop and pull it off, giving Chamberlain not only time to pass him but also warning of the danger ahead. By the time Roger had gotten back in stride, his opponent was ten yards in front. He soon discovered also that he had badly wrenched his knee. Try as he would, he could not shorten the gap, but in spite of his injury he finished second, well ahead of the third-place man.

Apparently Chamberlain was the only other one to see what happened, and naturally he would say nothing about it. Roger made no complaint either, even to his coach. The injury was not serious enough to require hospitalization, but, though it bothered him little in walking, it did cause pain in running.

"I only hope—" Coach Olds was obviously worried.

"I'll be all right," assured Roger. "It's still two weeks away."

The last and most important test of the season was coming up, the AAU National in Jersey City. Last year the Hurons had come home from Cincinnati with the junior championship. This year they were making an attempt at the higher laurels of the senior division. And it was on Roger that most of their hopes and those of the whole Midwest rested. One of the big dailies frankly voiced this hope:

"Moore, the American ten-mile champion, may encounter his stiffest opposition from Roger Arnett, captain of the Michigan State Normal College team. Arnett, in his section, is regarded as a possible point winner for the United States in the coming Olympic meet at Los Angeles."

Roger refused to pamper his injury. He had to run that race in Jersey City. Chamberlain would undoubtedly be entered in the national senior event, and he would have another chance to turn his recent defeat into victory. Then, too, the newspaper buildup of his Olympic possibilities both fed his ego and whetted his appetite for success. In these depression years, when even a college education by no means assured a teaching position, what opportunities might be opened by a gold medal in the Olympics!

33

Roger went to Jersey City. He was entered in the six-mile race of the AAU National senior meet. It was a bitterly cold day in early December, and the course was wholly strange, but for the first five miles he ran a good race, keeping side by side with Zepp, one of the front runners, all the way. Then his injured leg failed him. Stricken with cramps, he dropped far behind, finishing finally in the twentieth place. Defeat itself was disappointing enough, but to be beaten so badly, even with a good excuse, was both crushing and humiliating. The Huron thinclads, who had come East with such high hopes, placed only seventh in the meet. Roger could hardly look Coach Olds in the face. Humiliation was followed by self-pity. The sympathy of his teammates only aggravated the emotion. "Don't feel bad, feller. You were just running a handicap race, with all the odds against you."

Roger brooded. Even a handicap race was supposed to be fair, based on skill, not accident. Fate had played him a mean trick. Could a man's whole career be blasted by a shingle? Frightening thought! Then life wasn't what you made it, as he had naïvely believed. It was what blind chance made of you!

"Well," he vented his moodiness on Norm, "there goes all hope for the Olympics—if there ever was any."

"Nonsense!" Norm hooted. "Cripes, man, it's almost two years to Los Angeles!"

But not to the end of his college track career, Roger amended silently. It was for Coach Olds' sake as well as his own that he was anxious to qualify. Every coach dreamed of having one of his athletes make the Olympic team. Roger fretted impatiently at the enforced rest period. The indoor track season came, progressed, and the injury persisted. The first time he tried running he aggravated it, so he was again out of commission. In February, Ypsi lost to Ohio Wesleyan, its first dual indoor track defeat in eight years.

"The loss of Roger Arnett for indoor track season, because of a pulled tendon in his leg," lamented the *Normal College News*, "has greatly weakened the varsity strength in distance runs. Probably his presence would have defeated Ohio Wesleyan."

But after two more weeks of rest Roger ran creditably in a meet at Ann Arbor, and his leg seemed completely healed. Coach Olds was wary, Roger confident. On March 7 the Central Collegiate Carnival was to be held at Notre Dame, and, although Roger was not included among the eight squad members Olds planned to take

34

to South Bend, he determined not to let himself be pampered any longer. His time as an undergraduate athlete was running out.

"OK," the coach agreed with some reluctance, "we'll enter you in the mile. That should be safe enough. But the first sign of trouble, and you fall out, understand? We can't take chances on losing you altogether."

There was another reason why Roger was eager to go to Notre Dame. Alice was teaching at St. Joseph, just forty miles from South Bend. The meet would provide one of their rare opportunities to be together. He would drive to St. Joseph the night before, take her with him the next morning to South Bend, then spend part of Sunday with her.

Tentative plans were already made for this trip, for in late February Alice spent a weekend in Ypsilanti. Roger arranged a double date for them with Elizabeth Willman, who was in nurse's training in Ann Arbor, and one of her friends, a young graduate student in medicine. It was the two men's first meeting, and once Roger would have been tongue-tied with shyness, but no longer. It gave him a peculiar satisfaction to appear confident and at ease in the presence of Elizabeth, who had so generously taken pity on a gauche and bashful youth.

"Remember," he could not help reminding as he guided her expertly around the dance floor, "when you gave me my first lesson?"

"Do I! And now look at you!" Her warm glance of pleasure and admiration paid unmistakable tribute to his athletic fame, his beautiful and brilliant fiancée, and, most satisfying of all, his social adequacy.

It was well that he savored this moment of pardonable pride. It was one of the last he was to enjoy for a long time to come.

Roger drove to St. Joseph as planned on March 6. The next morning the weather looked threatening, and snow was predicted, but he reassured Alice and her roommate Gladys Greenhoe, who was accompanying them to Notre Dame.

"Worry wart!" he chided his fiancée affectionately. "There's not a flake in the air. And if we get caught in a snowstorm in South Bend, I promise I'll put you both up in a hotel overnight."

The storm was upon them before they had gone many miles, first a few lazy flakes, then gently teasing swirls, soon a steady barrage which developed rapidly into a snarling blizzard.

"D-don't you think we'd better turn back?" broached Alice nervously.

"Wouldn't do any good," returned Roger. "We've gone halfway already."

"But—we seem to be going into it, don't we?"

"Maybe. But it's just a squall, must be. It couldn't come down like this very long."

He was wrong. As if the sky had been slashed open, snow continued to tumble. Whipped by gusts more resembling January than March, it bombarded the windshield, shrouded the big rounded hood, massed itself in uneven patches along the narrow, curving road. The big high Dodge touring car with its rattling side curtains could not keep it out. Huddled under blankets beside Roger on the front seat, the two girls gamely joked about the virtues of ice packs for the complexion and vied with each other as to whose teeth could chatter the louder. But, sensing the tenseness of the slender shoulder touching his, Roger knew they were chattering as much from nervousness as from cold. He took his hand from the wheel just long enough to press Alice's cold fingers.

"Don't worry. It's really not so bad driving, as long as we go slowly and carefully. I'll get you there all in one piece."

But driving demanded all his grim attention. The road was winding, coated in places with ice, and the covering of new snow would have made it treacherous even without the blinding swirls obscuring his vision. They crept along for what seemed like hours but was probably only a few minutes. They must be getting close to Niles, he thought, and decided they would stop there if the storm did not let up. Occasionally there would come a slackening in the snow, and he could travel as fast as thirty. It was at one of these times that it happened.

The slight curve in the road seemed to be perfectly open and clear, nothing to show that under the drifting of snow there was a thin coating of ice. When the car skidded, he expected to bring it quickly back under control, but, slewing to the side of the road, it encountered some sort of obstacle—stone, hump of ground, ice mass?—which it hit sideways. The girls' screams were mingled with those of the tires. In the split second while the high old car remained upright, Roger reached out with a subconscious reflex, pushed Alice and her friend down and toward the dashboard. Then he was flung back over the seat. The car overturned, its frail top crumpling. His

36

world reeled, exploded, fell on him, crushed him. Time was compressed into a knife edge of blinding, splintering pain. Then, mercifully, he lost consciousness.

A newspaper item of that same day gave the details with simple brevity:

YPSI ATHLETE IS NEAR DEATH
Roger Arnett Suffers Double Fracture of Back
When Car Overturns

NILES, MICH., March 7. Roger Arnett, nationally known athlete at Michigan State Normal College at Ypsilanti, was probably fatally injured near here this morning when the car in which he was driving to South Bend to attend the Central Collegiate track and field meet overturned, crushing him and causing a double fracture of his back.

With Arnett at the time of the accident were Miss Gladys Greenhoe and Miss Alice Barber, teachers in the St. Joseph schools. Miss Greenhoe is seriously injured, but hospital attachés say she will recover. Miss Barber, aside from minor bruises about the head, is not injured.

Arnett has regained consciousness, but doctors despair of his recovery.

Arnett and his companions were riding through a heavy snowstorm, which is believed to have been responsible for the accident.

3

Strange how others could keep on living your life after you yourself had seemingly relinquished it! In the following hours, days, a score of people assumed vicarious control of his being, suffered his agonies, determined his destiny.

Soon after the accident a car came along and its occupants, shocked but eager to help, rendered the best aid they could conceive. Extricating the victims from the wreckage, they crowded them into their own car, propping Roger's unconscious body upright as they rushed with all the speed possible to the nearest hospital in Niles, a few miles away. If the spinal cord had not already been severed by the two crushed vertebrae, surely during the jarring ride over the rough road the jagged bone fragments must have finished the job.

Apprised by phone of the accident, Roger's father and mother started immediately from Owosso for Niles, driving the 140 miles through the fury of wind and snow and mounting drifts. But, difficult though the trip must have been, so great was their sense of daze and shock that they were scarcely aware of its hazards. Arriving in Niles, they saw Roger, talked to him, said he talked to them, although he had no memory of it later. They met a Dr. Henderson, who had examined Roger's X-rays and discovered the extent of the damage. Very wise and kind, he did not tell them the whole truth, that there seemed nothing possible to do, but recommended that their son be taken to the University of Michigan Hospital in Ann Arbor. Gratefully, hopefully, his parents agreed. Since the roads were too blocked with snow to trust to an ambulance, late that evening he was placed in the baggage car of a passenger train and was carried the hundred miles during the night.

Roger's sister Vivian and his brother Irving left Owosso about six that evening, with the storm still raging. When they arrived in Niles, Roger had already left for Ann Arbor. The hospital attendants could give the brother and sister little information and less hope. Vivian and Irving endured the exhibition of blood-stiffened clothes, heard that Roger was "seriously injured," and understood that he was not expected to live. They tried to counter the shocked helplessness of their parents with comfort, encouragement, and practical suggestions.

"I think," Vivian was to say long afterward, "Mother lived in shock for the rest of her life."

Early the next morning, when the storm had slightly abated, they all started for Ann Arbor.

Valden Criger, one of the track team who had gone to Notre Dame, rode in the baggage car with Roger. Val was a good friend. Roger had often gone to his apartment in Ypsilanti and shared a meal with him and his young wife. He would have been glad of his presence now had he been conscious of it, but only once, vaguely, was he aware of sensation, of throbbing, jiggling motion, of terrific pain so intense that he slipped immediately back into unconsciousness.

In his next brief awareness he sensed that he was lying on something very hard, probably an X-ray table. Later he heard a voice speaking from an immense distance.

"We're going to perform an operation, son. We must try to remove the pressure on that spine. We can't use regular anesthetic because you're not in good enough condition. We're going to use a new kind."

It was the last moment of near-consciousness he was to know for days.

Len, a junior intern on duty at University Hospital that Sunday morning, scrubbed, donned mask and gown, and entered the operating room. Another emergency operation, some poor devil who had been in an accident. Nothing unusual in that. They were always being brought in, especially on weekends, and with the storm this one had been worse than most. Broken legs and arms, cuts and bruises, concussions. . . . He had held so many retractors, snipped so many stitches that he could almost make the routine motions in his sleep.

The patient was already on the table, face down. Len noted the lean virility of the long, muscular body, the knotted strength visible in the broad shoulders, the powerful limbs. Too bad, such a young guy. Probably out on a Saturday-night joy ride with his girl. He hoped it was nothing serious, just a routine job.

But the grim faces of the surgeon, Dr. Peet, and his assistant, Dr. Kahn, refuted the hope. And in the grueling hours that followed Len found himself more and more emotionally involved in the desperate struggle to salvage that youthful strength and virility. The operation was an emergency laminectomy, removal of the laminae from the spine to release pressure on the cord, crushed and torsioned by fractured vertebrae. It was one of his first experiences with this delicate and crucial surgery, and he watched with all the novice's fascination, plus a tense awareness of the crisis involved. The thin, glittering knife edge had suddenly become something more than a tool. It was an instrument of human destiny, determining whether a young man like himself would be able to walk and move normally again.

"Clamps . . . knife . . . retractor . . . sutures . . ."

Mechanically Len followed the clipped orders. While his steady hand held the retractor, he watched the skilled fingers move swiftly in their desperate race with time, laying bare the delicate network of blood vessels surrounding the bruised and avulsed spinal cord, probing deeper and deeper into the injured area with infinite care and painstaking precision. He could feel the surgeon's tenseness of concentration, hear his measured breathing, sense the tightness of his clamped lips beneath the mask as the moment of crisis came nearer and nearer. Then—it came. Len caught a glimpse of the ominously narrowed spinal canal, the crushed cord, its torn edges nakedly revealed. Then Dr. Peet raised his head and turned to his colleague with a sigh of defeat and resignation.

"It's no use," he announced wearily. "The cord is almost completely transected."

Len's fingers gripping the retractor felt numb and cold. To be young, strong, and know that forever after more than half of you would be dead! Paraplegia, heretofore little more than a word in a medical text, became suddenly flesh and blood—the warm, hard flesh and singing blood of this poor devil of a stranger on the table. Mechanically he performed his duties through the remainder of the operation, saw the incision closed and sutured, the patient turned finally—no need now of such consummate gentleness!—to be lifted to the stretcher.

He looked down into the upturned face, then uttered a cry of shocked, horrified amazement. It was the student with whom he and Elizabeth Willman had gone on a double date just a few days before!

Len called Elizabeth early that afternoon. "Could I see you? I'd like to tell you something."

They met, and he told her, as kindly and gently as possible. "I couldn't believe it when I saw who it was. We all had such a good time together! And I knew you'd known him a long time and been friendly. I wanted to tell you myself instead of having you hear it from others."

"Th-thanks, Len." Elizabeth was so shocked and distressed that she could hardly speak. "I—I can't believe it. Not—Roger—never walk—" She choked. "It—it's almost as if Kreisler lost his fingers!"

Len took her to a movie—the first one she had ever attended on a Sunday—to try to take her mind off the tragedy. But it was little use. The picture seemed only a blur of happy lovers, dancing couples, swift running feet. But it succeeded in unloosing her shock and distress into words.

"They made such a beautiful couple, dancing together, remember? Both of them so tall and straight and handsome and full of life! . . ."

"Len, this will kill his folks. They're so proud of him! And they're such wonderful folks, salt of the earth!"

"I've worked on a ward where there were paraplegics, six of them, all young, with their backs broken in motorcycle accidents. There's nothing, absolutely nothing, that one can do for them!"

"He used to play the violin so beautifully. I wish you could have heard him. I played, too, in the church orchestra that he directed. That was how we became friendly. He used to enjoy the concerts so much, have so much fun, but always on the way home he would be so blue and depressed! I never could understand why."

"Len, I'm afraid for him now. What will he do? This will be after

41

the concerts. There'll be no more of them, ever. Will he be able to *take it?*"

The young intern groaned. "Heaven knows! I guess only time will tell."

It was two days later that Roger knew another few moments of consciousness. Suddenly he became aware of a pressure on his chest. Foggily the impression grew that it was somebody's head; finally that it was Alice's and that she was crying. He knew he should reach out and try to comfort her, tell her that whatever the matter was, it would be all right. But the effort was too great. He felt himself slipping away. Sometime later he heard a commotion somewhere, people moving about, voices. Some of them sounded familiar —his teammates. Must be getting ready for a meet. . . . Hadn't he been going somewhere to a meet? Then what was he doing here— lying on his back—of all places, in a bed! Must get up and join them. This time he made a strenuous effort, managed to lift his head, was rearing himself on his elbows when firm hands pushed him down.

"Please, you must lie still. Don't try to move."

He stared up into a strange face framed by a white cap. "What— where—"

"You're in University Hospital at Ann Arbor. You were in an accident on the way to Notre Dame University at South Bend. Remember?"

Remember. . . . It came slowly, like wavelets creeping up on sand and then receding, each one rising a little farther. . . . No, like snowflakes . . . floating, swirling, beating, becoming icy fury, grinding, crushing. . . . Yes. He remembered.

Occasionally other faces drifted through the limbo of his half-consciousness, some strange, some familiar. His mother's, looking both strange and familiar with all the color drained from her cheeks and the glints from her eyes. Norm Hagen's, smiling as always. Elizabeth Willman's, kind and—was it pitying?—framed in another white cap. Innumerable nurses', doctors'. Usually their appearance was accompanied by voices, often meaningless but sometimes cutting through his stupor with knifelike clarity.

"Your father had to go home, dear, but I'll be with you every day. I'm staying nights in your room over at Mrs. Squiers'. I promised Father we'd let him know if—if you should get worse."

"You're going to be all right, feller. Get that through your thick head."

"Amazing! A week ago I wouldn't have given a red copper for his chances, but now the crisis seems to be past. I believe he's going to make it!"

Slowly his world took shape again. The foggy limbo became four white walls. The faces grew bodies clad in white uniforms, suits, slacks, sweaters blazoned with the familiar "Y," his mother's familiar cotton dresses. And as he came to full consciousness life began to stir. Pain slashed through his head, his arms, his shoulder blades. Try as he would, he could not maneuver them into comfortable positions. Sheets and pillow pricked like barbs. The hospital gown grated like sackcloth. His awakening body clamored at the portals of all his senses.

Part of it, that is. Just when he realized that he was partially paralyzed he could not have told. At first there seemed to be a weight on his limbs. He couldn't feel it, yet he knew it was there. So heavy was it that it was impossible to move them. Then, looking down, he saw that there was nothing . . . just the long, narrow mounds and the arch of his feet under the bedclothes. Curiosity changed to bewilderment, to alarm, to panic.

"What's the matter with me?" he demanded of nurses and doctors. "How badly am I hurt?"

They were smiling, encouraging, evasive. "Come now, don't worry, you're doing fine." . . . "A concussion, lots of bruises, rather a bad injury to your back." . . . "Just be patient, it all takes time." . . . "We're doing everything possible." . . .

It was to Norman Hagen that he first voiced his fears.

"Tell me, Norm. Give it to me straight. How bad am I?"

Norm did not evade. Neither did he smile. "Bad enough so you're lucky to be alive."

"Lucky? Are you sure?" Roger drew a deep breath, then plunged. "I—I can't move my legs, Norm. Does that mean—"

The blue eyes did not waver. "I don't know, Rog. I honestly don't know. I doubt if the doctors do."

Roger clenched both hands. "If I can't be myself, Norm, I—I don't want to live. There's nothing to live for."

Norm still looked him straight in the eye. "You'll be yourself," he said quietly. "Whatever happens, feller, you'll be yourself."

Day after day the tests went on, interminably. Roger both dreaded and anticipated them. Each time at the beginning there was such hope, at the end such disappointment.

Each day one of the doctors would come, accompanied by a nurse with tray. The bedclothes would be pushed back. Obediently he would close his eyes. First there would be the "light touch," with cotton, to test the level of sensation.

"Tell me, do you feel this, Arnett? . . . This? . . . How about this?"

"No . . . No . . . No . . . Do that again, it almost seems . . . No."

As hope plummeted with each successive "No," lips tightened, breathing became more strained, until the last one was barely more than a whisper.

Then would come the "heavy touch," with pinpoint or other sharp instrument.

"Now tell me, please, just when you begin to experience sensation."

"Yes. *Now!*"

Each time when he felt the prick there would be the triumph, the violent hope, the swift opening of eyes to detect some encouragement in the doctor's face. Surely the reaction had come at a little lower level than yesterday!

"Sorry. No change yet. Still at the level of the accident. Better luck, perhaps, tomorrow."

And they would go away, leaving him limp and exhausted, his hospital gown clinging like a damp compress to his chest and shoulders.

Tomorrow! The word came to possess body, personality. He could feel its presence, see its face staring at him, now fascinating, now frightening, like a two-headed Janus, even hear it arguing with itself.

"He'll walk again, maybe even run again. Tomorrow will be different . . ."

"No. All his tomorrows will be like today, only worse. Tomorrow and tomorrow and tomorrow . . ."

On March 19, twelve days after the accident, a crisis arose. The catheter tube providing bladder drainage became plugged, causing not only congestion but danger of serious infection. The next day Dr. Nesbit performed a cystostomy. And only six days later, to Roger's intense surprise, he was discharged from University Hospi-

44

tal. His mother traveled with him in the ambulance to Owosso, where he spent two days in the Memorial Hospital enduring more tests to make sure the seventy-mile trip had not impaired his condition. Then he was sent home on an air mattress, a clumsy thing like a big rubber raft, perhaps six inches in thickness, just one huge air pocket the size of a hospital bed.

Roger was elated. Surely his being permitted to go home was an encouraging sign. Amid familiar surroundings, with the loving care only a mother could give, his splendidly strong body would renew itself. Some tomorrow he would wake up with a tingling of sensation in his limbs, perhaps even the blessedness of pain. There would come again the glorious awareness of *motion*. It was now near the end of March. Perhaps by May he would be able to *feel* the grass under his feet. He would walk barefooted in it, slowly, just exulting in the sense of *feeling*. Or if not by May, surely by August . . .

His parents seemed to share fully his joy and hope. Returning from work, his father would greet him with a jocular, "Missed you today, son. None of those new hands can work like you. Hurry up and get that lazy hulk off that dad-blamed rubber raft!" His mother smiled and sang about her housework. Little did he know what the pretense of optimism cost them. Not until years later would he learn the truth, that he had been discharged from hospital because there was nothing more the doctors could do for him, that his parents had been told he would certainly have no more than a year to live.

Nor was Roger's disability the only problem they were facing. Suddenly their second son Irving, apparently for no reason, left home. Proud of his brother's athletic prowess, which had raised one of the town's humbler families to enviable status, he must have been bitterly disappointed as well as grieved by the accident. "You already have enough on your hands without me," he wrote back later. The breach was never to be quite healed. Then, too, these were the deep depression years, and James Arnett, reduced to part-time employment, was earning barely enough for necessities, to say nothing of expensive medicines, doctors, luxuries for a helpless invalid.

But gladly, for his sake, Roger's father and mother changed their whole manner of living. A hospital bed was set up in the living room, the only place large enough to provide room for tending him. His parents slept in an adjoining bedroom. There was no furnace, so a coal burner was used to heat the room. Often it was stoked with coke salvaged from discarded heaps at the foundry. At night the fire would go down, and the house, old and draughty, would become cool. The air mattress, adjusting to the room's temperature, also cooled, and to their surprise it took as many blankets underneath as over him to keep him warm.

Although Vivian and her husband Adolph Beyer (usually called Abie), lived upstairs, she worked during the day, and it was Roger's mother who had to assume most of his care. She gave it lovingly, constantly, and to the nth degree. Since she insisted on changing his sheets every day and boiling them for at least an hour, the tiny kitchen was usually spouting steam, her roughened fingers grating almost constantly on the old hand wash-board. She gave him a bath every day, turned him at frequent intervals, got up often in the night to tend him. The daily enema, the twice-daily bladder irrigation, the frequent bowel accidents in spite of them, all added to her labors.

Roger's father was equally, if not always as practically, helpful and protective. Occasionally he carried his role of anxious guardian to absurd extremes. At some time he had seen a movie, *The Unholy Three*, its theme suggesting the possibility that doctors often use criminal tactics to secure their human guinea pigs. Afraid that someone would try to steal his defenseless son for such purposes, he kept a loaded shotgun beside his bed.

Roger found this dependence on others not only galling but nearly unbearable. He could not even turn in bed without help. Minor problems became major, such as the trivial matter of getting a haircut. Finally a barber was persuaded to come from downtown —at a premium; whereupon worry over the expense made the problem greater. He became morose, snappy, even critical of his mother, and hated himself for it. Once by accident the irrigation solution, which had to be heated to body temperature, got much too hot and, feeling it against his wrist, he snapped at her in irritation. She made no comment, just looked hurt. In all the time she cared for him he never once saw her cry or heard her complain. Only when he complained there came that look of hurt in her eyes.

His parents were not the only ones who helped. Doctors had suggested that the joints of his legs should be exercised every day. Dan, the younger brother of Roger's old friend Bill Carmichael, heard of this and offered his services. Walking to the house after school each day, two miles out of his way, he spent an hour exercising and gently massaging the paralyzed limbs. Because of that labor of love the joints would remain supple all his life.

But in spite of the air mattress, the baths, the careful turnings, the massagings, the irrigations, physical complications kept developing. Tubes became plugged, infections set in, pressure sores appeared. Even Dr. Parker, their physician, did not know how to cope with them, for these were still the dark ages in terms of medical knowledge and treatment of paraplegia. Few, if any, survived such spinal injury for any length of time. Heat was suggested, and an infrared lamp was secured. Placed too close to his insensitive side, it caused burns. Various medications brought no results. After a month he developed a severe kidney infection, and his temperature shot to 106, stayed there for three days. All Dr. Parker could prescribe were baths, aspirin, much water to drink, alcohol rubs. Before the attack subsided Roger lost an alarming amount of weight, and his legs shrank to spindles.

But torments of mind were far worse than those of body. Galling as was his present dependence, despair for the future was far worse. Looking out the window, he could see the Noonans' house across the road and up a side street. One of his poignant childhood memories was of the Noonan boy, who had become paralyzed. The shock and pity he had felt then now turned to envy.

"Why couldn't I have died like him!" he brooded silently.

Comforting platitudes from visiting friends fell on deaf ears. Although he had joined the church when in high school, his faith had never probed deeply into the realities of life. God? If there were really a God, He couldn't have let a thing like this happen! Or He would perform a miracle now and make these dead weights move, walk—yes, and run again. *Run!* The very thought set his temples pounding and his pulses racing.

But hope vied with despair. Perhaps the miracle *would* take place. Often he experienced intense pain at the level of the accident. Time and again he was certain the sensation at these nerve ends came, not from chest, but from hips, knees, legs, feet. The disappointment and frustration that followed were shattering. Or—"Maybe this paralysis isn't a physical thing at all, but mental," the thought kept nagging him. He would reach down his hands, lift his leg up as high as he could reach, then, removing his hands, strain with every nerve and fiber and by sheer force of will to keep it up . . . up . . . up . . . but always it would flop back again.

47

His parents were constantly hopeful, looking for improvement, especially his father. One night, when some dance music was coming over the radio, Dad happened to be watching Roger's foot, which was uncovered.

"It moved!" he shouted jubilantly. "I swear one of your toes moved. It was keeping time to the music!"

Nothing could convince him that he was mistaken, or that, if there had been motion, it was but a spastic reflex not uncommon in cases of paralysis. He was almost beside himself with joy, certain that the paralysis would pass. It was years before he gave up that hope.

If doctors, in their inexperience with paraplegia, were reluctant to prescribe remedies for his physical complications, not so the numerous friends, old and young, from school, church, athletic teams, who flowed with faithful regularity through the small living room. Each one, it seemed, had a different suggestion to make.

Diets were a favorite category. "You must eat lots of cheese . . . yogurt . . . yeast . . . fish, it's good brain food and builds nerves, but when you eat fish you mustn't drink milk at the same meal . . . lots of juice, fruit juices, you know they have vitamins . . . apples . . ." One person recommended watermelons and secured a luscious one from Florida via a helpful friend. It tasted delicious. Cod-liver oil was another favorite. Many suggested heat lamps and ultraviolet rays.

Some of these visitors were helps, others hindrances. The pitying ones were among the latter ("Such a shame, I'm so sorry!"), also the disciples of the adage, "Misery loves company," who told long stories of someone they knew who had been paralyzed all the rest of his life. Even Mr. Trythall, who had been his physics teacher in high school and was now a medical student at the university, failed to score a hundred per cent of encouragement with his, "Now you've just got to be patient, Rog. It's going to take a long, long, long time. You know nerves heal at the rate of only about a millimeter a day."

At that rate, reckoned Roger wryly, who knew more about millimeters than his guest suspected, in a hundred days the healing should have amounted to ten centimeters, nearly four inches!

The loyalty of team and college mates did much to make these first months bearable. Student friends, coaches, fellow trackmen,

48

even his competitors from other colleges, especially Michigan State, came to visit or wrote him letters. In May, Ralph Young, director of athletics at Michigan State College, awarded him a beautiful gold medal in recognition of his high standing in scholastic and athletic achievement. Soon after his accident the Men's Union at Ypsilanti sponsored a "Sports Night" for his benefit, a program of basketball games, clogging numbers, a gymnastic exhibition, and a pair of boxing matches. More than a thousand persons packed the gymnasium for the occasion, and about six hundred dollars was raised. The "benefit," however, contributed more to his morale than to his financial gain. Placed in a bank in Ypsilanti to await his more urgent needs, the fund was to fall victim to the numerous bank failures which swept the country two years later.

The arrival of the college annual, *The Aurora*, brought bittersweet satisfaction. There was a whole page entitled "For Roger Arnett," detailing the story of the accident and all his track triumphs. Its phrases drummed the high points of his career like spiked track shoes—or like nails being driven into a coffin.

". . . will never again don spiked shoes for Michigan Normal . . . was captain . . . set new records in state and conference runs . . . records from mile to five miles repeatedly smashed by this great distance star . . . rose to supreme heights in state, Midwest, and national competition . . . had won 23 A's, 18 B's, and 3 C's . . . no telling how far he might have gone . . . To say the least, he would have been a candidate for the 1932 U.S. Olympic team . . ."

Never again . . . was . . . set . . . smashed . . . had won . . . would have been . . . All in the past, nothing in the future.

Perhaps the most memorable of all the tributes received was a letter dated May 14:

Dear Roger,

For a long time I have been trying to think of something that you might like and at last I have thought of something I wish you would accept. It was the first time I ever met you that I got it, and it seems fitting to send you this token.

You pushed me to the limit and without you I would not be where I am today. Furthermore, I think you are one mighty fine, clean chap and if you do not accept this token I will feel very bad. I am not rich, so I thought I would send you one of my most prized possessions.

When I was at the Illinois relays I determined to beat Chamberlain for you. Two weeks before the meet the slogan "One for Arnett" was framed in the door of my room and it is still there. I would like your permission to be considered my buddy in all my coming races so that it will not be just me running, but you also!

Perhaps I am very crude in the phrasing of this tribute; it is true that I have never talked to you very much, but I do not always gain my impression of a person in that way. . . . I'm just a plain young fellow who takes to heart his friendships and hobbies and in this capacity I extend to you my right hand and along with it go my very highest regards to a "Real Fellow." Many happy hours.

Your slightly known friend,
Ray Swartz.

With the letter from his strongest competitor at Western State Normal College came the gold medal which Roger had failed to win in the state collegiate meet in East Lansing just a little more than a year before.

But if it was friends like Ray who made life bearable, it was Alice's visits which, infrequent though they had to be, made it for a little time worth living.

She managed to make the 200-mile trip by bus about every third week, spending the weekend. She was always hopeful, cheerful, encouraging. She was sure that in time he would be able to walk. All they had to do was be patient. If he was not able to go back to college this fall, then surely he would by the next. And she was sure he was going to love teaching. She was finding it fascinating. Roger and his mother conspired to spare her the more sordid details of his confinement. He shared with her only the encouraging ones: the letter from Professor Norris commending the paper he had written to complete the requirements of the winter term, with the final grade of A; the new courses he was planning to take by correspondence; his growing proficiency at the typewriter, an old-fashioned Underwood of Vivian's which, propped on his chest by pillows and a board, he was learning to operate by means of an instruction book, practicing hour after hour, flat on his back.

Her visits were flashes of sunlight in a dark wasteland. The afterglow would remain for several days after she went back to St. Joseph, fade, then be revived in lesser glimmers by her letters. They seldom mentioned his disability. It was almost as if by refusing to put reality into words she felt that she could deny its existence. She wrote of her pupils, of Gladys Greenhoe, who had completely recovered, of her plans for the summer, of things they would do together in some distant future. She came to visit him after school closed in June, then went home to Tecumseh.

This time the afterglow lasted longer. She was nearer now, less than a hundred miles away. She would come oftener. And certainly the letters would be more frequent. He waited impatiently for the first one. A week passed . . . two.

It came. This time there was no avoidance of reality. A spade was a spade, smooth and sharp-edged, designed for one purpose, to dig, to cut, to uproot, to lay bare naked earthy elementals lying deep beneath the surface. Roger must surely understand that all thought of marriage must be out. It was impossible under the circumstances. If he got well again, she would be waiting for him. But for the present . . .

It is a blessing that the first impact of every major shock brings an emotional numbness, often accompanied by an intensely rational perception. Roger read and reread the letter, the hands holding it seemingly as devoid of life as the lower half of his body, but his mind keenly conscious of unwritten words between the lines. It was all too obvious. She was using this polite way to break off their relationship. She wanted *out*. And of course he could not blame her. Probably he should have insisted on severing the ties long ago. But he had been so certain he would get well—he still was!—and she had seemed always to share his expectancy. Well—so be it.

Fortunately then there were things to do. He wrote a letter.

"O.K. Let's call it finished. It's much better that way. I'm not going to tie you down. When—*if* I recover, it may be a long time. It's better that we end it now and not even think about the future."

Then, because emotions, emerging slowly from numbness, were beginning to prickle and throb and smart, he had his mother bring him numerous bags and boxes and bureau drawers, rummaged through them until he found all the things Alice had given him— books, ties, pens, even the silk scarf she had bought for him last Christmas—bundled them into a package, and had them sent to her, quickly, before he could repent of the impulse to hurt her as she was hurting him.

And then, inevitably, came full comprehension. He had the shades of his room drawn. He would not see callers. He refused food. Burrowing into darkness, he sank deeper and deeper, wallowing in despair and self-pity. Surely his was the greatest misfortune that could happen to anybody, not excepting death. At least death took the whole of you, didn't leave you half a person, the top half worthless without the other! Why had God let him live? But it wouldn't take long to remedy that. His life wasn't dependent on God. It was in his own hands, no farther away than his bedside table where his razor lay, untouched since the letter came. It would be easy, just a neat, simple slash at the artery in his leg, and the irony was that he wouldn't even feel it! If he wanted to punish her, what better way than to drive her to remorse? But, no, how much more perfect a punishment to live and get well, to run again, to win, perhaps even go to the Olympics, and then to reject as he had been rejected! Both thoughts left him sick with revulsion. As if he wanted to punish anybody—or could! He was the one being punished—and for what? What had he done to deserve this greatest misfortune that could happen to anyone? And why had God let him live? . . .

Around and around went the wheel of self-torture, dragging, lacerating. But after three days in this shadow world he emerged, had the shades raised, ate the food brought to him, and again received visitors. Not that he experienced any spiritual resurrection! He merely came to the conclusion that such indulgence of self-pity didn't do him or anybody else a particle of good. Instead, it was bringing immeasurable hurt to the two people who were sacrificing everything for his welfare.

On July 4 Dr. Parker told him that he was ready to get up in a wheel chair. The family secured one at cost through a funeral home, a big wooden four-wheeled affair with a cane bottom and back and a reclining feature so he could lie down when he got tired.

Hope sprang anew. "When you get out in the sunshine," friends had told him, "then you will get well."

A whole new world opened, also a whole new set of problems. On his first time up the resurgence of blood to his limbs made him faint. He could sit up for only a minute. But soon he was able to do it for half an hour. He was dependent on others to dress him. New functional problems were presented for which no one in those days had even suggestions. He had to figure out the solutions himself—a large bottle, a rubber tube to provide bladder drainage, big and firm enough to keep from kinking or plugging, regulation of eating habits, and daily enemas to minimize the frequency of bowel accidents.

The conjunction of wasted flesh and hard cane seat soon caused dangerous pressure sores. Some sort of cushion was indicated. They tried a folded blanket. No good. Then a pillow. That also didn't help. Finally somebody suggested an air ring. Blown to capacity, it was hard as a cane seat. More pressure sores. They reduced the air. Finally he discovered that it would take two air rings at moderate pressure, plus a cushion beneath, to give adequate protection. Even this arrangement was not perfect. He was to be plagued by pressure sores the rest of his life.

Thanks to the iron castings, Dad was strong enough to lift him from bed to chair, but the chair was too heavy to be lowered down the three steps at the back door with him in it. At first Dad had to take the chair down, then carry Roger through the house, down the steps, and place him in the chair. The only solution was to build a ramp. Dad constructed one at the front door, too steep at first. Roger wanted to be able to wheel himself up and down. They finally built one elevated about one inch to the foot in length and found it successful.

Unable to get close enough to a table to eat from it, write, use a typewriter, and finding a board inadequate, Roger himself designed a desk made to slip on and off the arms of the chair. It was such an effective though crudely simple device that thirty-five years later he would still be using one of the same design.

Once in the wheel chair he was determined to live as normal a life as possible. His parents eagerly cooperated. With his father's help he traveled to summer ball games a half mile away, to church, to the movie theater a mile across town. Wheeling down the side aisle, he would slip over into a seat; then, to leave the aisle clear, Dad would pull the chair back out into the lobby. Of course there were set-backs, embarrassments, like the first time he went to a ball game and was talking with many eagerly welcoming friends when a terrific bowel accident caused a humiliating and chagrined retreat. But with grim determination he went back again to the next game.

Next he wanted to go for an automobile ride. The wheel chair would not fold, so Dad bought a rack for the back end of the car. He would lift Roger into the front seat, tie the wheel chair on the rack, and off they would go. One of the first places they traveled to was University Hospital. The doctors seemed surprised that he was still alive. They checked him again to see if the level of sensation had gone down. It had not. They made a few suggestions, advocated again that he exercise his joints to keep them from stiffening, that he use a board at the end of his bed at night to avoid drop foot and arrest the pressure sores beginning to form on his toes. They had no other help to give.

Others believed they had. One day Clifford Boyd, a track mate and friend at college, came to call on him.

"I wish you would see my father," he said earnestly. "He's performed some wonderful cures, even on people with broken legs."

"What kind of doctor is he?" asked Roger.

"He isn't exactly a doctor. He—I suppose he's what they call a faith healer. But I could give you the names of lots of people he's helped."

Roger was excited. Suppose this was the answer to his question: Why had God let this happen to him? Suppose it was so a miracle could be performed! Then if he were really cured, he could maybe run again right away, perhaps even in time for the Olympics. And what an advertisement that would be for religion! He told his father.

"O.K. Sounds like a bit of hogwash. But—I'd try anything."

Dad drove him up to Ithaca the next Monday. Mr. Boyd was a modest, kindly man who took no personal credit for anything he had done. He said God had given him the power to tell what was the matter with anybody just by putting his hands on the patient and using the Bible. "But you must believe, son, believe God can heal you." He laid his hands on Roger and prayed.

Roger tried to do his part. He closed his eyes and told himself over and over, "I can walk, I can walk." He strained with every nerve impulse in his brain to lift his legs, first one, then the other. Nothing happened.

"Oh, well, better luck next time—maybe," Dad encouraged.

He took Roger to Ithaca on four succeeding Mondays, often driving the forty miles and back after work. Then he balked.

"It don't look to me as if it was doing one blamed bit of good." For James Arnett it was mild language, but Roger had not heard his father utter a word of profanity since the accident. That *was* a miracle. "And I'm not going to take you eighty miles after work on a wild-goose chase."

But he spared no time or energy taking him much farther distances on other expeditions. That summer he bundled Roger into the car, tied on the wheel chair, stuffed the air mattress, tent, and cots into the back, and took him up north camping. Roger was almost as comfortable as in his own bed, and exuberantly happy. He was *doing some of the things he used to do.* True, he was unable to get into a boat, but they found a place where he could sit in his wheel chair and fish from the bank.

The accident had not killed his interest in sports. That fall he attended some of the track meets and without any feeling of bitterness watched his old teammates run. The trips usually meant that Dad must take the day off and travel at least 150 miles, but he did so without a word of complaint.

The *College News* commented: "A fractured spine has not killed the interest in cross-country running of Roger Arnett, perhaps the best distance runner ever developed at Normal. Arnett attended some of the cross-country meets sitting on the side lines in an automobile. He was on hand for the National AAU cross-country run last Saturday and was among the first to congratulate Clark Chamberlain of Michigan State, the winner. Last year Arnett took part in the same race placing well among the leaders."

He was without bitterness, yes, but hardly without envy. This was the biggest race of the year. It would have been his *chance,* and he believed—*knew*—he could have at last beaten Chamberlain. It took all the guts he possessed to smile and pump his old rival's hand.

Winter brought new problems. Roger still wanted to get out-of-doors. But how was he to know when his legs got cold? They might be frozen, and he would be as unaware as if they were a couple of fence posts. His mother designed a pair of heavy wool leggings to cover his feet and legs completely. But still he was extremely cautious. Everything depended on his own ingenuity, on experimentation by trial and error. And error might well be fatal. There was no one to give aid or suggestions. For this was 1931, with little knowledge of medical procedure and less of rehabilitation techniques to cope with problems of paraplegia.

Roger found this out increasingly when in December he became severely ill with pressure sores and serious bladder and kidney infections. Dr. Parker tried everything and said finally, "Well, there just isn't anything I can do. You'd better go back to Ann Arbor."

Three days before Christmas Roger entered University Hospital, to remain there for the next six months.

4

It was a new era in Roger's life. Once the infections were cleared up by the use of stronger irrigation solutions, the doctors decided that he should be put in the bone and joint department. To clear up the pressure sores he was put on a Strycker frame, an ingenious device made in two separate parts, enabling the patient to lie sometimes on the back, sometimes on the face. Roger was in a ward with about twenty patients. Every so often the orderlies would come and turn him. If he was lying on his face, on the anterior frame, they would place the other frame on top of him, strap the two together, then turn him over. The frames, simple structures of plain rods covered with muslin and cotton, were a great improvement over a bed. Being on his face half the time, he had freedom of hand motion, so he could read and, under the tutelage of a therapist, do handwork. He passed the time making pocketbooks out of leather, carving, weaving reed trays, as well as reading and writing.

It was here that he met Orville Mitchell. Orville also had attended Michigan State Normal but had been out teaching for several years. About two months after Roger's accident he and a girl friend had been driving to Toledo with two other couples after a jolly party. Getting out of the car on the way, Orville, stupefied by liquor, had fallen on his head and been knocked unconscious. His friends had lifted him, put him back in the car in a sitting position, and rushed him to a hospital. Now paralyzed from the neck down, he could do nothing except talk. Immediately he and Roger developed bonds of friendship. Both were from the same college, both had prepared for teaching careers. And both fully expected to recover. Also both had a penchant for fun, and they kept the ward alive. Mitch was a prolific storyteller, and each night he and others would spend hours spinning yarns. They manufactured balls from paper fastened with adhesive, and threw them from bed to bed. Those able to get up would rescue the ball when it misfired. One time a boy operated on for appendicitis was picking it up, and the lone nurse on duty, surprising him, exclaimed in despair, "I can't do a thing with them!"

But Mitch had a way with women, including nurses, and was able to get almost anything he wanted. Although late-night snacks were forbidden, he persuaded a midnight nurse to bring him each night a large onion sandwich. Roger soon learned to relish them also. However, Mitch's attraction for women got him into trouble. Having two girl friends, he tried to arrange it so one would come to visit him on Saturday, the other on Sunday. But occasionally their visits coincided, and the ward derived great glee from poor Orville's sufferings while the two girls glared at each other across his bed.

He and Roger also shared a fondness for dancing. The Women's League of the university, only a block away, held a dance every Friday night. When the windows were open the patients could hear the dance music. On one night in particular Roger was close to a window and enjoying the music, but Mitch was out of range. Roger inched his bed over to where he could reach Mitch's and was pulling it closer to the window when there was a great splash. Mitch, who was a prolific water drinker and always slept on his face, had a bedpan elevated on a block under his Strycker frame! Meekly Roger watched the patient orderly remove Mitch from his bed, put him on a stretcher, Strycker frame and all, change the bed, and mop up the floor.

Hope flared afresh as the doctors reevaluated Roger's condition, examined his charts, asked many questions, gave him endless tests with pinpricks. If they really believed there was no hope, would they bother with so much detail?

One day Coach Olds and Dean Brown came over to visit him from the college. Roger greeted them gaily from his bed and asked for all the athletic news.

"I'm getting along fine," he told them. "For quite a while now one of my toes has been moving. I may be up around again sooner than some people think!"

The two men turned their heads away and left very quickly. Not until long afterward did Roger understand that they were too over-come with emotion to face him.

As soon as he arrived in the hospital that December he was started on physiotherapy, which included being fitted to leg and back braces. The entire staff of the Department of Physical Medicine of the University of Michigan consisted of two men, Dr. Beslock and Mr. Terry. Neither was a trained physiotherapist. But both were good-humored, creative, and intensely interested in people. Every afternoon, five days a week, they would come to the ward and take Roger and Mitch down to the physiotherapy department, one small room containing a big bathtub. Hard to believe then that this bathtub was the first step in a program which during the next ten years would make University Hospital one of the world's foremost pioneers in rehabilitation for paraplegics! At that time most hospitals wouldn't have had even the bathtub! There the two patients would soak in a salt solution for a quarter to half an hour.

"Rub-a-dub-dub, two men in a tub," Terry would improvise gaily.

Then Roger would practice walking. It was a sorry experiment, and he hated it. Slowly, teeth gritted, shoulders and face dripping sweat—he had found to his discomfort that he could not perspire below the accident level—inch by painful inch he would drag himself along with the help of crutches. Every inch, it seemed, took as much energy and will power as a lap of the gym had once done.

"Fine, fine!" Terry would encourage him. "Now just a little farther, all with the shoulders, you know. Bravo! That time you went all of six feet! Yes, and in four minutes plus. I was timing you."

Roger's grin was crooked. Six feet in four minutes plus! Just the time it had taken him to run a mile!

By the end of five months he was able to walk—no, not walk—move, *crawl*, perhaps half a block on crutches. Having done everything possible for him, the hospital decided to send him home.

"Be sure and practice your walking," urged Terry, "and get up every day. You've really made wonderful progress. I'm proud of you."

Roger was grateful to him, but less for instruction in walking than in woodcarving and playing chess. Perhaps it was stubbornness, but he failed to see the advantage of crawling when he could get around so much faster and more easily in a wheel chair. The doubtful dignity of passing as *homo erectus* seemed scarcely worth the loss in efficiency. Time was to vindicate his opinion. Many paraplegics who learned to walk, he later discovered, developed sores on their feet. One whom he came to know well and who developed skill in walking returned to his wheel chair with both legs amputated.

The braces were an improvement, however, not only providing rigidity but serving as anchors for the big bottle which was his constant accompaniment.

His parents welcomed him eagerly, extra work, financial burden, and all. One big improvement had been made in his absence. In January Vivian had bought a little black velvet bag with rhinestones at one of the local stores. A numbered ticket had come with it. She had won an electric washing machine, with wringers attached. It sat in a corner of the dining room, carefully protected when not in use by a white-painted plywood cover which Mother called the "elephant," her pride almost exceeding the more practical enjoyment of its possession. It made the excessive washings seem almost like child's play.

Roger came home on his Strycker frame, and it was placed on his high hospital bed in the living room. At night he slept on it lying on his back. In the daytime, when not in the wheel chair, he used the anterior frame, lying on his face. The thought still possessed him, haunted him as he lay awake at night, that his inability to walk might be all in his mind. Time and again he would dream he was running a race, feel the steady pumping of his legs, then waken to lie sweating and straining, certain that if he could only *will* hard enough, think the right thoughts, he could stir his limbs into motion. One night, when he wakened from such a dream, he found himself on the floor. Instantly his parents came running.

"What's the matter? What happened, son?"

Dazed, Roger looked up into their frightened faces. "I—I don't know. I—guess I must have been walking in my sleep."

"Walking!"

"No, of course not. I—just fell somehow."

"Are you hurt?"

No, he was not hurt. Even though he had fallen from the frame, six inches higher than the hospital bed, he was unhurt. In body, that is.

His father lifted him and put him back on the bed. There was still a wild hope in his eyes. "But—you must have moved your legs, son."

Roger shook his head. "No. Just strong shoulders and arms. Like yours."

He knew what had happened. Often a sleepwalker in childhood and youth, he had tried to do the same thing now. And if ever a person could walk without mental inhibition, surely it would be in his sleep! So—there went the hope that it might be all in his mind.

Dad was out of work that summer, and, since they could live as cheaply camping as at home, they packed up and went to Lake Leelanau, a beautiful long, clear lake 200 miles away in the northwest corner of the lower peninsula.

"I'd like to go swimming," Roger said one day.

His parents always encouraged him to make new ventures, so one afternoon, when the lake was perfectly calm, they helped him put on his bathing trunks, and Dad picked him up and laid him in the water. Paddling carefully out until he was sure his legs could suffer no damage from the lake bottom, he discovered that, though the breast stroke he had previously used was unpractical for one unable to kick, he could swim easily and normally on his back. It was a glorious feeling! So elated that he almost lost contact with the world, he swam out and out, until his mother became panicky and called to Dad, who jumped in the canoe and hastily paddled out.

"Far enough," he cautioned. "Better turn around and go back."

Only then did Roger realize what he was doing. After that he was more careful.

The thing he missed most was boating. Even he admitted that a canoe was a hazard for a person with heavy braces. That fall Roger came across plans for a combination sail and motorboat, fifteen and a half feet long and small enough for oars. Mother had a nephew, Herbert Wood, in Cleveland, a carpenter who had built sailboats. He agreed to build it if they would furnish the materials. Dad was working again spasmodically, so they managed to scrape together the necessary seventy-five dollars. It was something to look forward to during the long fall and winter.

Gradually his world widened. He was asked to conduct the Methodist orchestra again. Here was one activity where a wheel chair was no liability. Most of the participants were seated, like himself. It was one of the things he had done before and could do now equally well. Sometimes, especially in familiar associations with old friends, he could almost forget that things were not as they were. Then something would happen, perhaps a word or a gesture, as on one night in December. . . .

A young woman whom he used to date occasionally in high school came to call, then asked if he wouldn't like to go for a ride. The night was bitterly cold, but his mother bundled him up, his father carried him out to the car, and they started out. It was a pleasant ride, full of high-school reminiscences and the bantering give and take which had always characterized their relationship. Roger felt almost a man again. At least a young woman found him attractive enough to seek out and enjoy his company. He was sorry when the ride was over and they sat waiting for his father to come out after him. Although there had been little of romance in their relationship, just as a gesture of friendship and gratitude Roger had often put his arm about her briefly after a date. He reached out to do so now, and instinctively she recoiled. He said nothing, pretended not to notice, but the coldness which enveloped him as his father lifted him from the car was not all from the bitter December night. So she had taken him to ride out of pity, not because she wanted his companionship!

During that winter and spring he felt a growing sense of futility and frustration. Small satisfactions and triumphs had little meaning: the young schoolteacher who seemed to enjoy coming to play chess with him, the first girl he had found who didn't shy away from his company; the spring concert of his orchestra combined with the church choir, for which he had made a special arrangement of "Onward, Christian Soldiers." Even the arrival of the sailboat and the vacation in July at Lake Leelanau brought enjoyment but not the sense of fulfillment he had expected. He was like a runner crouched at the starting line all set for a race—life? death? who knew what?—waiting for a gun that never went off.

And then one day he was sitting out in the yard watching his mother hang clothes. Somehow she managed to make poetry, beauty, out of the commonest, even the ugliest things. It had always been so: the birds she used to make out of seed pods, feathers, and pine cones; the Christmas turned into golden magic merely by an orange in one's stocking; the songs as they rode along in the rattling old car; the way she stooped, separated a sheet from a tangled wet mound, mated its corners, fitted it into smoothness and straightness with a few deft motions, and then, arms stretched high and wide,

61

flung its pure whiteness against the blue of the sky, as if in triumphant climax of an act of worship.

It was like her to have planted morning-glories at the foot of one of the clothes posts, and like flowers to have bloomed their best for her. They had climbed up the rough old post, crept along its weather-beaten arms, and turned it into a living cross of heavenly blue.

But it was at the other post that Roger found himself staring, ugly, bare, gaunt, nothing but two pieces of dead wood. Like a pair of useless legs.

And then suddenly he knew. Perhaps he had known for a long time but had not been willing to face it. Now suddenly he did face it, met it head on.

This is it. I'm not going to be able to walk again. Not ever.

He could take his choice, be one or the other of the two posts, remain just dead wood, or plant something which might give at least a semblance of life. But what? Not morning-glories. They were beautiful but would hardly earn a man a living. Perhaps—pole beans?

There was a Mr. Whitehead who owned several drugstores in Owosso and who was known to have helped crippled children. Roger had known him a long time. The family had bought drugs at his store. Roger called him and made an appointment. One evening his father drove him over to Mr. Whitehead's house, and the druggist came out and talked with him.

"I thought you might be able to give me some advice," Roger told him. "I want to find something to do, something to earn a living."

Mr. Whitehead nodded approvingly. "What would you like to do?"

"That's just the trouble. I don't know. All I know is I have to do something. I can't go on like this, just a stick of—of dead wood."

The other man considered. "How about writing?" he suggested. "With your education, you ought to be able to do that."

"No!" Roger's reaction was violent with distaste. He remembered his horror of English composition. "Anything but that."

"Well," said Mr. Whitehead after more thought, "it seems to me the first thing you've got to do is go back to college and finish up your work."

"Go back—" Roger gasped. "B-but—have you forgotten? I'm paralyzed!"

The businessman's eyes were shrewdly appraising. "Then you don't think you could do it?" he asked bluntly.

Roger's head swam. "I—I don't know. I'd—never thought of it. Anyway, I couldn't." He discarded the idea almost with relief. "I haven't any money."

"I think that could be arranged," said Mr. Whitehead.

They talked for an hour. Roger went home dazed, elated, and— terrified. He felt like a young bird about to be pushed out of a comfortable nest, with one difference: he had no wings to fly. How could he possibly take care of himself, without parents or nurses? Who would do his excessive washings? turn him on his bed? nurse him when he had fever? help him up and down curbs and up the stairs into classrooms? check every inch of his body every day to detect the slightest redness or abrasion, every thread of his clothes for the tiniest piece of metal—pin, hook, or eye—which might cause a pressure sore? *Who*—

But elation banished terror. To go back to college, get his degree, perhaps even teach! And why not? He had learned to do other difficult things, largely through his own ingenuity and the trial-and-error method. Here was a chance to plant some seeds to cover up the dead wood, and who knew? There might even be some morning-glories mixed with the pole beans!

One by one the problems were solved. First the finances. The Vocational Rehabilitation Department of the state was contacted. Yes, they did help the handicapped get better education, but only if a patient was a feasible candidate. A paraplegic was not. But they would agree to take care of tuition and the cost of books. These were but minor expenses. Board, room, medication—these made the dismaying total. But Mr. Whitehead took the matter up with his Rotary Club. It was arranged that they would send Roger fifty dollars a month as long as he was in school. He wrote to Ypsilanti, and the college authorities agreed to do everything possible to help.

Next came board and room. Suppressing their anxiety and reluctance, his parents drove him down to Ypsilanti before school opened.

"We'll never find the right place," worried his mother, almost hopefully. "Ground floor, wide enough doors, board with room, and—and some woman who wouldn't mind seeing after you a little!"

But they did. Mrs. Tabor ran a rooming house for men only a block from the college. Yes, she did have one room on the ground floor which she used herself, but she would willingly move to the third floor. She would be glad to let him eat with the family. And—yes, she *was* the sort of person who wouldn't mind seeing after him a little. They could tell that just by the warmth of her motherly face and the look of keen interest in her eyes.

A ramp was built to the Tabors' back door. The first time Roger used it he tried it alone. Since it was too steep to go down front-ward, he went down backward, gaining momentum faster than he had expected. Unable to stop at the end, he tipped over on his back. Mrs. Tabor was petrified. Calling some of the other lodgers, she came running, and together they helped him back into the chair. After that he waited for assistance in going up and down.

At the college there were three steps just inside the main building, so the authorities built a ramp along one end of the large hallway. One of his classes was on the second floor of the science building, but arrangements were made for Louie, the janitor, to meet him there each day at class time and take him up on the hand-operated dummy elevator, used to haul equipment between floors.

They brought his hospital bed from home, with the posterior section of the Strycker frame. Since he would be in his wheel chair all the time he was up, there would be no occasion to lie on his face. The rod was fastened above his bed so he could get himself in and out. By meticulous planning and prearranging each night, he could perform all necessary procedures without help: morning enema, bladder irrigation, even dressing himself.

There were problems, of course. The door into the adjoining bathroom was too small to admit the big front wheels of his clumsy old wheel chair. He had to back in as far as possible, then reach around the high chair back to use the facilities. One night, getting up about two o'clock, he was reaching backward to wash his hands when the chair overturned, and he found himself lying, feet in the air, head and shoulders flat on the floor. It was a real crisis. After yielding for some moments to panic, he saw some humor in the situation and began to laugh. A ridiculous predicament, but he would find himself in many worse ones, and he must learn to get out of them *without help*. Grimly he struggled to extricate himself. How he managed it he never quite knew—probably by reaching the doorframe and pulling—but somehow he righted the chair.

When the weather was good, there was no difficulty in getting to school, but snow and ice and sleet brought problems. The other fellows in the house were always glad to give him a push when necessary. They also saw to it that he attended all the sporting events. Kenneth Yeoman, the son of a Methodist minister, was particularly helpful.

"Roger, come to the show with us," they urged one night.

"Oh, no, I couldn't. It would be too hard on everybody."

"Oh, come on. We'll take you."

And they did, even carrying him up a long flight of stairs into the balcony.

Always his goal in returning to college was to become a teacher. Realizing that conventional teaching might present problems, he conceived another idea. Why not become a teacher to the handicapped? Who better for the job than one who so completely understood their problems? Michigan State Normal College had at that time one of the leading departments of special education in the country. Full of enthusiasm, Roger went to the head of the department and suggested the possibility.

"Oh, my, no!" The professor looked shocked. "That would be impossible. One handicapped person wouldn't be allowed to teach another. It's one of the rules."

Roger was dumfounded by the logic. It seemed like telling somebody he couldn't be an optometrist because he wore eyeglasses. And to his further amazement and dismay no one in the college had anything practical to suggest. They were all glad to have him back, thought it was wonderful for him to show such enterprise and bravery, gave him all kinds of verbal encouragement to develop his mind and continue his education, but could think of nothing useful for him to do with either of them. Nor had they done so at the hospital. Oh, he could weave baskets, do woodcarving, make pocketbooks, things that would make any red-blooded man say, *So what!* Nobody had ever suggested any *work* except Mr. Whitehead, who had mentioned writing.

But he persisted doggedly with his studies and graduated from college in late March, 1934, with a record for the two terms of five A's, four B's, and one D (in Physical Training). There were no graduation exercises, no fanfare. He was simply handed his B.S. degree diploma and his life certificate for teaching. Only one thing made the event unusual. The registrar gave him a letter he had received complimenting Roger on completing his education and graduating from college. It was signed by Franklin D. Roosevelt, President of the United States.

The second practical suggestion of a useful occupation came from his long-time friend, the superintendent of schools for Owosso. Roger went to him immediately after his graduation, presented his diploma and life certificate, and asked him about a teaching position.

"You know what I would advise?" said Mr. Willman, regarding him with fatherly solicitude. "Why not open an insurance office downtown?"

"But I'm trained to teach," protested Roger, "not to sell insurance."

The superintendent hemmed and hawed. He was sorry, but there just wasn't any opening that fall in Owosso for a science teacher.

"I could teach other subjects, even a grade. I've had an all-round teacher's training."

Well—Mr. Willman was sorry—but, as a matter of fact, there wasn't any vacancy anywhere.

"And I suppose there never will be," Roger returned quietly. "For me, that is."

Well—surely Roger must realize the difficulties—

"You mean because I'm a cripple, a paraplegic" said Roger frankly.

The superintendent flushed, averted his eyes, toyed with his fountain pen. Queer, thought Roger, how people always tried to avoid mentioning your handicap! They would talk all around it, indicate that they were conscious of it by every nuance of word and gesture, yet be shocked and embarrassed if you mentioned it, especially if you called it by name.

"A man doesn't teach with his legs, you know," he continued while the other man cleared his throat and hesitated. "He uses his hands, his voice, and, most of all, his mind. Am I lacking in any of those qualifications?"

"Oh, no, no, no!" Once the superintendent had found his voice, words came with a rush. "Nobody knows your mental ability better than I. You had a splendid record in high school, and I know your grades in college. I hope you understand that we have nothing against you personally. We'd like nothing better than to help you"—he flushed again—"that is, to give you a chance—I mean—"

"I understand," said Roger. "Please don't be embarrassed about having to refuse. I do understand perfectly."

So teaching was out. Roger consulted with Mr. Whitehead, who, knowing his interests, suggested chemistry work in a laboratory. Together they contacted the Parke-Davis Company in Detroit and the Dow Chemical Company at Midland, knowing that both used laboratory technicians, but there was no opening.

"Well," said Whitehead at last, "it may not be much to start on, but I think we can get you a job in the welfare department."

Being chairman of the commission and well acquainted with officials in the department, he proposed that his young protégé be hired as a clerk, and Roger accepted the position with alacrity. A job was a job, even if it was a lowly one which paid only twelve dollars a week. He began work in the bookkeeping department, checking over invoices, filing, performing other simple directives.

His father took him to work each day, lifting him in and out of the car; then driving while Roger held the heavy wheel chair on the side. Thank God for strong arm and shoulder muscles that hard work in a foundry had developed! They would prove a big asset the rest of his life. Soon after starting work Roger made an important discovery. One day he wheeled himself out to the car ahead of his father. He was sitting beside it looking in when the thought dawned, "Why, I can get into the car myself!" No sooner thought than done. Reaching his right hand on the doorframe and placing his left on the seat cushion, he could swing himself into the seat with a minimum of risk and difficulty. A small achievement, it would seem, but for the paraplegic a tremendous discovery! For it was another step to independence. Again thanks for strong arms!

His work in the office was congenial and satisfying. Although he was starting at the very bottom with almost menial tasks, he sensed no feelings of patronage or inequality among the fifteen or so employees. Perhaps there was more of friendliness, less of dog-eat-dog competition, among workers in these depression years. Even Mr. Donovan, the director, was more comrade than boss.

"You should get out in the air more, Roger," he said one sunshiny spring noon, and insisted on taking him out-of-doors and pushing him around the block.

Although his fellow workers seldom mentioned his disability, their silence seemed due less to embarrassment than to a sense of its unimportance. Always before whatever he attempted had ended in frustration: music at Northwestern, track, teaching, romance, teaching the disabled, a job in chemistry. Life seemed to thwart him in everything. Here, for the first time, he felt at ease, unpressured, accepted for what he had to offer, even capable of increasing success.

Three weeks after starting work he came to a decision. He would make office work a career. And since he was starting at the bottom as a clerk, so he would have to start at the elementary level to get a business education. He must become proficient in typing, study shorthand and bookkeeping.

"I'll be glad to teach you typing and shorthand," said Mrs. Weatherby, head of the high-school commercial department, when Roger consulted her. "And if you want bookkeeping, I would recommend Miss LaVerna Bowen. She's a very capable teacher, and she has a car. I'll give you her address if you wish."

Roger's father drove him that evening to the teacher's apartment, and she came out and talked with him. Yes, she knew very well who he was. One couldn't have taught in the Owosso High School for six years and not heard of Roger Arnett. And, yes, she thought it would be possible for her to come to his house and teach him bookkeeping, although the idea of teaching a college graduate was rather frightening. And, if it was satisfactory to him, she would plan to come to his house on Tuesdays and Thursdays in the evening.

"Sounded as if she knew her business," remarked Dad as they drove home. "And not a bad looker, either. Didn't you think so?"

"Yes," said Roger, finding the agreement wholly inadequate to express his feelings. Not a bad looker, indeed! She was beautiful! His paralysis had by no means dimmed his appreciation of the opposite sex! But the picture he took with him was not so much of a daintily slight figure, blond hair, blue eyes, and a warm but shy smile. It was of a game little person walking toward the car at a slightly awkward, unbalanced gait, slender shoulders straight and erect, obviously making the best of what must have been a long-time handicap. The sight had for some reason brought to his senses a rush of tender protectiveness. The irony of it twisted his lips. Protectiveness! For a girl who walked with a slight limp from a man who couldn't walk at all! Nevertheless, all that evening a warmth of anticipation possessed him, as if fortune, having capriciously frowned on him time after time, might possibly be getting ready to smile.

It just happened to be April 30, the day before his twenty-sixth birthday.

5

It happened the summer she was six. It was the same summer that Grandfather Bowen, who lived with them, had said, "It's time LaVerna saw a circus." They had driven by horse and buggy to Ashley, Michigan, taken a train to Alma, where the Ringling Brothers had set up their tents, spent the day there, then returned to the farm near Ithaca. It had been by far the most exciting day in LaVerna Bowen's life, except possibly the one a few months earlier when she had wakened to find she had a new baby sister, Vivian.

It began on a Monday morning, when her mother was washing. Not feeling well, she would lie down on the bed and go to sleep. Then when she wanted to get up she would slide to the floor. After taking hold of the bedpost and pulling with all her might, she would cry for her mother, who would stop her washing, pick her up, and put her on her feet; then off the child would go. But if she sat down in her rocking chair and rocked, when she moved forward her legs would not come. Soon she became delirious. Frantic with worry, her mother called the doctor, but by the time he arrived the delirium had passed.

"Walk across the floor for me, will you, LaVerna?" he asked. Then when she did, "That's fine, now you can come back."

But when she tried to turn around, she fell to the floor.

There followed long weeks and months in bed, with what the doctor called typhoid. Even a pillow under her head hurt. She was constantly in pain. But it was an equally painful ordeal for her mother, with the agonizing worry, a small baby to tend, a fretful and demanding child, and no modern conveniences, not even water in the house. One day she read in the paper about an epidemic in New York City, and she said to the doctor, "Could LaVerna have had anything like this 'infantile paralysis'?"

"Yes, Mrs. Bowen," he said gravely. "I believe that's just what she's had."

Out of bed for the first time in November, she was at first unable to stand, much less walk, but finally, by hanging on to the furniture and moving from one piece to another, then balancing by the wall, she could move about the house. The doctor had told her father it might help to massage her right leg for twenty minutes a day.

"If twenty minutes would be good," her father had decided, "an hour would be better." So as soon as the fever subsided and all winter long he massaged the limb an hour at a time, three times a day. The doctor was amazed when she finally did walk again and always said when he saw her afterward, "You owe the fact that you can walk to your father."

Not that she could walk normally. She never would. It tore her mother's heart to see her struggle over the rough ground and grass, constantly falling. A curious child, it seemed that she was always being chased by animals in the farm barnyard—two big geese when she tried to pick up a gosling, a snorting horse when she wanted to pat its colt, a black cow when cattle were being driven through the yard. Always her parents arrived in time to protect her, but the experiences haunted her sleep even into adulthood. She would dream of being chased by black cows and horses, of being down on her knees and unable to get up. Doors never stopped them. Once in her dreams a horse came into the house and followed her up the stairway.

The next fall, when she started school, her father had to stop his farm work, hitch the horse to a buggy, and drive her twice a day a mile and a half. It so interfered with his work that he decided to move the family to Ithaca, about twenty miles away, where for two years he drove a delivery wagon, then, having taken a civil-service examination, became a mail carrier.

Now LaVerna could walk to school. She found for the first time that she could not walk as fast as other children. Although she soon found friends who were willing to wait for her, there was no defense from the small boys who tried to imitate her ungainly way of walking. It had never occurred to her before how different she must look. All that had concerned her was keeping on her feet, moving. Now she realized for the first time that she had something to be ashamed of. In school she could forget her handicap, for she was a good student, had learned to read when she was three. Only when she started to go home did she become timid and self-conscious.

Once during her early childhood she believed a miracle was going to happen. Her parents were very religious people and involved in many church activities. One night they were entertaining in their home a missionary who had spoken in their church. LaVerna sat listening as the adults talked, gathered about the dining table. The missionary had a dramatic story to tell. While working in her Oriental mission station she had developed symptoms of leprosy. LaVerna had heard the word, read about it in the Bible. The very sound of it sent shivers running up and down her spine.

"But I prayed," continued the missionary, her face glowing with more light than could possibly come from the kerosene lamp on the table. "I knelt on the steps of our little church there in the jungle and asked God to remove the leprosy. And—I was instantly healed."

LaVerna found it hard to go to sleep that night. She was thinking about the missionary rising from her knees the way Naaman had come up out of the river Jordan pure and clean as a little child. Then, suddenly, the thought came, "If she could do it, I could, too!" It was hard for her to kneel and get up again, so her parents had told her that God could hear her prayers just as well after she got into bed. She closed her eyes so tightly that the lids hurt.

"Please make me well again, God," she prayed. "Make me walk the way I used to."

It did not occur to her to doubt that her prayer would be answered. She got out of bed fully expecting to run across the room with all the vigor and zest of her pre-sickness days. When she found that nothing was changed, she was more dumfounded than disappointed. The incident did not destroy her faith, merely taught her at an earlier age than usual that God was not Santa Claus.

She developed compensations. An intense perfectionist, she became an ardent and skillful croquet player. Finding that her cousin was taking piano lessons, she practiced with fierce concentration at the wheezy old organ which was their sole musical asset. Watching her struggle with the creaking foot bellows, Grandfather Bowen, who was visiting, ran his fingers through his shock of white hair, which made him look a trifle taller than his diminutive five feet, and his blue eyes brightened. Having cleared eighty acres and built a set of farm buildings all with his own hands, he admired courage and persistence. After he returned home LaVerna received a card, saying, "Have your dad watch the freight office. I'm sending you a little package." But why on earth by freight, they all wondered. The "little package" proved to be a piano.

Her father, William Bowen, missed the soil. Since mail carriers drove horses in the winter, cars in summer, the pair of horses must stay idle all summer, their feed a useless expense. So when LaVerna was thirteen he bought a farm about a mile out of Ithaca. Now in the summertime he could farm in the afternoons. LaVerna would ride to school with him in the morning when he went to the post office. Then she would walk home the mile and a half in the afternoon, except in winter when, driving horses, her father would finish his mail route about the time school let out.

LaVerna was intensely proud of her father. Diffident and stage-shy herself, she admired his ease and self-confidence, whether singing in the choir, acting as Sunday-school superintendent, or giving dramatic readings in public. Fortunately she did not know when he was going to perform and never heard him practice, for she suffered agonies whenever he appeared on the stage. But although she shared her mother's shyness, in many ways she was the embodiment of her father—short, compact body, vivid blue eyes, quick gestures, haste to get things done—while Vivian, a bit plump, calm, always smiling, was more like their mother.

High school contributed little to LaVerna's social ease. All the parties seemed to be dances. Again she compensated, this time by excellence in scholarship, but its rewards were bitter, for the announcement that she was to be salutatorian of her graduating class came on the day she returned to school after her mother's funeral. It seemed a hollow victory, without her there to know about it. She was sixteen, her sister Vivian eleven. The shock of loss was somewhat lessened by their beloved Aunt Eunice, their father's older sister, who gave up her good position in Toledo to come and live with them for a year.

Since she had never expected to go to college, LaVerna had taken a commercial course. But the school superintendent convinced her father that she should have further education. That fall she entered Central Michigan Normal School at Mt. Pleasant, thirty miles from home.

She hated to miss classes when her father wrote that he had been advised to take her to a polio specialist from Grand Rapids who was holding a clinic in Ithaca. The dean of women looked skeptical when she could not even tell the name of the doctor but finally gave her permission to go. When the specialist examined her, both her father and her own doctor were present. To her amazement it was found that one of her legs was two inches shorter than the other.

"But her shoulders are even," protested the family doctor. "How could they be with two inches difference?"

"By will power," answered the specialist with a grim smile.

Extensive surgery was indicated. As soon as school was over that year she went into the hospital for three weeks. The ankle was stiffened. Much dead bone was removed. A wedge was put in the back of her knee in a cast and every day or two made larger until a two-inch wedge was introduced. It was an excruciatingly painful process. Aunt Eunice came to Detroit to take her home in a wheel chair. The last of August she returned to Detroit to have the cast removed.

"Now, LaVerna," said the doctor, "you'd better limber up that ankle because you've got to walk across the room and back before you leave." She tried to exercise the ankle until he returned. "All right," he said, taking her arm. "Let's go."

She did it, but they were the most agonizing steps she had ever taken. When she had finished, the doctor said, "LaVerna, I have told every one of my patients to do that. You are the first one who ever did it."

It had no more occurred to her that she could get out of doing it than when she was a child and her father had wakened her in the middle of the night, telling her to go outdoors and pick up the toys he had previously told her to put away.

Two days later she went back to college, leaving her crutches behind. Although she lived just a block from the campus, it took her twenty minutes to walk it. When snow came, its unevenness made every step painful. But she finished the semester and made up the courses missed in the summer session.

During her third year in college her father remarried. Her step-mother also had two daughters. Pauline was near Vivian's age. Dorothy, who had just finished high school, came to Mt. Pleasant and became LaVerna's roommate. Now her father had four girls to educate instead of two. That summer he gave her $300. "This is for your final year. It's all I can spare." By working in the college cafeteria as check girl—a task which she learned to execute with incredible rapidity—she managed to defray the cost of books, tuition, clothes, and graduation.

But in that last year there came a chilling disappointment. Her critic teacher advised her to give up the idea of teaching. Physical frailty plus the difficulties of a handicap, she felt, would create impossible problems of discipline. LaVerna's dismay changed quickly to stubborn determination. After the sacrifices her father had made for four years so that she might become a teacher, she was not going to announce that she wouldn't even attempt it. Her mother and three aunts and an uncle had been teachers. She had had no other goal since deciding she was going to college. And she was certainly not going to give it up without trying.

She took the first job offered her, at Custer, a little town of three hundred, near the eastern coast of Lake Michigan. The high school had only seventy-five students, with three teachers: the superintendent, a young man who had once been in her trigonometry class, herself, and one other. A commercial course was just being initiated, which pleased LaVerna. A new course, a new teacher! This was ideal, because now she could make up her mind whether she wanted to teach math or commercial subjects. The pay was small. The snow was deep from fall to spring. A visit home meant an all-day trip. But she loved both the work and the community. She knew every student not only by name but by personal traits and problems. She played the old reed organ for church services, taught a Sunday-school class of high-school students, was active in the PTA.

The first year she was in Custer, when the inspector came from the University of Michigan, the superintendent was gone for the day. As principal LaVerna had to handle the situation. "I've never had this experience before," she told him frankly. "What do you expect of me?" He told her exactly what he wanted.

The next year when a Professor Rich came, also from the university, she was grateful that the superintendent was there but a bit chagrined when the inspector came and sat in her trigonometry class. "At least he can't be a math professor," she thought, "like the one last year!" It was the last class day before exams, and she was reviewing the entire course. She discussed every formula and process, and the class did remarkably well. Only once a boy made a mistake, and she thought, "I won't bother to correct him. The man won't know the difference." But *she* knew. She stopped and cor-

74

rected him. So sure was she that the inspector could not be a mathematician that she was perfectly relaxed.

When the class was almost over, the professor rose and went to the front of the room. "Miss Bowen," he said, "I teach trigonometry at the University of Michigan. And I've never had a class at the end of a semester that handled everything as well as this class has."

When later she applied for a position in the Owosso High School her superintendent told her, "In my letter of recommendation I told him what Professor Rich said, and that if he wanted verification he could write to Rich himself."

LaVerna was dumfounded. As if the professor could possibly remember her!

She went for an interview with Mr. Willman, superintendent of schools in Owosso. "I have written Professor Rich a letter," he told her. "If out of all the teachers that he inspected during the year he can remember you enough to recommend you, the job is yours." But he continued, "I have many other applications here from much more experienced teachers and frankly you look too small and shy to stand up to some of these bullies we've got here in school. I really don't believe you could handle them, do you?"

"Well," replied LaVerna, "I always have."

Professor Rich did remember her well, and she got the appointment.

But on her first teaching day in Owosso she discovered that she had never known the meaning of the word "bully." When she went home that noon she realized that if she had not taught before, she would give up then and there. But she knew the pupils were only testing her. If she could survive this first day, all would be well. It was. All her classes were in math, and she found them fascinating. She was always imaginative in her teaching. For instance, having found the usual methods of teaching positive and negative numbers cumbersome, she suddenly thought of an easier way.

"Have you played games in which you kept score?" she asked the class. Of course they had. "How did you designate it when you lost or went in the hole?" They drew a circle around the number. "Suppose you gained ten points and then lost fifteen, what was your score?" Of course they could tell immediately. "Then suppose we call the winnings positive, the losses negative." Before the period was over they were adding positive and negative numbers like professionals.

75

"And my brother told me how hard algebra was!" she heard one pupil say.

The friends she made in Owosso helped compensate for the void left by her father's remarriage. Although she liked and respected her stepmother, her father's house no longer seemed like home. For some years she had spent vacations with Aunt Eunice in Toledo. Now she became one of a close-knit little group of teachers. There were Margaret Finch and Treva Zinn, both in the math department, and Theresa Combellack, who taught English. After Treva married and moved to Detroit, LaVerna often went to visit her.

Then after a time her sister Vivian came to Owosso to attend the Business Institute, and the two took an apartment together, sharing it until Vivian married Eldred Waters and moved to his family homestead not far from Owosso. The next fall LaVcrna started sharing an apartment with an eighth-grade teacher, Letah Stewart, a happy arrangement which terminated only with the next major change in her life.

On March 8, 1931, she wrote in her diary: "Roger Arnett, a graduate of 1927, was in an accident yesterday, and his back was broken. He may never walk again."

LaVerna felt as if she knew Roger Arnett, although she had never seen him. During the last year his name had been on the lips of every high-school student in Owosso. Every time he won a race there had been headlines in the local newspaper.

"I can't remember walking any differently," she thought with poignant sympathy. "But here he has been a trackman and has known all that glory. How can he, a young man of only twenty-two, take it to never walk again!"

To her physical handicap she had long since learned to adjust. When she fell down, which was frequently, she picked herself up, usually with the help of friends more concerned than herself. She wore out pair after pair of gloves, skidding on them when trying to save herself from falling. After she bought a car and learned to drive it, a poor pair of legs became even less important.

Her handicap had never quelled the spirit of adventure. After a trip taken with Margaret and Theresa in the early summer of 1931, she went to visit Treva in Detroit. She was telling that she had just traveled 2,200 miles at an expense for car of only thirty-one dollars, including a new muffler, when Elroy Scheifele, Treva's husband, said, "How much money could you spend on another trip?"

76

"Oh," reckoned LaVerna, "about sixty dollars."

"Good!" he said. "Let's all take a western trip. You give me your sixty dollars, and I'll pay all the expenses."

They left on July 15 in Elroy's 1926 Packard, traveled through South Dakota, with every bit of vegetation eaten bare, slipped and slid over roads covered inches deep with grasshoppers; went on through the Badlands and petrified forest to Yellowstone, to Salt Lake City; visited the Grand Canyon, crossed the desert to Hollywood, stayed in a beautiful cottage in Los Angeles which cost them just two dollars. Uusally they slept in cabins costing only a dollar a night. The road across Arizona was only a dirt trail. Hitting a rainy spell in New Mexico and Texas, they plowed through mud for days, often at no more than ten miles an hour. These were depression years, and all of them were living on a shoestring. But they had a marvelous time. The good-natured and voluble Treva, always brimming with fun and energy, could have turned the voyage of a slave galley into an excursion.

But for LaVerna the depression had barely begun. In 1933 math was taken off the required list for college entrance, and the commercial department was expanded. To her deep regret she gave up her beloved math and became again a commercial teacher. Classes kept getting larger and larger, pay checks smaller and smaller. She and Letah had to move to a cheaper apartment. In one month they received only ten dollars.

Financial problems were compounded by physical ones. Soon after school started in the fall she went into the hospital for an appendectomy. Her students were loyally concerned. One whole class wrote notes of sympathy. When Letah was reading them to LaVerna, she was stricken speechless by one which read, "Now, Miss Bowen, don't worry. Nearly everyone lives now through an appendectomy."

She lost a month of school without pay. The week after she went back she caught a severe cold, which lost her another week. Then the school board ran out of money and closed the school on December 8 until the first of the year. It was the worst year she had ever spent financially.

No wonder that when her father suffered a cerebral hemorrhage in April and she went home, not expecting him to live, she was near the breaking point. He was prostrate and blinded for about three weeks, then slowly began to recover. In spite of her relief the experience left her with a sense of loneliness and insecurity. The loss of her father would mean that she had no home to call her own. Friendships were at best tenuous and transitory. A brief semi-romance with a young associate who had paid her special attention had aroused emotions which could culminate only in frustration, for she soon discovered that the young man was committed to another girl. But the episode had left a deep and sensitive scar.

On April 27, 1934, she wrote in her diary: "Felt good. The boys' quartet from Albion gave a nice program. Received an unexpected letter from Howard P. Why can't I get a break and find someone I could be interested in?"

It was that same day that Roger Arnett decided that he was no longer content to be just a clerk and as a first step in advancement he must take lessons in stenography, typing, and bookkeeping.

LaVerna had expected to feel pity at sight of Roger Arnett. For the three years since his accident she had thought of him as a wan and tragic invalid: *Poor boy! What a terrible loss and waste! To have one's hopes, ambitions cut short on the threshold of fulfillment! To be half alive, half dead!*

The shock of having to revise this picture left her breathless. Poor boy? He was not a boy at all, but a man, and one of the most attractive men she had ever met. Hope, ambition gone? His every word vibrated with them. Half dead? She had never seen anyone more alive. Life glowed in the blue eyes, the dark, curling, wind-blown hair, the ruddy cheeks, above all in the sudden smile which lighted up the sober, intense face like sunlight on rugged granite.

"Good! Two nights a week, then, Tuesdays and Thursdays. O.K.?"

"O.K. But—don't expect too much. I'm used to teaching high-school sophomores, not college graduates."

"I'm not worried."

Looking after the Arnett car, LaVerna felt a confusion of emotions, doubt, anticipation, excitement. Tutoring an adult with all that practical and business experience? But the prospect intrigued her, for its promise more of adventure than of extra income. The feeling of excitement persisted during the following days.

The next Tuesday was the date of the teachers' banquet, so she could not go for the first lesson until the following Thursday. The night before, she received a message from home that her father had suffered a relapse. Worry dispelled any nervousness or personal interest she might have felt in this first encounter. She found Roger Arnett an eager and able pupil and knew that she had handled the lesson competently. Afterward one of the students drove her home to Ithaca, where she found her father still seriously ill but out of danger.

The next few lessons proceeded with similar businesslike efficiency. Another employee from Roger's office wanted to share the instruction and sat in on the next two sessions. Then her interest waned, and she did not come again. Still worried about her father, LaVerna felt little inclination to respond to Roger's overtures of friendly conversation or his mother's invitation to stay for a bit of refreshment. There was always a good reason for rushing away. But on Sunday, May 13, when she went home again, her father was so much better that the tension of anxiety dissolved. With all the four girls at home and Aunt Eunice visiting from Toledo, the household was almost gay again. She returned to Owosso with a zest for teaching which she had not known for months. She could hardly wait to check on the progress made by her star pupil.

"At this rate you'll finish a whole semester in a month!" she marveled. "And you're working full time and taking typing and stenography, too!"

"I like bookkeeping," replied Roger. "Maybe it's because figures have always been my specialty. Or"—his glance shot out to enfold her in a sudden blue intensity—"maybe it's just because I like my teacher."

LaVerna flushed, then felt foolish when the intensity became absorbed into an engaging grin; a bit relieved also to discover that he was just teasing her.

"Come on, stay awhile," he urged. "Surely you don't have to rush off every night. Let's talk, get acquainted."

LaVerna yielded. *Of course,* she thought, *he must be lonely. Every evening in that wheel chair, with no one his own age to talk to.* She had papers to correct, but decided she could spare a few minutes. Roger did most of the talking, explaining why he was so eager and interested to get ahead in his studies. He simply had to learn, and *fast.* He had already lost a lot of time. He liked his work but was certainly not content with being just a clerk. By learning shorthand he might become a court recorder, of if he kept on with advanced bookkeeping he might even be an accountant.

79

After subsequent lessons they had other talks. On May 31 La-
Verna wrote in her diary: "Roger told me about his accident, his
operation, his outlook on life. He is not soured in the least. Part of
him is dead, but he is a new person leading a new life."

For the first time in her memory she found herself talking frankly
and without embarrassment about her own handicap, the little hurts
and deprivations which she had never shared even with her own
mother. At first she was almost ashamed to confide them, they all
seemed so petty beside his overwhelming problems, but his gentle
probings and swift understanding responses were irresistible.

"I know . . . That's just the way I've felt, too . . . Funny, isn't it,
how being handicapped yourself makes you know how every other
handicapped person feels! Like you and me, it's a bond between us.
Don't you feel it?"

"Yes, oh, yes," agreed LaVerna, so stirred by a sudden discovery
that she quite missed the electric-blue warmth of tenderness leaping
from the deep-set eyes. "I never thought of it before, but I'm sure
it's helped me understand some of my pupils better."

Although these final school days left her more physically drained
than usual, she found the evenings with Roger more stimulating
than exhausting, as much from their conversations as from the
phenomenal progress made by her pupil. She was almost sorry it was
Thursday, and she must wait five days for another session.

But on the next Tuesday she received a message from her father.
He was in Toledo. Aunt Eunice had just been operated on for a
burst appendix. She was acutely ill. As usual, LaVerna kept this
further cause of worry and depression to herself. She would not
have mentioned it if Roger had not chosen this evening to ask her
for a date.

"I can't exactly ask you to 'step out' with me, because you'd have
to do all the stepping. The driving, too, worse luck. But I'd like
very much the pleasure of your company. How about this Saturday
night?"

LaVerna was amazed. She had deliberately forced herself to consider their relationship impersonal and professional, partly because
she had heard a rumor that he was engaged. Now, looking into his
face, frank, honest, expectant, she knew he was not the type to date
one woman when committed to another. But—where could he
possibly take her on a date, she wondered, and how? No matter, he
would find a way, she knew instantly. A gay recklessness possessed

her. Why not? They were both lonely. It would mean nothing except that they enjoyed each other's company. She told him about the message and her anxiety over her aunt.

"If nothing happens by Saturday," she agreed, "I'll go."

Wondering if she had done right, she asked Letah's advice.

"Probably it will be all right," her friend answered, "provided you don't get serious." Both of them laughed at the very idea.

Thursday came, and still no word from her father. "It must be good news," she told Roger. "It looks as if Saturday would be O.K."

But when she came home from school on Friday, Letah looked grave. "I had a call," she said. It was all she needed to say.

The shock was devastating. It was like losing her mother all over again. She felt that now she had no home. "I'll be looking for you as soon as school is out," Aunt Eunice had told her just a week ago. Her aunt's death also brought fresh worry for her father. He had been told to avoid any shock, and Aunt Eunice, two years his senior, had always been close to him.

LaVerna drove over to tell Roger she would not be able to keep their date. He came to the door and swung it wide, smiling from ear to ear. "At last," he exulted, "you've come just to see me, not for a lesson!" Then he saw her face, and the smile disappeared.

"I'm on my way home," she told him, too immersed in her own problems to fathom the depth or significance of the disappointment in his face.

When she returned from the funeral on Sunday she was near collapse. At Letah's first words she burst into tears. She was able to eat nothing. Lessons were a farce that week. She was too sick to keep the appointment on Tuesday. On Thursday she wrote in her diary: "Roger's mother had varnished all the chairs, so we had the bookkeeping lesson in the car. Afterward we went for a ride. We had a long talk, and I think each knows now where the other stands."

That evening, for the first time, LaVerna suspected that Roger might be falling a little in love with her. She was touched, excited, and disturbed. But she could not believe it was at all serious. There had been other episodes of pupils getting a "crush" on her, a temporary infatuation. They were just teacher and pupil, as she tried to explain to him, and whatever friendship developed from the rela-

81

tionship must be on that basis. Besides, she was too tired and sick even to think clearly.

She was still sick on Saturday, but she had promised Roger a date and she could not disappoint him a second time. They went to Carrothers Grove for a picnic with a Mr. and Mrs. Pratt who were connected with the welfare office. Then they went to the Pratts' home and played bridge. For LaVerna the evening was sheer agony. She still could not eat. Although bridge was one of the few recreations in which she could compete without a disadvantage and she usually enjoyed it thoroughly, tonight she merely wanted to get home. Leaving as soon as possible, she drove Roger straight to his house. She was in no mood to talk, and all the way Roger was unnaturally quiet. But when she started to get out to help him with his wheel chair, his fingers closed about her arm.

"Wait—please, not yet. My darling, I can't wait any longer. I have to tell you something."

His voice was low and urgent. It set her taut nerves vibrating like sensitive wires. She began to tremble. *No, no!* she wanted to cry out. *Don't tell me. I couldn't bear any more, not tonight.*

But before she could speak, he *was* telling her. Surely she must know how he felt about her. He had loved her from almost the first time he saw her. When she had come to the house and he had seen her get out of the car that first night, he had suddenly seen more than a teacher. He had seen a beautiful young woman. And the fact that she walked with a slight limp had made her even more beautiful. It had created a bond between them. Heaven knew he didn't have much to offer a woman, but if she would be willing to accept what he had, he would spend all the rest of his days trying to make her happy.

Afterward LaVerna could not remember what she said or how she got away. She was near hysterics when she got home. But she did not blame Roger. He knew little of the pressures she had been under, how close she had been to the breaking point. Now the burden of this added problem seemed more than she could bear.

"What on earth!" cried Letah. "LaVerna, what *is* the matter?"

"It's n-nothing," she wept, her teeth chattering. "I'm—just so—t-t-terribly t-tired and sick."

Her physician, Dr. Arnold, had given her some nerve pills to take when necessary. She took one and crawled into bed. She remained hysterical. Then she remembered that the doctor had also given her some sleeping pills. She had to get relief. The prescription was half a pill, but she took a whole one. Then suddenly she was blessedly calm. The world seemed to slow down. She thought, "I'm dying," then, very vaguely, "Well, maybe that's the only way."

LaVerna had always been the alarm clock for the two teachers. Not this morning. Waking, Letah discovered that it was nine thirty. Church was at ten and they always attended. When LaVerna failed to respond to her numerous shakings, Letah became alarmed. But finally she roused her, and they went to church, arriving late. Standing for the first hymn, LaVerna became deathly sick and left, Letah following. She gave her friend the car keys. "You drive us home." Letah called Dr. Arnold and told him what medicine LaVerna had taken. He was confounded. "That sensible girl do a thing like that!"

Following his directions, LaVerna soon recovered from the medication, if not from the tension and anxiety. With her sister Vivian's help, she was able to get through her teaching. It was the week of final exams, each lasting two hours. She would pass out the papers and make explanations, then rest in the lounge while Vivian, a business-school graduate, supervised the test. They corrected them together at night. She saw Roger several times. Now that he understood the situation, he was remorseful. But he could not take back what he had said, even though it had been impulsive and ill-timed. He had meant it from the bottom of his heart.

On Friday Dr. Arnold asked LaVerna to come to his office for a checkup. He was much more than doctor. Chairman of the school board, deeply sensitive to the problems of all his patients, he had long been her personal friend.

"Now give," he said. "Whatever possessed you to take those pills?"

Unprepared for this approach, she stammered, "I—I guess I was just overwrought. And I had exams the next day. I had to sleep."

The keen eyes under the shock of red hair were shrewdly appraising. "No. It won't do. You're too clearheaded a mathematician to disregard prescriptions just for a few exams. Something was bothering you. Give!"

LaVerna drew a long breath. "Do you know Roger Arnett?"

His eyebrows lifted. "Why, I know about him. I was never his doctor. Why?"

"Could—could a girl be happy married to him?"

She thought he was going to jump out of his chair. "No!" Then slowly he relaxed and emitted a soft whistle. "So—that's the way the land lies. I—begin to see." He was quiet for some time, considering, his shrewd eyes never leaving her face. "Let me take back that 'no.' You know I'm too quick on the trigger. I suppose—that would be up to the girl. Let me explain."

He did so, and that night she told Roger what he had said. She wrote in her diary, "Roger and I enjoyed our evening by ourselves. I really think we can be happy together as friends, although we both realize that's all there may ever be."

She decided to keep her apartment for the summer, and she saw Roger frequently. He tried to teach her to play chess, without success. They took pictures together and developed them in his improvised darkroom. She went with him and his family on camping and fishing trips. They spent many evenings either at his home or at her sister Vivian's. Following Dr. Arnold's advice, they went to see Roger's doctor at Ann Arbor. He assured them that there was no physical reason why a paraplegic should not marry, that there was even a possibility they could have children. LaVerna came back and told Dr. Arnold, but she knew he was not satisfied.

"We'd hate to lose you," he said. "You're one of our best teachers. But—why not go somewhere else this fall? We'll help find you a position."

Others were even more determined to break up the relationship. None of her Owosso friends except one teacher, Emily Osmer, was at all sympathetic. "You're utterly crazy!" "Stop it now before it goes any farther!" "Somebody's going to get hurt, and we don't want it to be you." Although Vivian and Eldred welcomed them in their home, LaVerna knew they did not approve of the friendship. And although she had written Treva about Roger, she was not sure of even her support.

"Would you mind if I brought my boy friend to your home for a date?" she wrote her friend in July. "Your husband will have to be there to carry him up the steps. Just say yes or no. If it's no, I'll understand."

"Come ahead," wrote Treva.

The trip was clumsy with the wheel chair tied on the side. LaVerna found it hard to pass other cars. But they had a delightful weekend. Treva's husband, a big, strong man who gloried in his physical prowess, carried Roger easily. Treva, with her exuberant friendliness, could be counted on for hospitality, if not approval.

And Roger, with his charming manners and yen for photography, delighted the Scheifeles. One of his favorite pastimes was to sit in his wheel chair and snap LaVerna in the most ridiculous of poses.

It was her father's violent disapproval which most distressed and confused LaVerna. On her few visits home, when she tried to tell him about Roger and show pictures of him, William Bowen would explode.

"That cripple! I tell you I won't have it. You shouldn't be wasting your time with him. Wait for some able-bodied man who can support you. Oh, I know how much you've been seeing of this fellow! Vivian has told me. Together almost every day! No good can possibly come of it."

"Don't forget," LaVerna reminded him once quietly, "I'm a cripple, too."

He snorted. "No such thing! It's not to be mentioned in the same breath, that little lameness. And even if you were, that's all the more reason. You should find yourself a man who can help you with the things you can't do."

If her father could only see Roger, thought LaVerna, he would feel differently. So in August she wrote and asked if she could bring him home for her birthday. She received a telegram from her stepmother: *Come home and talk to your father before making any plans*. LaVerna drove home immediately, both hurt and angry. She found her father had known nothing of the telegram. Her stepmother, afraid the shock would be too great, had not shown him the letter. It was no use. He would scarcely let LaVerna mention Roger's name. She returned to Owosso and spent her birthday on a sailing trip with Roger and his parents. For her birthday he gave her the gold medal presented after his accident in honor of his scholarship and athletic prowess, one of his most precious possessions, made into a necklace. It was beautiful, she told him, but she could not wear it because that would mean that she was engaged to him.

Through all her uncertainty Roger was patient, undemanding, understanding, even self-sacrificing.

"Darling," he wrote when she was at home before her birthday, "you have made me more happy than I had ever dared hope I could be. I am going to continue to love you just as long as you want me because my loving you and your loving me means happiness and contentment. With our love goes the hope and desire for life. It makes me smile in the face of the future. Whatever happens, remember I love you and will sacrifice everything for your happiness, even to giving you up if that will make you happy."

But he left her with no doubts as to what the price of such sacrifice would be, for in the next letter he wrote: "With you I feel I can overcome every handicap and face all the world with a smile. I want to live!"

For LaVerna it was an ecstatic but agonizing summer. For the fact that she had come to love Roger with a deep intensity solved nothing. Not long before school was to begin she knew that she must come to a decision. She must decide either to marry him or to leave Owosso. The uncertainty was tormenting them both.

She and Emily Osmer planned a trip to Cleveland the last week in August. Emily had a brother there, LaVerna a teacher friend, Viola, who had married and moved there with her husband. It would have been a delightful holiday if she had not been so tortured by the necessity for decision. It was at the end of an exciting day that the moment came. She had been downtown with Viola. They had gone to the park and, after waiting two hours, seen Colonel Lindbergh, not heard him, for after a lengthy introduction he had merely risen and bowed without saying a word. But they had felt it was worth it. They had seen Gertrude Ederle, who had just swum the English Channel, give a swimming exhibition in a tank.

"I must end it." All day she had been slowly coming to a decision. "I must go back to Owosso and tell him that it's all over. I must leave there and never go back."

Then, when she came into the house, there lying on the table was a letter addressed to her in Roger's handwriting.

She didn't need to open it. Just seeing it was enough. She knew, suddenly, that she would never have any more doubts or misgivings. They belonged to each other. The future was unimportant as long as they faced it together. If she ever got back to him, she would never go so far away again without him. And she could not get back to him quickly enough.

6

Rumors of the engagement aroused a shocked and excited uproar in Owosso. The whole idea was incredible. That one of the town's most popular and capable and highly respected teachers, possessed of an excellent job, a good salary, and a promising future, should even think of throwing herself away on a pitiable cripple, a has-been, a hopeless ruin of manhood, was beyond comprehension. To be sure, the town liked Roger, respected his past record, pitied him, admired him for his remarkable courage in returning to school and going through the motions of working. But of course the job wasn't really important and had probably been given him out of sympathy, and he could no more support a wife on the pittance he made than when he had been a schoolboy delivering the *Argus-Press!* Comments ran the gamut from disbelief to ridicule to right-eous indignation.

"You're joking! It's impossible!"

"What's the matter with her? She can't be *that* crazy! And she always seemed so levelheaded!"

"Why, she'd have to support him all his life! Not that he's likely to live very long!"

"That wonderful teacher, turning herself into a nursemaid—or worse!"

Even "Abie" Beyer, Roger's brother-in-law, who had often worked on LaVerna's car in the garage where he was employed, was shocked into crude protest. "What in heck! If she wants a man, she certainly can do a lot better than marrying him!"

Dr. Parker, Roger's physician, heard the rumor when he was going up in the hospital elevator. "No!" he exclaimed. "Good heavens, he can't do that!"

Mr. Willman, superintendent of schools and therefore LaVerna's employer, was one of the most vocal critics, possibly because he was such a good friend of both of them. Roger could never teach, he maintained. Most schools would have stairs, no facilities for such a handicap. And the same liability would apply to other well-paying jobs. LaVerna, on the other hand, was one of his best teachers. There was a rule in Owosso that a married woman could not teach. She would be giving up security for heaven knew what.

It was Letah Stewart who had to bear the brunt of the criticism. People kept coming to her adjuring, "You've got to do something!"

"But what can I do?" she would counter helplessly.

"I don't know. But *something!* You've got to stop them."

Life was made miserable for Letah. As LaVerna's housemate she was the target of her friend's confidences as well as of her critics' constant barbs. While she did not approve of the engagement, she admired Roger and respected the maturity of LaVerna's decision. Although she dutifully protested more than once, she knew there was nothing she could do to stop them.

If LaVerna was conscious of the turmoil about her, she did not let it fret her. She had made up her mind. She was disturbed by the opposition of only one person: her father. The last time she had seen him during the summer vacation he had wept and begged her to promise not to see Roger any more. Knowledge of the pain she had caused him, the greater pain she was going to cause him, was a physical sickness. Waking in the night and remembering, she felt nauseated. In the middle of a meal she would all at once see his face, hurt and accusing, and she would choke, unable to eat. Even in the warmth of an embrace the thought of her father's disapproval would make her suddenly cold with misery. Fear that her defiance of his wishes would turn the precarious balance of his health drove her sick with worry, and memories of all his tenderness to her through the years—the hours of massaging, the sacrifice to send her to college, his insistence on her operation—rose continually to haunt her. She was torn between two fierce loyalties. Sometimes she could actually feel the physical pain as if members of her body were being ripped apart. Although she tried to keep Roger from knowing the extent of her anxiety, their relationship was too close for secrets on either side.

88

"If only he would agree to see you—come to know you!"

"You really think that would help?" he returned moodily.

At such times Roger's own doubt and uncertainty became almost unbearable. He knew what people in the town must be saying. Were they right? Was her father right? Was he taking unfair advantage of her love by accepting it? Could he really make her happy, as he usually so confidently believed? And suppose he never got a better job but had to let her continue to earn the major part of their support, as she obviously must do at first! What would that do to their man-woman relationship? Already the very thought jabbed nagging barbs into his masculine pride. But of course he *would* get a better job. It was only a matter of time. And how could either of them even think of giving the other up? It would be like tearing apart two members of the same body! No. It was right, whatever people might say. They belonged together, and he knew she was as sure of it as he was.

LaVerna knew finally that she could wait no longer. On the day before Thanksgiving she went home and told her stepmother what had happened.

"I am going to be married in June," she said. Then, drawing a long breath, "Please—will you talk to Dad," she pleaded, "and try to do something with him? It's no use my talking to him. And—I'd so like to have Roger here with us sometime during the Thanksgiving holidays."

Reluctantly her stepmother agreed. "Though I'm sure I don't know what it will do to him." The next morning she said, "It's all arranged. You may bring him for Sunday dinner."

LaVerna drove up and got him. At first the day was agony. Roger was strained and sober, far from being his usual sparkling and genial self. William Bowen was politely distant. But as the day advanced tensions eased. Roger's usual charm of manner broke down barriers. The two men found interests in common—a farm background, church activities, and, most important, a consuming love for La-Verna. Roger warmed toward the man to whom she bore such marked resemblance, with his short but well-proportioned body, his springing white hair, his startlingly blue eyes. Before the day was over they had become genuine, if slightly wary, friends.

"Sorry, darling," confessed Roger ruefully on the way home. "I'm afraid I didn't put my best foot forward—as if one of them were any better than the other!"

But LaVerna was well satisfied. She felt as if a great weight had been lifted. "We really had a grand time," she wrote that night in her diary. "Roger and I stayed until seven. He fixed two keys on the piano. We were both so happy to have the attitude at home changed ever so slightly."

Not that her father ever really approved of her marriage to Roger, much as he came to like and admire him! But, recognizing in his daughter a determination equal to his own, he merely decided to make the best of it.

One person who did heartily approve was Norman Hagen. Visiting Roger just before Thanksgiving, he made opportunity for a private conversation with LaVerna.

"You should be married right away," he urged. "What say? I'll drive you two across the border where you can get a license without a three-day wait."

"Oh, no," said LaVerna after a moment's hesitation. "I couldn't do that."

He regarded her shrewdly. "Something's bothering you, and I'll bet I know what it is. You're thinking about Alice."

"Why—yes," she admitted, "I suppose I am. He was engaged to her for a long time and it was a terrible blow to lose her. I can't help wondering—"

"Don't," said Norm. "I've known Alice as long as Roger has, and you're much more the girl for him than she ever was. He was a top man in college, and she was the top woman. She didn't really love him for himself, nor did he her. Forget Alice."

Approval came from another surprising source.

"Dr. Arnold wants to see you," Letah told LaVerna one day. "He says if you don't come he's going to take drastic steps to break up your marriage."

"He couldn't do that," said LaVerna calmly.

She went to the doctor's office after school. Red hair bristling, he talked to her a long time. She listened patiently, then said quietly, "We know exactly what we're doing. I assure you, Dr. Arnold, we're going to be all right."

He leaned back in his chair and studied her, blue eyes narrowed, lips pursed. "All right," he said finally. "I guess you do know. O.K., LaVerna, I'm with you from now on."

His approval brought even more relief to Roger than to LaVerna. Always before he had had some doubt as to the wisdom of their decision. But Dr. Arnold's opinion carried weight not only with LaVerna but with many others in Owosso.

Roger had no illusions about the difficulties he would encounter in marriage. One galling experience that fall underscored his humiliating dependence. They went to Ypsi for homecoming. A long trip was always both a trial and a hazard. He had figured out a way that his wheel chair, big, wooden, uncollapsible, could be fastened on the side of the car. By putting two wheels on the running board, tying a rope from the door hinge around the outside of the chair and back through the top of the window, it could be fastened securely. But, projecting at least twenty inches from the side of the car, it was a big traffic hazard, especially at night, and made driving for LaVerna difficult.

However, they made the trip safely, met many old friends, saw Ypsi win the game, stayed for the football banquet, and started home. It was near midnight when they pulled into the southern edge of Morrice, about twelve miles from home, and raining. The car stopped. Roger groaned. He could tell by the way it stopped that it had run out of gas. No good telling himself that it was LaVerna's car and she should have watched the gas gauge! He was a man, and he should have noticed. A man? Never had he felt more keenly his male inadequacy. He was forced to sit in the car, dry and sheltered, despising himself, while LaVerna limped down a lonely, deserted gravel road in the driving rain and awesome darkness, at least a half mile to the nearest gas station. The first one she came to was closed, and she had to go on to another. He knew it was only the fore-runner of many such bitter reproaches to his manhood.

He gave her a diamond in December, and she wore it for the first time at school just before the Christmas vacation. "It's the most beautiful one I've ever seen," admired Letah. But most of the teachers didn't even see it, and the pupils didn't dare to mention it.

Roger went home with LaVerna before Christmas and stayed overnight. He played the violin, LaVerna the piano, and for two hours her father sang to their accompaniment, obviously with great enjoyment. For the first time Roger sensed a genuine, if reluctant, warmth in Dad Bowen's acceptance. He was on top of the world. Not so a week later when LaVerna had gone to Detroit for a few days to visit Treva! He was desperately lonely. She had planned to come back on December 31, so they could start the New Year together. On that afternoon he received a telegram saying that Treva had something planned and LaVerna could not come as she had promised. It was a bitter disappointment. On New Year's Day his emotions hit an all-time low. He was beset with more doubts and, worse, with self-pity. Could he really hope to make her happy? Didn't she deserve a better fate than being tied to a wheel chair? But late in the day she arrived, having traveled through a snowstorm over treacherous, icy roads, and all doubt and disappointment vanished.

Immediately they began making plans and looking at houses and furniture. Since her contract became void if she married, LaVerna would have to give up teaching and take an office job. Certainly they could not live on his fourteen dollars a week. Meanwhile she must save all she could. But June seemed a long way off.

It was Dr. Arnold who wrought the miracle. One Sunday afternoon when Letah was sick he came to make a house call. He saw on the dresser an enlarged picture of Roger and LaVerna taken when they were sailing the preceding summer. He began to question Letah. How often did they see each other? How much time did she spend with him? At her answers he shook his head in shocked disapproval, then asked bluntly, "Do you suppose she'd marry him right away if she knew her job was secure?"

"Why, I—I can't answer that," replied Letah.

"Well, you find out. Then you call me."

Soon after he had gone, LaVerna came in with Roger, and Letah started questioning her. Suppose a married woman were allowed to teach in Owosso, would they get married right away?

LaVerna laughed. "You're daydreaming. Why dream about the impossible?"

"I know, but—would you?"

"Why, of course we would." LaVerna turned to Roger. "Wouldn't we?"

"I'll say!" he replied fervently.

The next Friday LaVerna received a note from Dr. Arnold asking her to come to his office. She went in some trepidation. What now?

"The school board has asked me to tell you, at Mr. Willman's request," he announced formally, "that if you want to get married, your job is secure." Then he added severely, his eyes twinkling, "I hear you're spending far too many evenings away from home. Both your health and your teaching are likely to suffer. As your doctor and as chairman of the school board, I am ordering you to get married as soon as possible."

LaVerna drove directly to Roger's. They could hardly believe their good fortune. Deciding that three weeks were the least possible time to complete their plans, they set the wedding date for February 23. Letah offered to find another place to live, for the apartment was ideal for a person in a wheel chair. It was on the ground floor. The car could be driven to the end of the porch, and Roger could swing himself from car to wheel chair without the need of a ramp. All the rooms had wide doors. It seemed made to order.

The three weeks passed in a flurry of showers, luncheons, dinners, with a host of friends and groups entertaining—Letah, Emily, the high-school teachers, the YWCA girls for whom LaVerna had been adviser, her Sunday-school class, Roger's orchestra, his welfare department. They visited LaVerna's parents to announce the news, but were too far out on Cloud Nine to gauge their reaction. At least William Bowen seemed relieved that his daughter need not give up the security of her teaching job.

The wedding was in the apartment at four o'clock on a Saturday afternoon. Letah was maid of honor, Norman Hagen best man. Only the immediate families and a few friends were in attendance. Roger insisted on standing up for the ceremony. Once on his feet, he locked his braces so they would hold him upright. LaVerna, a bare five feet tall, felt strange with his six-foot height towering above her. It was the only time in their lives that they were to stand side by side.

Afterward they all went out to Vivian's, LaVerna's sister's, for a wedding dinner. It was not an entirely happy occasion. LaVerna was afraid her father would break down. She was sure of it when someone turned to him and asked, "Is this your last daughter?" But fortunately Letah saved the situation by breaking in impulsively, "I wish my dad could say that!" William Bowen, after a brief hesitation, only laughed. Norman Hagen, too, helped ease the tenseness by reading a long, foolish poem he had written and throughout the evening playing the part of a buffoon.

"Remember the bet we made," he reminded Roger. "First one married would owe the other a box of chocolates. I just won. You lost."

"Thank heaven!" responded Roger fervently.

"But barely by the skin of your teeth, feller." Norm's words were prophetic, for just six weeks later he was to marry Jo, with Roger his best man.

LaVerna wrote in her diary that night: "We came back to the apartment extremely tired but infinitely happy."

There was no wedding trip. Next Monday morning they were both back at work, LaVerna in her classroom, Roger in his welfare office.

Roger could scarcely credit his good fortune. Certainly if there was a Janus guarding the portals of his future, both of its faces were smiling. The song they had called "theirs" during the courtship continued to be the theme of the first months of their marriage and, indeed, of the rest of their lives. A quarter century later, whenever its strains came over the radio, perhaps once a year, they would turn the volume clarion high, as if to let the whole world know how they felt:

> They'll never believe me,
> They'll never believe me,
> That in this great big world,
> You've chosen me.

His new wife adjusted to the necessary demands of his condition with remarkable ease and competence. In fact, it was Roger who had to make the most drastic adjustments. Up to this time he had been fairly self-centered. Now, suddenly, he had acquired another self, very personal, very precious, for whom he was uniquely responsible; a self that could not be absorbed into his more aggressive personality but must be respected as well as cherished, treated as an equal partner in this man-wife team.

There were few personal services now that he could not perform for himself, but to compensate for the extra work that a paraplegic must inevitably create in a household he made his own contributions to the ménage. One area in which he excelled was cooking. His specialties tended toward the exotic, such as chilies and grilled-cheese sandwiches with sliced onions. His culinary pride suffered a blow, however, on one occasion when LaVerna's parents, with her sister and husband, were invited for dinner. Roger volunteered to cook. Wanting something unique, he purchased a fine large goose and cooked it according to directions, as he supposed, with all the fixings; then, with the guests seated and expectant, bore it proudly to the table and prepared to carve. To his chagrin it was nothing but

94

a hollow shell. Partaking of canned corned beef, he vowed never to cook for a big meal again.

LaVerna also paid the price of errors. One came near being tragic. It happened soon after their marriage, on a Thursday in April. As usual, they had allowed minimum time for her to drive him to work and then go to her school. It was Roger's custom to pull over to the side of the drive in his wheel chair and wait while she backed out of the garage. Being in a hurry, she did not notice that when driving in the night before she had cramped the wheels. It was too late to yell when Roger saw her coming straight toward him. Crash! He was knocked to the ground, one wheel of the chair bent, and its footboard broken. She slammed on the brakes, and the car tire stopped within inches of his foot.

"Are you all right?" she called quaveringly. After an ominous silence she called again, "Are you—"

"No," he replied testily, but with reassuring volume. "I'm not all right."

Miraculously he was unhurt. A hasty call to a funeral home provided them with another chair. Roger was a little late to work. LaVerna, still white and shaking, arrived in her classroom five minutes after the last bell had rung.

Although the apartment was fairly satisfactory, they wanted a home of their own. LaVerna had saved a little money and had inherited a bit from her grandfather, enough in all for a $500 down payment on a house and some furniture. They asked the bank for a list of houses which might have been forfeited during these depression days for inability to make payments, and started looking. Having almost decided on an old one that needed many repairs, LaVerna asked her father to come and examine it. Immediately he found a dozen imperfections and insisted on seeing one that they hadn't dared look at, a fairly new bungalow.

"This is it," he decided immediately, and refused even to look at others.

To their delighted surprise the unpaid balance on the house was only $1,800, plus back taxes. Dad Bowen, abhorring interest charges, insisted on paying for the house himself, with the agreement that they should pay off the debt in monthly rent. The newlyweds were ecstatic. Less than a month later, on May 4, they moved into their own home, scrubbed clean by Roger's mother and equipped with scant but brand-new furniture. It was their second "high day" of this eventful year.

The house needed adjustments to fit the needs of a paraplegic. Like most houses, it had steps. Just building a ramp over the steps did not suit Roger. It would have been too obvious. It happened that at the back door there was a hallway about twelve feet long and thirty inches wide, with three steps just inside the door. Roger's father, an amateur carpenter, came over two weeks after they moved in and installed a new floor in this hall, dropping one end of it to ground level. Roger could easily negotiate it under his own power, another important step toward independence. With block and tackle Dad Arnett also pulled the garage twenty feet forward and built an enclosure between it and the house so Roger could get to the car easily in bad weather.

The basement presented a worse problem. How was he to get downstairs to do his man's chore of tending the coal-burning furnace, to say nothing of utilizing the space for shop, photographic darkroom, and other purposes? He got an inspiration. In the center of the house was a hallway, a good six feet wide. Why not use half of it for an elevator shaft? Since there was no money to invest in an expensive, power-operated one, Roger designed one with Tinker Toys and demonstrated to his father how it could be worked with a hand rope and pulleys. Dad built it that August. It was an awkward, lumbering contrivance, but it worked to perfection and cost much less than a tenth of one bought and installed in the usual way. For Roger it spelled "open sesame" to furnace, darkroom, carpenter shop, attic storage space, and, on one occasion, near death.

He had built LaVerna a big fruit cupboard in the basement. All that summer she canned bushels and bushels of vegetables which Dad and Mother Arnett brought from their big garden. Each morning she would load the elevator with the jars canned the day before and take them down to the storage closet. One day she had taken down twenty-one quart jars of dill and bread-and-butter pickles. Then, too tired to think straight, instead of coming back via the elevator, she walked up the stairs. It was a Saturday, and Roger worked until noon. After lunch he prepared to go down to the basement to work. He always backed onto the elevator. LaVerna sat at the table watching him. Just as he took hold of the wheels to make a last push backward, she screamed. Whirling, he stared down into the empty space. One more turn of the wheels, just another second, and he would have plummeted twelve feet to the bottom of the cellar!

That summer brought another "high day" to Roger. Up to this time LaVerna had had to do all the driving. This affront to his masculine ego had always smarted. After much thought he designed hand controls for the clutch, brake, and foot throttle and gave the specifications to a mechanic employed by the welfare office. They were successfully installed. Not long afterward he drove home alone for the first time, then took LaVerna for a ride.

"Boy, does this feel good!" he exulted over this new step toward an independent life. "Now I'm really a *man* again!"

But the triumph was only surface deep. He knew very well that he would never feel himself a *man* until he was able to provide for his wife as a normal husband should. As the months passed his economic dependence became more and more galling, especially since he had to keep his mounting frustration to himself. His meager fourteen dollars a week were a mere token contribution to the household expenses. They were really living on LaVerna's salary. Secretly he fretted and fumed under the humiliation.

And as time passed the gnawing frustration turned into fear. Would he always be dependent on his wife for support? Every way he explored to increased income led to a dead end. The door to teaching was slammed shut again and again. His new knowledge of bookkeeping and typing, while enhancing his efficiency at the office, opened no new opportunities. He earned less pay than a secretary. Society refused to dissociate a man's facility with head and hands from that with feet. A ditch digger without brains was apparently less expendable than a college graduate without legs. The only answer seemed to be self-employment. Roger toyed with many possibilities, photography among them. But, though he did some amateur work for friends, he knew it would take years of further training and experience to qualify as a professional. Meanwhile he accepted his wife's support with outward cheerfulness, but inwardly he felt like a "kept" man.

Little did Roger know when he answered the magazine advertisement how that simple act was going to change his life. Twenty small gladiolus bulbs, it offered, for a dollar. He sent for them. To his surprise and delight every one bloomed. Beautiful though they were, however, in their variety of colors, they looked pale and ordinary beside a bouquet that Treva Scheifele brought when she came to visit, all of the same color, a gorgeous dark violet. Aïda was their name, he discovered. With growing fascination he began poring over catalogs.

The first summer they had only a small garden. LaVerna planted most of it. But during the following winter and spring Roger turned into an ardent would-be agriculturist. In March he hauled boxes of dirt via the elevator into the attic and planted seeds in boxes in the south window: cabbages, tomatoes, peppers, many kinds of flowers. As soon as the ground was spaded he was out planting, cultivating, weeding. It was amazing how far one could reach from a wheel chair! He developed an ambitious plan for landscaping the big four-by-eight-rod lot, with Lombardy poplars at the two back corners, tall shrubs for background on the south and east sides, shorter ones in front. With his dad's and LaVerna's help these were all planted in the early fall.

He had always been a great lover of tulips. Why not have a big bed along the driveway? He ordered 500 bulbs of different varieties and colors. One day in early October, with the help of a hired schoolboy, he planted them, digging trenches, lining them with sand, placing the bulbs at exactly the right distances from each other. It took them all day.

But this driving energy soon flagged. For some reason Roger began to tire easily. He lost weight, started to cough frequently, sometimes ran a temperature, awoke from sleep drenched with perspiration. "Oh, oh!" he thought. "Another bout with kidney infections!" He was used to them by now. They were the bane of the paraplegic. But somehow these symptoms were different. He finally went to Dr. Arnold for a checkup.

The doctor gave him a thorough examination, took X-rays. When he came back from reading them, his face looked grave, its skin unnaturally pale under its heavy peppering of freckles. He began pacing the floor.

"Tell us," said Roger finally. "We can take it."

"Well—" the doctor hedged—"I'm no expert, and I can't say for sure. But—I'd like to send these pictures to the sanatorium at Howell and let the experts look at them."

Roger dared not look at LaVerna. *Dear God, not that! On top of everything else, don't let me have TB!* He wet his lips. "O.K. Do that, Doctor. How—how soon are you likely to get a report?"

"Soon, I hope. A few days. They don't usually take too long." He clamped his hand on Roger's shoulder. "Now meanwhile, you two, don't worry. As I say, I'm no expert. My diagnosis may be wild. And if it should be what I think it is, it may be a very mild case."

They waited . . . and waited. During the following days they went about their routine life as usual. LaVerna taught, cooked, cleaned, attended PTA. Roger worked at the office, developed pictures in his darkroom, rehearsed with his orchestra, directed them at Church School on Sunday morning. They entertained, played bridge with friends, went visiting. They planned trips they would take when the new car they had ordered arrived. Roger had picked a Terraplane, a car he thought he could drive easily because it had what was called an "electric hand," a device on the steering wheel which controlled the clutch. Carol, the high-school girl who lived with them, earning her board and room in return for the household help she could give, never suspected that anything was wrong. But for Roger and LaVerna the few days moved with the relentless precision of a slow-ticking time bomb.

Roger recived the call at the office. "Dr. Arnold, Rog. Er—the report is here. Er—How about you and LaVerna coming over?"

They went during the noon hour. Again Dr. Arnold paced the floor . . . and paced.

"I take it the news isn't good," said Roger calmly.

It wasn't. The doctors in Howell had examined his X-rays. They said he had an advanced case of TB in one lung and it was breaking out in the other. He should be hospitalized immediately. The fact was—the doctor was blunt—he was a menace to society.

"I see," said Roger. "Then—I suppose I go to Howell."

Go to Howell. The words reverberated in his ears like a tolling bell, a death knell. He had heard them on other lips before. "Those who *go to Howell* never come back." *Go to Howell . . . never come back . . . go . . . never . . .*

But it seemed he was not to go to Howell. At least not for the present. There was no bed available in the tuberculosis sanatorium, so Dr. Arnold advised that he go to the University of Michigan Hospital-until Howell should have a vacancy.

They left the doctor's office together, drove away in silence, then separated, Roger returning to his work at the welfare department, LaVerna to her teaching. She thought she could get through the afternoon, but when she went into the teachers' lounge she met Theresa.

"How's Roger?" asked her friend casually.

LaVerna opened her mouth to answer, found she couldn't, and burst into tears. Then she rushed from the room, went out to her car, and drove home. Roger managed to finish the day. When she went after him, he looked white and strained but threw her a game smile. Again they drove in silence. Only when they got into the house and were alone did the flood of pent emotion break. LaVerna wept and clung to him. Even Roger shed tears. Then, suddenly remembering, he pushed her gently but resolutely away.

"No, darling. I'm a menace to health, remember? Don't come too close."

This only plunged them both into a deeper flood of emotion.

To Roger the future looked completely blank. His associations with tuberculosis had all been somber. There was the neighbor girl, Dorothy, who had died of the disease. Another acquaintance had been helpless for years. At best he could look forward to months, years, probably at least two of them, flat on his back away from home. Then, if he should come home, uncured, there must be isolation, no work, precautions of sterilized dishes, no human contacts. He must leave everything: LaVerna, their beloved house, the new car, the yard. *I'll never see those tulips blooming in the spring!* Hadn't the paraplegia been enough? Was he like Job, that curse after curse must be thrust upon him? And just when he had begun really to live! At first it seemed more than he could take.

But slowly his indefatigable spirit asserted itself, outwardly, if not in actuality. He had not conquered a broken back just to be defeated by tuberculosis!

"I won't be gone long," he told LaVerna cheerfully the morning Mr. Coe, one of the welfare workers, came to drive him to Ann Arbor. "I'll be back soon."

LaVerna wanted to believe him, but she didn't dare. She did not go with him. It was a school day, and she taught classes as usual. Fortunately she was not alone during the week. Carol was with her. But Carol, one of a family of twelve children that lived in the country, went home from Friday night to late Sunday each week. That first weekend, after trying to sleep in the house by herself, LaVerna got up, went over to her friend Emily's, and crawled into bed with her for the rest of the night.

Not that she was able to sleep soundly at any time! The emotions of loss and loneliness and futility were compounded by a helplessness and uncertainty. Dr. Arnold would make no prediction. She figured that even if Roger came back, it might not be for a year, probably two or more. What should she do? Find somebody to live with her, rent rooms, rent the house, sell it? She remembered a teacher friend who, having lost her husband very suddenly, had been completely at sea. She would think she wanted to teach, then, when the opportunity came, refuse it. All her friends had become discouraged and disgusted. Suppose she should be like that! LaVerna came to a decision. She would go to summer school, train herself better for commercial teaching, which now she might have to do the rest of her life. Not to Ypsi where Roger had been a student, but to some distant place where no one would ask about him, to— perhaps to Chicago! That was it. She obtained a circular about a Gregg summer school that she might attend. Every night when she went to bed, she would say to herself, over and over, "I'm going to Chicago this summer. I'm going to Chicago." It was a rudder to keep her from drifting, perhaps foundering.

Nine days passed. Each day she received a letter from Roger, and each showed the same almost superhuman determination. He was "doing fine, gaining weight all the time." He had "licked it already." He "would be home before she knew it."

Thanksgiving was coming. *Thanksgiving!* But a pretense of cele- bration must be made. LaVerna planned to go with Roger's father and mother to Ann Arbor. They would eat dinner somewhere on the way, then spend the afternoon at the hospital. But at noon the day before Thanksgiving she received a telephone message. It was from the hospital. Mr. Arnett, she was informed by a crisp official voice, was ready to come home. He would like his family to come and get him.

LaVerna's head whirled. Hope struggled with bewilderment. Immediately she called Roger's mother, and they agreed to meet as soon as his father could be summoned from work. A little later the Arnetts called for her at the school, and she got excused for the afternoon. All the way to Ann Arbor they wondered, conjectured, hoped.

"Surely if it were a hopeless case," LaVerna kept telling herself, "he wouldn't be allowed to come home and mingle with his family. But—you can't cure tuberculosis in nine days!" What could the news mean? Was it bad or good? Was he being sent home because they could do nothing more for him, as after his accident in 1931?

As soon as they saw Roger's face, they knew the answer. It was good. His cheeks were ruddy, his eyes bright, his smile wide and beaming. No, he objected when LaVerna tried to kiss him, he couldn't let her do that. Things weren't all that good yet. But he was going home, and he would explain it all later.

He did, in the car on the way home. Of course, when he arrived at the hospital, they had X-rayed him again and given him all kinds of tests. Then a day or two later they had started doing it all over again.

"What's the matter?" he had asked jokingly. "Can't you find anything wrong?"

Without giving him any satisfaction, they had repeated the whole process of examination. He had known by the way they acted that they were puzzled.

"You can't find anything wrong with me, can you?" he had challenged them.

Finally they had admitted that he had many healed scars on his lungs but they had been unable to find any active areas. Of course he had immediately asked about going home, and finally they had agreed to let him go provided he would stay in bed for six weeks and follow the same routine as in the hospital. His temperature must be taken and recorded three times a day, he must eat so many times a day, and follow a strict diet.

Of course he had to stay in bed Thanksgiving Day. Nothing had been bought or prepared for dinner, but his mother was equal to any occasion. She brought over the dinner and they ate it together, so happy that they scarcely knew what they ate. Turkey was quite unnecessary. They could have made a thanksgiving feast out of corned beef and cabbage.

During the following six weeks Roger's mother stayed with him during the day while LaVerna taught. He put the enforced rest to good use, answering every ad he could find for florist catalogs, and studying them by the dozens. He also decided that this would be a good time to have his toes amputated, since he had been having difficulty with their infection.

Thankful though she was, LaVerna found it hard to adjust to their new good fortune. Occasionally she even found herself caught in the same tangled mental web which during his absence had so involved her thinking. As once when Roger was talking of plans for the summer . . .

"Why, I have to go to Chicago this summer," she heard her-self saying.

"You *what?*"

She repeated, parrotlike, "I have to go to summer school in Chicago this summer."

He stared at her. "Well, what am I going to do, then? Am I supposed to go back and live with my folks?"

She laughed, shamefaced but infinitely relieved. "But I don't have to go now, do I? You're home!"

After six weeks Roger went back to Ann Arbor for further examination and X-rays. The doctors found nothing changed, and he was given a clean bill of health.

How did he account for his "quick" cure? He didn't, although he was sure it had some rational explanation. Had there been an error in reading his X-rays? It had been done by the best experts in the state. Had the doctors at Howell deliberately painted a dark picture because they wanted to get him out of contact with other people? It would always remain a mystery, but one for which he had no words to express his gratitude.

He was convinced, however, that he could account for some of the symptoms. Worry over his financial dependence on LaVerna had become a gnawing canker which had not only consumed peace of mind but had more and more sapped his physical strength. He had brooded over it by day, lost sleep at night. Frustration, self-depreciation, resentment because he felt his potential was not recognized, all had preyed on his mind and body until both had reached a point of nervous collapse. Around and around the unhealthy thoughts had spun until somehow the vicious cycle had spiraled to its nadir. The days in the hospital had brought release. He had learned that financial dependence was a minor flaw in the wealth of values already attained: home, love, life itself. Not that he had relinquished the ambition for independence, merely refused to become its slave.

Another person believed he could account for Roger's remarkable comeback. Not long after his return home Mr. Boyd came to the house one day. He said to Roger, "You have had a very severe illness. I knew it, and I prayed for you. I prayed continuously. And finally I knew that you were healed of it. But you know, I've been wondering ever since what that illness was. So I've come today to find out."

One by-product of the six weeks of enforced idleness was a diary. Carol gave it to him for Christmas. Roger kept it for exactly one month and ten days. On the first page he listed his worldly possessions: "Home with nice fat mortgage. Six rooms and bath. Houseful of furniture, simple and cheap but all paid for. Lot which house stands on, four by eight rods. One car, Chevrolet. Six kinds of iris, 487 tulip bulbs, 20 varieties, one empty fish and lily pond, 30 shrubs, 20 small evergreen trees, 18 peonies, 30 varieties of roses."

"Looking forward to prosperous year," he wrote jubilantly on January 1, 1937. "Am resolved to get a much better job during this year. LaVerna and I each made up an order for five dollars' worth of flowers and bulbs for my wedding anniversary present. Maybe if I try hard she will get interested in gardening." Little did he realize that the last two sentences were to prove the answer to the first two.

The January diary sprouted and bloomed like a summer flower garden.

"Yesterday twelve hardy lily bulbs, six oratum, six specio, came from Burpee's. So this morning Dad and Mother came over and helped plant them. Dad had his pickaxe set for a real job. But to our joy the ground wasn't frozen. I could have done the job myself."

"Made three plant starting boxes today, ten by twenty-one by five, just the size to put on the arms of my wheel chair. Eleven seed and bulb catalogs came. Took all the music out of the piano seat to make room for my seed catalogs."

"This afternoon the garden bug got me, so I put thirty-six muffin holder papers in a box, filled them with dirt, and in each placed a glad bulblet."

"This morning I got wire to make frames for my home-made hothouse for the garden. LaVerna is getting the flower bug in earnest. Hooray!"

"Hurrah! Got my O.K. from the doctor today. Fit as a fiddle and ready for the dance of life. It sure is a glorious feeling to be healthy. This afternoon I filled furnace with coal, banked it good, and we drove out to Vivian and Eldred's. And what do you think? Yeh! She had a new seed catalog!"

"Joyfully went to work this morning. Office seemed just like home, and I stepped into the harness without a hitch. The folks brought the Terraplane tonight, which we hope will be ours someday. Bargained for it before I got TB. Couldn't take it. Folks took it over until we could get straightened out."

"Banner day, as I received eleven catalogs. Took a peek at the glad bulblets, but not showing. Guess you can't fool them into thinking winter is over."

"LaVerna sick with stiff neck. Went to school to help mark her grades. Very embarrassing situation developed. Roomful of many teachers. Paying too much attention to work, let urinal bottle run over. Huge puddle, terrible odor. Horribly embarrassed. Oh, well, that's one of the social handicaps of the paraplegic."

(The notation did not tell the half of it. He was to remember the incident with shame for the rest of his life. Always he was to wonder if it was not this episode rather than the paralysis which caused Mr. Willman to keep saying he would never be able to teach. For the paraplegic such social problems were far greater than the inability to walk! No wonder so many were unable to take the possible humiliation and preferred to ostracize themselves from society! It was years before he learned never to concentrate on a job so hard that he would be impervious to the telltale signal of odor.)

"Drove the Terraplane to Ithaca, and what fun! Freezing rain, roads a glare of ice. When we drove into the garage wheel chair on side was coated with a half inch of ice!"

"Boy, would I like a job teaching! Two white shoots in gladiolus pot."

"Saw Mr. Willman today about a teaching job. No soap. But I'm not discouraged. My day is coming!"

"Went to bed this afternoon for the weekend. Have to cure pressure sores on my heels. Spent time on glad catalogs."

Even LaVerna caught a mild case of the fever. On January 14 her diary recorded, "Nothing like counting your chickens before they are hatched! I find myself trying to place beautiful bouquets of anticipated glads and iris about the house, wishing for more mirrors to reflect them."

Just when Roger made the decision to specialize in growing glads he could not have told. Certainly the idea germinated during those six weeks of convalescence. After the TB scare he realized that photography as a possible occupation, even as a major hobby, was out. Work in a darkroom would be too confining. He must get out-of-doors. As he lay in bed, the snow blowing and the wind howling outside, he remembered his glads of the preceding summer, and the bouquet of purple Aïdas, how beautiful they had been. Somebody gave him a book about Luther Burbank, the miracles he had wrought in crossing plants, and Roger became tremendously excited. In his mind's eye he saw the glads, all twenty varieties of them, tall and luxuriant, easily reached from a wheel chair; imagined all the hundreds of variations in shape and color that crossing might produce. He thought, "Now this is something that I might try."

As the weeks passed and he studied more and more catalogs, planted more and more seeds, bought more and more bulbs and bulblets, he became more and more excited. Perhaps the pole beans —a routine job in an office—could be dug up and discarded. Maybe the old dead wood would sometime blossom into something just as beautiful and creative as morning-glories!

7

So Roger did see the tulips that spring, after all. They were such a blaze of glory along the driveway that people came from miles around to admire them.

In fact, he could hardly wait for spring to come and the ground to get soft and dry enough to be plowed. On his birthday, May 1, he hired the boy Charles again, and they planted glads all day long. It was the hardest physical labor he had done since his accident.

They planted the bulbs in beds four feet wide and the length of the garden. The rows, spaced a foot apart, ran across the beds, with eight inches between the bulbs. A walk three feet wide was left between the beds, wide enough for his wheel chair, so he could do his own weeding, hoeing, and cutting. He would be able also to reach over and cross-pollinate the different varieties. The wire stakes he had made during the winter were set at the end of each row and name tags attached. There were close to five thousand bulbs.

"Better stop now and rest," urged LaVerna near the end of the afternoon. "Besides, you need to get cleaned up for dinner."

"Not on your life!" retorted Roger, stubbornly resolved to plant as many as possible this first day.

He was still working hard at five o'clock, tired, sweaty, face and arms and overalls begrimed and bedraggled, when who should walk into the garden but his old high-school crony Bill Carmichael and his girl friend! LaVerna had invited them to drive over from Grand Rapids to help celebrate Roger's birthday and spend the night. It was too genuine a surprise party.

"And I thought I was coming to visit an invalid!" joked Bill, seeming to derive great sport from his friend's predicament.

It took two more Saturdays to get all the bulbs planted. Then every evening and every Saturday Roger worked constantly in the garden. He watched and nursed them with the tenderness of a mother caring for her first baby. When it rained on them, he rejoiced. When a dry spell turned the earth to powder, he spent hours watering them. And when after two months the first spike appeared, he felt the pride of a mother over her child's first tooth. It was the end of July when the first bloomed, a yellow one called Gold Dust. Each morning he would wheel through the garden before going to work, noting each new bloom. All varieties were new to him except for his intensive study of the catalogs, but it was not long before he knew every one by name.

He attempted considerable crossing of varieties that summer, becoming more and more excited about the possibilities of creation. For the first time work became self-fulfillment, not mere self-subsistence. Who could tell? Other men might leave books behind to bear their name—or music, or paintings. Suppose he also could create a lasting memorial, something of rare beauty uniquely his! Life received a new impetus.

After a crossing he would watch with avid interest to see whether the seed pods filled out. If the plant developed a seed pod of about two inches long by a half inch in diameter, the crossing had been successful. Most of his attempts that year were hit or miss, but out of them one variety, a very early yellow, developed which many years later he was to market under the name of Candlelight.

News of the garden spread, and soon people came to view it. About the middle of August the blooms were at their peak, and Roger decided to hold a glad show. LaVerna placed bouquets at points of vantage all over the house. (Oh, for the extra mirrors!) She filled milk bottles with the 200 different varieties, labeling each one, and turned the basement into a huge display room. Central to the display was Roger's prize Golden Goddess, with its fourteen blossoms on a single spike. A couple of hundred people came, poured through the rooms, "Ohed" and "Ahed," and were soon coming to LaVerna with bouquets and demanding to buy. The intention had not been to sell flowers, only to take orders for bulbs for next spring delivery.

LaVerna went to Roger. "What are we going to do?"

"Let them go," he replied.

Soon all the flowers were sold, breaking up the glad show. Out of this experience came the idea of selling cut flowers to cover expenses.

That August they attended as well as gave their first glad exhibition, a state affair held in western Michigan. Enraptured by the wealth of unimagined varieties and colors, Roger became even more enthusiastic about his avocation. He immediately began making plans for enlarging his business the next summer. Their small plot of a tenth of an acre was the merest beginning.

The end of the season was only the start of an even harder job. The tender bulbs all had to be taken up and stored. Roger worked every night as long as he could and again hired Charles to help him all day on Saturdays. It was thrilling to discover the increased size of all the bulbs and the numbers of little bulblets.

Every variety had to be stored in its own container. If there were fifteen or more bulbs of one variety, he would put them in one of the boxes he had made. If only one, it would be put in a small paper sack; if two or three, in a three-pound sack; and so on. Roger was meticulous about saving every single bulblet, for they were as precious as gold. After all were dug and classified, the containers must be left open to let the wind dry the bulbs. If it looked like rain, they must be taken inside at night, then taken out again. After drying, they were placed first in the garage, later in the basement.

The crossed varieties demanded special care. If the seed pod was collected too soon, it wouldn't be ripe enough. If he waited a day or two too long, the pod would open, and some of the seeds would blow away. He stored the seed pods in half-pound paper sacks. Later, during the winter, would come the threshing process. The pods must be taken out, all seeds removed, then placed in tiny sacks and fastened with a rubber band, with the name of the cross on each sack. For it was just as important to keep track of the mother and father of the crossed seeds as it had been to list each separate variety.

But the endless detail and multiplying hours of labor only whetted Roger's enthusiasm. That fall he wrote to all the leading glad growers in the country for catalogs. He spent every spare minute studying all the literature he could find on the growing of glads and the business of selling blossoms and bulbs. At last he was engaged in a creative task, something which would contribute to the world's beauty and the enrichment of human personality.

It was well that his body seemed to choose the fall season for its bouts of rebellion. Last year it had been TB. This year it was the usual series of infections and abscesses common to the life of the paraplegic. No doubt they were aggravated by the long hours without respite in the wheel chair.

Then late in 1937 his temperature began soaring for no apparent reason. Examination of his body revealed no inflamed areas, no abrasions. But finally as the infection developed they discovered a red streak on his right leg extending from ankle to knee. Somehow, inadvertently, he must have scratched himself. LaVerna started the usual treatment for such infections, soaking in solutions of epsom salts, and called the doctor.

Roger spent many days in bed. His mother came and cared for him during the day while LaVerna taught. In spite of all remedies, the infection persisted. LaVerna got little rest at night. Sometimes Roger perspired so profusely that she had to change the bedding every half hour. After five such nights her principal noticed her fatigue and sent her home to rest. But she found Roger so much worse that weariness was forgotten. She called Dr. Arnold, then waited in an agony of worry and desperation. It was four in the afternoon when he came running in. Seeing Roger apparently in deep sleep, he looked relieved.

"Good! I was afraid your message meant that it might be serious. Sleep can do him a lot more good than I can."

"But—are you sure it is sleep?" LaVerna was almost surprised to hear herself asking.

The doctor looked startled. On further examination he discovered that Roger was in a coma. "He must go to the hospital immediately. Get him ready."

Roger's mother had seen him through so many illnesses that she refused to acknowledge that this episode was more serious than any other. That evening she and Dad Arnett came over to help get him ready.

"Now, Roger,'" she said when he had roused somewhat from the coma, "if you don't want to go to the hospital, you don't have to."

"Mother," he told her as firmly as if he were in full consciousness, "I'm going—to hospital."

He was in the last stages of blood poisoning. Only by working over him all night were the doctors and nurses able to save his life. But the siege was only begun. The infection kept progressing, finally moving up into the trunk of the body.

"Roger," said Dr. Arnold finally, "I hate to tell you, but—we've got to take off that leg. We don't want to do it yet, not until the infection is curbed, but you may as well know it. It's got to come off."

No! determined Roger, gritting his teeth. He wouldn't let them. As long as he had both legs, there was hope that someday he might walk again.

"But if it would save your life—" argued LaVerna tearfully.

He was stubborn as she had seldom seen him. Doctors had thought before that he was going to die, and he had fooled them. He would fool them this time, and with both legs intact. Frantic with worry, LaVerna told Norman Hagen about the problem when he and Jo came from Detroit to call on Roger.

"What's this about your thinking you know more than the doctors?" Norm lectured him severely. "What do you think you are, some sort of cosmic pet with a charmed life? Come on now, feller, you're not going to walk again and you know it. Why kid yourself? Isn't it better to live with one leg, than to let them bury you with two? If you're too pigheaded to do it for your own sake, then do it for LaVerna's."

Roger managed a lopsided grin.

A day or two later Dr. Arnold came again, looking even more worried. "Hang it, Roger, I don't know what to do. If we take it off while it's still infected, it's likely to be fatal, and if we leave it, it's pretty sure to be fatal. I'll have to leave the decision up to you, because you're between the devil and the deep blue sea."

"Then let's choose the devil," said Roger, too sick to care very much what happened. "Take it off, Doctor."

The question then was where to make the amputation. Roger motioned first below the knee, then above, finally with a feeble grin across his neck. "Take your choice."

The next morning they took him to the operating room. He was placed on the table with a sheet hung as a barrier in front of his face. Since the leg was insensitive, there was no anesthetic. However, he fooled them. Looking up into the large light with its shining chrome reflector, he could witness the whole operation. It was a peculiar sensation, especially when they started sawing. They had finally decided to amputate just above the knee.

Although the operation was successful, recovery was slow. His neighbor and friend, Charlie Dynes, who had moved into the house backing theirs only the preceding year, gave numerous blood transfusions. Roger came home at last, but his troubles were by no means ended. The baneful pressure sores kept recurring. No sooner was one healed than another one would start. Then again came near tragedy.

He was suffering from a severe abscess on his hip. Somehow they procured some stale dressings from the drugstore. They failed to drain away the poison. His temperature shot to a new high, and he became violently ill. Although he did not admit it at the time, Dr. Arnold despaired of his life.

"There's a new kind of drug," he said to LaVerna one Saturday night. "I've never yet used it on a patient, but if you're willing I'd like to try it on Roger. Under normal circumstances I wouldn't risk experimenting on a patient, but in this case—"

He did not need to finish. LaVerna understood. The new drug was a last slim hope of saving Roger's life. "Give it to him," she said tersely.

The doctor administered the new sulfa drug. He and LaVerna watched beside his bed. All that night Roger tossed in high fever, and his eyes were glazed. Neither of them thought he would live until morning. It was the darkest night LaVerna had ever spent. But in the morning Roger's temperature had gone down. His eyes were clear, and he was talking rationally. Within a week's time he was up and dressed, and the following Sunday he sat in his wheel chair and entertained twenty-two callers. The following Monday he was back at work.

Even the tuberculosis episode seemed no greater miracle. With the magic of the sulfa drugs a whole new world was opened. Infections which had often proved fatal could be conquered. Although one must still be eternally watchful for the insidious pressure sore and for the bladder and kidney infection, if they did develop there was a way now of keeping them under control. For Roger and

LaVerna the future looked brighter than at any other time since their marriage.

A dream which had seemed but a hazy and distant possibility seemed suddenly capable of more immediate fulfillment. Perhaps they could have a child! One day when they were out in their back yard and their next-door neighbor came over for a visit, the dream assumed shape and substance.

The neighbor was a doctor, an old friend who had gone to high school with Roger. He was regaling them with a rhapsodic description of his new baby.

"You may think you're happy," he said, "but it's nothing compared with when you have a baby in the house. You folks should have one."

"Well," said Roger, "how about giving us a little help?"

The doctor studied them seriously. "O.K. I'd like to examine LaVerna."

After a careful examination with X-rays, he gave his report. It was doubtful if she could ever carry a child. She would have to remain in bed for the nine months, and even then the risk would be great.

"Even if you did succeed in having one," he summarized, "you might have to spend the rest of your life in a wheel chair."

That settled it. One wheel chair was enough in the family. They began to discuss the possibility of adopting a child. But this also presented difficulties. For the present LaVerna could not give up her teaching. They could not live on Roger's small income. So any child they considered must be of school age. Then another thought occurred to LaVerna. Much of her time had to be spent helping Roger with his various activities, for he was always busy. Even errands to the store must be her responsibility, for Roger could not enter most stores with his wheel chair. She thought, "If we had a child who was just big enough to go into the store for him or hold the boards when he was carpentering . . ."

One day she was sitting out in the back yard with another neighbor, Mrs. Rundell, while the latter's youngest boy played close by. "Now he looks big enough to help," she reflected, "yet he's just a child."

"How old is Jim?" she asked.

"Ten."

A ten-year-old, then, would be exactly right.

It was less than a week later that Roger's mother mentioned a nephew who had been left without a home. Picturing a small baby, LaVerna inquired casually, "How old is he?" When the reply came, "Ten years old," she glanced quickly at Roger, to find her own surprise and excitement reflected in his face. She lifted her eyebrows, and he nodded, then turned to his mother and said, "We'll take him."

This was March. Roger wrote at once to the county probate judge in western Michigan under whose jurisdiction the boy Dick was being cared for, but it was the last day of July before approval of their home was given and the child was brought to their house, a thin little fellow with a generous, unsmiling mouth, light brown curly hair, and a lost look in his big brown eyes. Instantly their hearts went out to him, and they adopted him as soon as possible.

There was pathos in his story. Before he was born his father had deserted his mother, leaving her with three older children. She placed her older son, Roger, in a home and, boarding out her two daughters in Alma, obtained work to support them. But when Dick was born she gave him up for adoption. A couple who had lost their first child took him. A year later they had twin girls. When Dick was three and the twins not yet two, the family was traveling to spend Christmas with a relative when Mr. White, standing by the car to fix a flat tire, was run over and killed. Mrs. White, left with three children and another one coming, was in poor health and desperate need. When the bank containing her small insurance closed, she was forced to live on welfare. She died when Dick was nine. Looking up his record, the welfare agency found that the Whites had never signed his adoption papers. They wrote to Dick's mother, Roger's Cousin Fern, but her income from work in a hotel was insufficient to care for her daughters. At this point Roger's mother had heard of his predicament.

For days the lost look in his eyes persisted. He desperately missed the twins, who had been so close to his age. He begged and begged Roger and LaVerna to take them. "You've got room enough," he pleaded, peering into the extra bedroom. It was no use trying to explain that they could not afford three children, that many people considered them reckless to assume the responsibility of one. It tore their hearts to have to refuse him.

His loneliness was not the only problem. LaVerna, who had never had brothers but thought she knew boys from her long teaching experience, found herself totally unprepared for this mother-son relationship. She was unable to anticipate his reactions or figure out what he might do next. The first morning, after an early breakfast, she heard the back door slam. Going out, she was unable to find him and was forced to inquire at the homes of all the neighbors before locating him in one of them. In spite of disciplinary measures such embarrassing episodes kept recurring. The child apparently thought he could go anywhere he wished at any time.

At first he seemed to prefer LaVerna's company to Roger's, doubtless because his home had been woman-dominated. He had spent much of his time sitting in the house embroidering with his mother and twin sisters. He seemed to resent any attention which LaVerna gave to Roger. But this phase soon passed, and it was not long before he preferred Roger's company, especially since the wheel chair was usually the center of some interesting male activity.

He was curious about the missing leg but unable to understand the paralysis. "You mean I could—could kick you in the leg, I could even stomp on your foot, and—and it wouldn't even hurt?" The big eyes were round with unbelief. "You really mean that, mister, honest to gosh?"

"Honest to gosh," replied Roger. "But you may as well start calling us 'Mom' and 'Dad,' because it looks as if we're going to be your parents."

It was the height of the glad season when he arrived, and he soon found to his shocked surprise that he was expected to contribute to the family labor. He had never worked before in his life, nor had anybody within his immediate circle. Subsistence had come painlessly from welfare. However, by dint of coaxing, sterner persuasion, and example, he was soon doing his share more or less willingly: weeding, carrying the glads to the car, moving trays from one place to another.

This second glad season was one of vigorous expansion. Early in the spring Roger planted the seeds from his previous crossings in prune boxes. Putting an inch of gravel in the bottom, filling the box within one-half inch from the top with a mixture of half peat moss and half dirt, he was able to get three or four hundred seeds in one prune box, all planted in rows with tiny tags to indicate the varieties.

But this was only the beginning of a long process. The first year the seedlings would look like little more than spikes of grass. The second year a few of them might come to blossom. The good bloom would come in the third year, and perhaps then only one bulb of the lot would be considered worth saving.

During the winter Roger had corresponded with R. J. Nitchman, an Ohio florist, about new varieties. One he had suggested was Shirley Temple, a very large cream blossom, which promised to be a sure hit. One day a letter had come saying that Mr. Nitchman had a special buy on Shirley Temples. For only $200 Roger could buy a whole pint of bulblets. It was a big investment, but they managed to raise it. In the spring Roger planted the bulblets very carefully, and they grew well. However, the spikes tended to bend over and grow crooked, so his first real investment was a disappointing and very expensive flop.

With so many more bulbs he needed more land, especially since it was not recommended that the same soil be used two years in succession. He rented a big lot on Adams Street, about two blocks away. That season he planted in rows rather than beds, and the yield was gratifying. Sales of both cut flowers and bulbs burgeoned. But prosperity was still around several distant corners, and he was in no position yet to give up his steady, if petty, income from the welfare office. At this level of his spiraling plans more sales merely meant more money to buy more glads.

It was during this summer of 1938 that Roger first called on Robert Cox, a meeting which was to have far-reaching consequences for both of them.

Robert was a paraplegic who lived in Corunna, three miles from Owosso. His paralysis had occurred at about the same time as Roger's, when he had been crushed between a barn and a tractor. But since that time he had never left his bed. In fact, staying in bed was the easy way out for the paraplegic at this time. Many of them did not realize that it was possible to sit up. Once a year, when the county fair was held in Corunna, friends would wheel Robert, still in his bed, to the fairground, and he would sell Christmas cards. This was his sole earned income. An article published about Roger and his glads in the local paper came to his attention, and he sent a message asking Roger to come and see him.

Roger found a young man some years his junior, thin as a rail, body stiff as a board from head to foot, but with eyes that looked literally on fire.

"Is it true, all those things they say you can do?" Robert demanded, scarcely waiting for an introduction. "You work, you're married, you raise glads, you drive a car, you get around all by yourself?"

"Well—see for yourself," said Roger. "I'm here. Nobody brought me. I would have come earlier, but I've been working all day at the welfare office. And here are some of my glads. I thought you might like a bouquet. It's one of my favorites, called Golden Goddess."

"And you're honest to God paralyzed, like me, from the waist down?"

"Honest to God."

The eyes glowed like two live coals. "Do you suppose I could get up in a wheel chair like that?"

They talked for a long time. As a result Robert Cox went down to University Hospital. The doctors did everything possible to make his hips bend. But he had been in bed too long, and no one had realized the necessity of massaging his joints hour after hour to keep them supple, or the possibility of his sitting up. It was no use. Finally they conceived the idea of breaking his legs. This also was unsuccessful because of infection and complications. But Robert did not have fire in his eyes for nothing. Only sheer will power saved his life. Once he had seen what another man could do, there was no stopping him. Finally he was forced to have both legs amputated at the hips. Before many months he also was in a wheel chair and, later, driving his own car. In years to come his wheel tracks and Roger's were to cross many times.

For Roger his first meeting with Bob Cox was also a startling confrontation with himself. The experience forced him into a troubling evaluation of his own achievements. Sure, he had made progress in conquering his handicap, enough perhaps to warrant a bit of secret smugness about his accomplishments! He had formulated a purpose for his life and stuck to it. But what was he making of that life? Face it honestly. A sequence as narrow and rigid as a nautilus shell! *Self*-survival, *self*-preservation, *self*-sufficiency, *self*-fulfillment. What else had he achieved? Even his concern for life and children—what had it really been but *self*-concern?

Now all at once the shell had cracked open. He had touched and changed a person unrelated to *self*. Through the crack he suddenly glimpsed with mounting excitement another world filled with infinite possibilities of self-*giving*.

117

But it was only a crack. And although it remained open, the pressures of living closed in to keep it from widening. The shell continued to bound his daily existence, enclose him in a tight spiral of problems related to self and family.

New problems arose with Dick when school started. He had much to learn. One night he wanted LaVerna to play a game with him. "I'm sorry, Dick. I can't now. I have these papers to correct."

"What do you have to teach for?" he asked curiously.

"Why, to earn money, so we'll all have enough to live on."

The big brown eyes were skeptical. "But you don't have to teach, and Dad needn't go down to that office every day. You could just as well live on welfare."

It was a formidable task teaching him the virtues and rewards of independence, but a triumphant day when the lessons showed signs of paying off. They had taken him shopping and bought him a brown suit—his first long pants—with bow tie, socks, shoes, and a natty little cap. It was the first full outfit he had ever had, and he was inordinately proud.

"But I ought to pay for it somehow," he worried aloud.

"O.K.," said Roger, "you can. There are lots of glad bulbs in the basement. I'll give you so much a tray for cleaning them." He named a good price.

They put a paper on the wall to record Dick's earnings. The boy wanted to know how much everything had cost, added the amounts, and figured how many trays would defray his debt, then worked diligently evenings and Saturdays and vacations until all the clothes were paid for.

It was even harder giving him a sense of security. Was it fear, wondered LaVerna, on a day so hot she had not worn even a light sweater to school, that made him come running to meet her wearing two heavy sweaters, the perspiration running off his face? Was he afraid it would turn cold or rain or snow? Or did he need these outward symbols of his new security to give it a sense of reality? She could never quite fathom the reason.

Nor could she understand why, each time he looked forward to something with great anticipation, when it came he was unable to enjoy it. That fall she took him to a football game. He had babbled excitedly about the prospect for a week. They sat in the bleachers with some of her fellow teachers, who derived great amusement from Dick's excitement. All during the first half he cheered lustily and jumped up and down. Then all at once he started crying. During the second half he never looked at the game, no matter how excited others became. When the game was over, he refused to walk home with LaVerna and all the way kept several steps behind. She said to Roger in exasperation, "I'll never take him to a ball game again."

It was the same way at Christmas. He was tremendously excited. But when LaVerna asked him to help trim the tree a week before the holiday, he refused. Oh, no, his mother always put the tree up the night before Christmas, and they never saw it until the gifts were all on it!

"We like to enjoy our tree ahead of time," explained LaVerna, who had been anticipating his pleasure almost more than Dick himself. He would not come into the room, but after she had disappointedly abandoned the decorating, leaving the ornaments on the divan, he peered through the door, finally stole inside, and began fingering the decorations. After a while he put one ornament on the tree, then another, until all were on, massed on a single branch. After he had gone to bed, LaVerna distributed them in more orderly fashion.

It was even worse on Christmas Eve, when Roger's family came to share their tree. Dick would not play Santa Claus. Since he had come to them with little more than the clothes he wore, relatives, neighbors, friends had outdone themselves in buying him gifts, but he took them all to his room, refusing to open them. It was a disappointing fiasco. Eventually, however, he made atonement. Before the evening was over he began appearing with one after the other of his gifts, raving about them, jumping up and down, displaying so much pleasure and excitement that it was almost impossible to get him to bed.

"But *why?*" agonized LaVerna. "What makes him act so?"

"Who knows?" Roger was less concerned. "Perhaps because his foster father was killed on Christmas Eve. We'll never know. But don't worry. Time will take care of it."

Roger was by no means an easygoing or permissive father. He expected his son to work as well as play—but not alone. Except when he was sick, he always worked with him. Raising glads was a year-round business. In the spring they must prepare the ground, soak the bulbs in bichloride of mercury to get rid of the little insects called "thrips," plant, hoe. In summer came the weeding, the spraying, the cutting, the carting to market, the waiting on customers, the hybridizing, using paper bags and tweezers and innumerable wired wood labels bearing the name of each parent, reminding one of the pedigree of a dog. Dick came to enjoy this part of the work, it was so full of surprises.

Fall and winter were not so enjoyable. The bulbs had to be dug, thousands of them, and the dirt sifted to get all the bulblets. Sometimes they dug through frozen ground, well into the fall. But Dick never remembered having to dig alone, except one season when Roger was sick. It was a winter's job to clean the bulbs after they had dried, to remove the old roots, check the bulbs for disease, separate the bulbs from the bulblets. But here again he never had to work alone. Roger always worked with him.

And there was time for play after work and on weekends. Often Roger played with him. He took him bass fishing on the Shiawassee, on camping trips to Lake Leelanau. He taught him how to play croquet and chess. Roger was tops at croquet. Using a sawed-off mallet, he would lean over the side of his chair, steady the ball with his hand, then send it flying. It was a long time before Dick could beat him. And as for chess . . . Once when Roger was sick in bed and Dick had become quite proficient, he and Bob McCarthy challenged Roger to a game. They lasted less than five minutes. Although Dick was his father's best pupil, he never did learn to beat him. In fact, most things that he could do, or that other people could do, Dad could do better.

As he grew older, Roger coached him in track. Dick also could run well. He would practice running to school and back, three-quarters of a mile. Then sometimes after school Roger would go to the athletic field and give him pointers. Dick was intensely proud of Roger's cups and plaques and ribbons and pennants.

"Oh, your father's O.K.," he might be heard to argue with a schoolmate, "but you should see my dad run!"

"Your dad! But he's in a wheel chair. He can't run."

"He don't need to. He's already done it. He broke all the records. Your dad didn't do that, did he?"

"Maybe not. But—my dad can walk now, and yours can't."

"Huh! I'll bet my dad could do anything your dad could do, except walk, and do it better!"

And with just a few exceptions, Dick was probably right.

The Arnetts working with the author
in their home at Belleville, Michigan.

Far Left: Young Roger Arnett with Coach Olds
at Michigan State Normal College.

Upper Left: Roger Arnett, champion runner.

Lower Left: Roger and LaVerna soon after marriage,
with his parents, Mr. and Mrs. James Arnett.

Above: Ready to take off on a pastoral call.

Photographs by Courier-Journal and Louisville Times

Upper Left: Weeding glads from scooter,
with Ronnie and Faye helping.

Lower Left: Getting into truck to take glads to market,
with Ronnie helping.

Above: Roger hoisting himself to the tractor seat.

Upper Right: Running the tractor.

Lower Right: Roger and his daughter Faye.

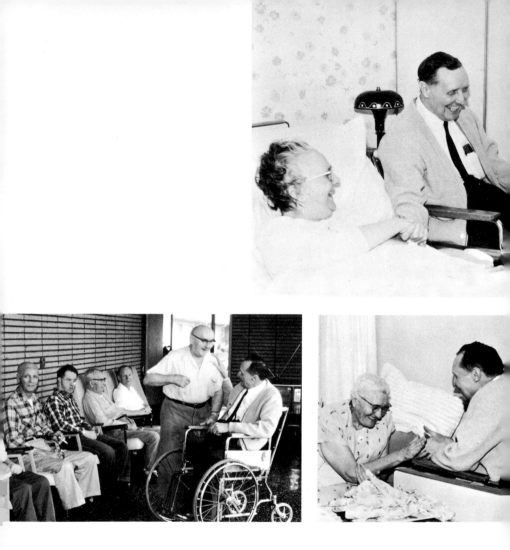

Upper: A pleasant call on Helen Eddy and Gayle Marland.

Lower Left: Calling on the men in a home.

Center: "The touch of a hand."

Right: Giving communion.

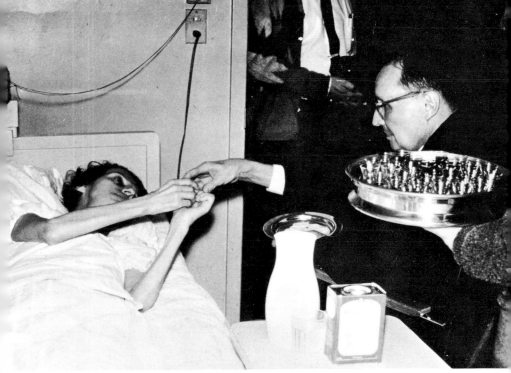

Receiving citation from Governor Schricker of Indiana
with Paul Schmidt and Ray Davis looking on.

The glad business grew. The year after Dick came, 1939, Roger had to rent an even larger piece of ground. In late May that year a hard freeze came after many of his early-blooming varieties were up, and the next morning he went over to look at them with heavy premonition. As he expected, they were all black as coal. But to his relief many of them revived, and the crop was not a total loss.

He made many more crosses that summer, and the first seedlings from his earlier crossings bloomed. Although he knew they were no world beaters, they were his own creations, and he was as thrilled as a parent with a new baby. He visited many more glad shows. And there were many, many more flowers to cut and sell. The drudgery of making the bouquets fell largely on LaVerna, and, though she did no complaining, she secretly began to hate the sight of glads. People came to the house for flowers every day of the week and at all hours of the day and night. She was almost glad when "vacation" was over and she could go back to the "work" of teaching school.

In the spring of 1940 Roger's father was thrown out of work because of the permanent closing of the stove foundry. There were no jobs available to a man of fifty-five. The glad business interested him, for he had always had a yearning to return to the soil, and he and Roger decided to go into partnership. Roger would go on working at the welfare office and furnish the stock. His father would do much of the field work. They rented ten acres of land about five miles from Owosso and purchased a small garden tractor for planting and cultivating. It was equipped with a hitch connected with the front of Roger's wheel chair, and he controlled it himself as it pulled him up and down between the rows. They started the project with high hopes.

The weather was beautiful for planting, dry and sunny, and it stayed so. Day after day passed with no rain. The glads germinated and grew, even produced flowers, but the blooms were short, the stems stunted. As summer progressed, with only one good rain, they seemed to get shorter. The Arnetts tried wholesaling the Detroit market. "Well, you can send them down, and we'll try to sell them on consignment." They did so, but there were too many blooms in competition. It was a disastrous year for all, including Dick, who, at age twelve, found the hoeing and weeding of the long, long rows interminable.

The year brought physical setbacks as well as economic ones.

Because of a failure to use proper cushions, in the late fall Roger developed a huge abscess on his right hip. The sulfa drugs, though effective, proved to be no cure-all.

"We might have known it," his brother-in-law Eldred Waters commented drily. "One of those mules took sick yesterday, and every time that mule of mine gets sick, you do, too. Never fails."

"That's because he's so stubborn," said LaVerna with affectionate candor.

This time, she discovered, it was no joking matter. The abscess was a very bad one. Two or three hours after it had opened she noticed that Roger's face was the color of the pillowcase. She threw back the covers and found him lying unconscious in a pool of blood from shoulders to knees. She felt like fainting, but instead called the doctor. Fortunately he was in and came on the run. He stopped the bleeding and helped her clean up the bed. LaVerna became irritated because he seemed to be watching her rather than Roger.

"I suppose you're expecting me to faint," she said acidly. "I'm not going to."

He looked at her in admiration. "Well, if you don't now, you never will."

And she never did.

Although Roger must have lost half his blood, to LaVerna's surprise no transfusion was suggested. When she thought he had recovered sufficiently to eat a good meal, she cooked a wonderful steak dinner and set the table in his bedroom, so that the family could all eat together. Before Roger finished giving the blessing, over came the pitcher of water, spilling into their laps. Raising her head, LaVerna was terrified to see him jerking and shaking, white as a sheet. She screamed at him, over and over, and he failed to answer. Frightened, Dick ran out of the room. The telephone seemed miles, years away. *He's dying*, thought LaVerna. *That's what happens when a person dies. Our married life, so short, and now it's over!* Somehow she called the doctor.

"He's gone," LaVerna told him, meeting him at the door. "I'm sure this time—" But as they walked down the hall they heard his voice. When they entered the room, he was conscious.

"He must have fainted," marveled Dr. Arnold, looking perplexed, "but the books say you don't faint in bed."

This time he did recommend a transfusion, and again Charlie

Dynes came to the rescue. Going to the hospital with Roger, he gave him a long, direct transfer. It was a painful process, for Roger had lost so much blood that the vessels had collapsed, and the doctor had difficulty finding the vein. Reaction was severe. Chill followed chill. The nurses covered him so heavily with blankets that LaVerna thought the bed would collapse. But Charlie Dynes, always keenly sensitive to others' pains, suffered from the ordeal worse then Roger.

"I wish we could have swapped places," he lamented.

Roger came home around midnight. Although LaVerna had thoughtfully put the beautiful steak dinner back in the oven, no one seemed to want any.

There was humor even in this near-tragic incident. Soon afterward a couple, man and wife, came in to call.

"I just told Ed," said the woman to Roger, "that we were going to call on people now, not wait until it was too—"

She stopped hastily, but not quite soon enough. Her flaming face showed her sudden awareness that in this instance it was already "too late."

Roger accepted this setback and the dry glad season with much the same philosophical aplomb. Both were natural hazards, one of being a paraplegic, the other of raising gladiolus. It was neither physical weakness nor discouragement which caused him to retrench in the glad business the following year, confining his planting to the home lot. Since James Arnett was depending wholly on the glads for income, and Roger was not, he gave his father all the name varieties and kept his own seedlings. By now he had thousands of them, grown from the hundreds of crosses he had made, and it was in them that his creative interest lay. The summer was full of constant delights and surprises as one variety after the other appeared. Even Dick became excited over the many new colors and combinations, especially since there was so much less work to be done.

When they took an exhibit to the Northeastern Gladiolus Society show in Bay City and won a cup for the best seedling, Dick was almost more thrilled than Roger. He carried the cup all over the neighborhood, proudly exhibiting it. Then he made a sign to place in front of the cans of glads displayed on the lawn: "EXTRA SPE-CIAL. ARNETT GLADS."

But this season also brought its disappointments. One of the crosses made in 1937—Candlelight, a seedling out of Gold Dust—was just now coming to full fruition. It bloomed very early in the year, at least a week ahead of most other varieties, and Roger had great hopes for it. This season it had produced an excellent crop of bulbs.

"I think next year," he told Dick when they were doing the fall digging, "we can put that on the market."

Being a new variety as well as early, it had excellent financial prospects. Roger was well satisfied with the tray of bulbs, carefully labeled. They started digging the next variety. What was Roger's horror to see Dick unwittingly dump the new set of bulbs on top of the tray of Candlelight! It was a major tragedy. A few bulbs that they were sure were Candlelight were salvaged, and new stock had to be propagated from them. But the mistake was a costly one.

"Oh, well," Roger comforted the stricken Dick, "that's just one of the little hazards of the glad business."

But with willful mistakes he was far less lenient. One day in August, at the height of the glad season, he had given Dick a job to do before going to work at the office. Returning, he found that Dick had not done it. Roger's blood pressure rose. Seldom had he been so angry with the boy. He gave him a blistering reprimand.

That night when he went to bed he discovered a bunch as big as his fist on the rear of his body. The result, he had not the slightest doubt, as much of mental as of physical irritation! And that, he told himself with some chagrin, was one of the hazards of a hasty temper as well as of paraplegia.

8

Adopting a ten-year-old boy, LaVerna discovered, would never fulfill her yearning for motherhood. She wanted a baby. So strong was the desire that it became almost an obsession. She envied every pregnant woman she saw. Frequent visits with Barbara, her sister Vivian's adorable three-year-old, only whetted the desire to knife-sharp intensity.

They applied to adoption agencies, but were frankly told that Roger did not have the life or financial expectancy to warrant their being considered as a possibility. LaVerna inquired of two doctors if they would try to find them a baby to adopt.

"Sure," said their friend Dr. Arnold, "I'll put you at the top of my list."

But twice during the following year LaVerna inquired of new foster parents where they had secured their baby, receiving the answer, "From Dr. Arnold." Evidently the "top of the list" did not mean much.

"Perhaps if I stopped teaching," thought LaVerna, "we might be considered better prospects." So in February, 1940, she announced to the school board that she would not teach full-time the following year. And, although she did much substitute teaching during the next two years, she remained free to give up work at any time. Still no baby.

Freedom from full-time teaching, however, meant no more leisure time. When she was not substituting or cutting and arranging glads, she was often nursing sick members of her family. In the fall of 1941 Roger had another bout with infections. He was just getting up again when her sister Vivian was threatened with a miscarriage and told she must stay in bed for the next few months. For some time LaVerna tried to run two households; then, thinking it would be easier to care for her sister in her own home, right after Christmas she moved Vivian into town. Soon afterward Eldred went to the hospital with an ear infection, and when he returned he was also at the house.

Vivian's son was born in January, prematurely, and lived only a few hours. LaVerna felt the loss almost as keenly as her sister. Finding vicarious satisfaction in Vivian's motherhood, it was as if she had lost a child of her own. There were more weeks of convalescence before Eldred could take his wife home.

The evening after they left LaVerna felt as if a tremendous weight had been lifted. For the first time in months they were able to have their nightly "constitutional," a rubber of bridge with their friends Charlie and Anita Dynes. There were the usual gay interchange of banter, the pretense of disgust with Roger for holding all the cards and playing them with irritating craftiness, and between Roger and Charlie the jolly, half-insulting badinage which can be ventured only by two people completely at ease with each other. Charlie knew, for example, that Roger had not the slightest sensitivity about his handicap. One could safely poke fun at it.

"Come on, Rog," he would goad when the bidding lagged, "quit dragging your feet."

LaVerna suddenly became deathly tired. The first stimulus of relief dissolved in an overwhelming flood of fatigue. She thought, "I'm not going to substitute again until I get rested. This week I'm going to spend as much time as I can in bed." It was at that moment that the telephone rang. She reached to answer it without getting out of her chair. It was the high-school principal's voice.

"Marshall Simpson broke his back this afternoon tobogganing," he said. "The new semester starts tomorrow morning. You've taught all his subjects. Can you take his work until we find out whether Marsh will ever be able to teach again?"

Stunned, LaVerna hesitated, and the principal misinterpreted the hesitation. "This won't be at substitute wages," he said quickly. "You will get the same salary as when you were a full-time teacher. And if you're willing to do it, we can hold Marsh's job for him."

LaVerna's head whirled. She couldn't . . . yet she had to. It was impossible to live on Roger's income, even though it had increased through the years to $105 a month. She of all people should not refuse this opportunity. Besides, there was Marsh Simpson. She could not let him down.

"I'll be there," she said.

It was a strange coincidence that during the preceding week she and Marsh had both attended a first-aid class, where accidents had been discussed.

"I'd like to stress," LaVerna had interpolated, "that in case of accident an ambulance must be called and the injured person taken to hospital on a stretcher, especially if he is unconscious. If an ambulance had been called when Roger was hurt, he might be walking today."

It was the following Sunday that Marsh and his wife and another couple were tobogganing. They decided to take just one more trip down the hill. Marsh was sitting in front. They hit a stump. The rest were able to roll off, but Marsh took the full brunt of the collision. He was conscious though in terrific pain. And he remembered what LaVerna had said. "No! Call an ambulance," he told his companions when they started to lift him. They did so. In time he recovered and, except for a slight limp, was able to walk as well as ever.

"Which I may very well owe to you," he told LaVerna later.

The next day LaVerna went to school so exhausted she could barely stand. As she walked down the aisles, she had to hang on to the desks. That night she went to an eye specialist to see whether her glasses needed changing. After examining her, he said, "You're in no condition to teach. Go home and rest."

But after she explained the situation he relented. "All right. Try it for one week. But you're only to teach. Give up every other duty."

She resigned her YWCA sponsorship, her Sunday-school class, canceled appointments right and left. She hired household help. The doctor let her continue for a second week. On the following Friday, since her last period of the day was free, she felt well enough to correct papers. In came the principal.

"Mrs. Weatherby would like you to take her last hour typing class," he announced, "so she can have the period free."

LaVerna opened her mouth to protest, then thought, "What's the use?" So, starting the next Monday, she had another class of forty-four students. It was weeks before strength returned, but by the end of the semester she was beginning to fret because she had promised the doctor: no housework. The white walls and woodwork, grimy in the sunlight, tempted her perfectionist zeal.

Came Friday of examination week. There would be another week for correcting exams, entering marks, and getting through graduation. Then, she vowed, tired or not, nothing would stop her from a furious week of housecleaning before the glad season started. But something did.

"Roger wants you to call him," said Wilhelmina, the principal's secretary.

She called him just before lunch. "Hi!" he greeted. "How would you like a six-weeks-old baby tomorrow morning?"

Her heart lurched. "What—you don't mean— Oh, Roger, not at last—"

No. He hastened to disillusion her. It was not a baby to adopt. It was just that the social worker at welfare had to find a place to board a baby for a couple of months, until his mother could take care of him.

LaVerna rallied from the first pang of disappointment. She thought, "Well, I'd get two months of a baby, anyway. Maybe that's all I'll ever get."

"I'll have to wait a week," she temporized. "All those exams to correct, no housecleaning done—"

"No. It's tomorrow or nothing. He has to leave the hospital in the morning."

"Tell them—tell them we'll take him," she threw back recklessly.

She tried to correct bookkeeping sets that afternoon, but the figures blurred into outlines of chubby arms and dimpled cheeks. That night she was too excited to eat. Suddenly she thought, "I don't even know how to bathe a little baby!"

"Let's go over to Vivian's," she said.

Vivian came back with them, bringing Barbara, a bagful of baby clothes, and numerous accessories, even to a set of baby scales.

As LaVerna opened the door the next morning to the baby's mother and the social worker, she thought suddenly, "Here I've been picturing a beautiful baby! Whatever gave me that idea? I'll bet it's the homeliest baby you ever looked at." As they came in and sat down. she was tongue-tied and deflated.

"Don't you want to look at the baby?" the social worker asked finally.

"Yes. Oh, yes, of course."

She flipped back the blanket, and LaVerna caught her breath. It was the most beautiful baby she had ever seen. Enormous brown eyes, fluff of brown hair, complexion like glad petals, and—he smiled at her! From that moment she was lost.

LaVerna found opportunity to talk to the social worker alone. Wasn't there a chance that conditions making it impossible for the young mother to take her baby home now might persist? Might not the baby become adoptable?

"Oh, my, no!" The response was emphatic. "She would never give him up. Take him with the idea that you will have him for just a couple of months."

LaVerna was stubborn. "I'll take him under this condition, that if he does become adoptable, we will have him. I don't want to take care of him two months just to hand him over to some other party." The social worker agreed.

For the next three days LaVerna corrected exams, while Vivian cared for the baby Ronnie. By Monday noon she had finished, so she went to the high school to mark her grades. By Wednesday she was ready to take over the baby's care.

Four-year-old Barbara was present when Ronnie arrived. She thought for years after that that that was the way babies came. "I was there. I know," she would say. "I saw Ronnie when he came."

The next Saturday the baby's mother came to see him. LaVerna had just given him a bath and changed his clothes. The girl grabbed him up and ran out to the car to show him to her parents. Watching, LaVerna thought, "Someday she will take him just like that, and it will be the end."

When the girl came back, LaVerna said, "I don't know as you're planning on ever letting this baby go, but if you ever come to the point where you feel you have to, we want him."

The girl's eyes filled. "Oh, I couldn't ever give him up!" Reluctantly she returned him to the bassinet. "But I can see he is having wonderful care, and I promise that if I ever do have to give him up, you can have him."

The summer was half ecstasy, half agony. LaVerna was torn between hope and fear. She *had* to believe something would happen so she could keep the baby, even while she knew she must adjust to the idea of losing him. It was an impossible conflict. She solved it by keeping constantly busy: cutting and sorting glads, canning mountains of fruits and vegetables. For if they did keep the baby, she could not teach, and income would be pared to the core. She dared not take time really to enjoy the baby. At night she would stand sometimes looking down at him, asleep, her arms aching to hold him, but she would not let herself.

Ronnie soon outgrew his bassinet. He would cry during the night, and LaVerna would find his head jammed against the bars.

"He's got to have a crib," she told the baby's mother on her next visit. Knowing the girl had not been working, she added, "Of course if we knew we were going to keep him, we would be happy to buy it. Otherwise, you should."

The girl shook her head. "I have no money," she said finally. "You'd better buy it." But, though the words caused hope fiercely to flare, LaVerna knew there had been no promise.

Dr. Arnold kept nagging Roger. "You know LaVerna can't stand it to keep on taking care of that baby, and then give it up. I'm warning you. She'll break. You'll have to get a yes or no answer on the child, and soon."

It was only two weeks to the opening of school. Marsh Simpson asked LaVerna to teach half time for him. Another school wanted her full time. Of course she could not accept either offer if she kept the baby. The torture of uncertainty became unbearable. One noon she sat down at the table and could not take a swallow.

"All right, this is it," said Roger with finality. "You'll have to write and tell her she must make up her mind."

LaVerna wrote to the baby's mother. "If I can't keep him," she said, "I have to teach. I couldn't stay at home without having him there."

It was the girl's sister who answered. She said they could have the baby. As soon as his mother had an opportunity, she would come and sign the papers. Still there was only hope, not assurance. They had nothing in the girl's own handwriting. But LaVerna refused her two chances to teach. It was not until near the last of September that the baby's mother came to the door.

"I've been over to the judge of probate's office and signed the papers," she said. "The judge wants you to come in tomorrow morning and sign."

LaVerna went back into the house and took Ronnie in her arms. She sat down and rocked and rocked him. She stroked and stroked the cheeks that were like creamy glad petals. She pillowed the small head on her shoulder, letting the fluff of brown hair tickle her throat and chin so that she laughed, and that made him laugh, and they both had a great time laughing together. Then, when the bright brown eyes had dulled into sleep, she still held and held him. She was like a thirsty traveler who, after glimpsing many mirages, finally finds water and drinks and drinks; or, more accurately, like a new mother who, after going through long months of waiting and much travail, finally holds her baby in her arms for the first time.

But even after the papers were signed, her worries were not over. One Sunday in December the baby's young mother came to the house with an older brother.

"He's leaving for the Army," she told LaVerna, "and he's just found out about my baby. He wants to see him."

LaVerna was entertaining company for dinner. Not wishing to make a scene, she led the two into the bedroom where Ronnie was napping and returned to her guests. When she carried dishes from the table, the girl came into the kitchen. Her eyes, huge and dark like Ronnie's, were defiant. "My brother says I have to take him home," she said.

LaVerna's heart lurched, but she tried to speak calmly. "But you know you can't. You know you signed the papers."

They went away then, but after a few days the Arnetts received a letter. "Since gas rationing," wrote the baby's mother, "I can't come to see Ron, so I'll just have to have him back. You'll have to give him up."

Roger and LaVerna penned the reply together. "You knew when you signed the papers that the adoption was final. Judge Matthews told you so. We are sorry to have to disappoint you, but the baby is legally ours."

LaVerna lived in terror for days, even though Roger laughed at her fears. "My dear, the papers have been signed. There's nothing they can do." Yet for weeks afterward she felt the presence of impending disaster. She would not leave Ronnie alone. She dreaded to open each mail. She trembled at the sound of the doorbell. But not until three years later was she to learn that her premonition had been well founded, or how close they had come to losing him.

When Ronnie arrived, Roger knew he must find a new job. The thought almost made him sick. Already he could feel the pitying but wary glances, hear the transparent excuses. Then, if the miracle happened and he was hired, there would be the inevitable difficulties of adjustment, including the temptation to most employers to take advantage of a handicapped worker. But, as his friend Charlie Dynes put it, he mustn't drag his heels. At least he had one advantage, he told himself grimly. Who should know better how to set wheels in motion?

There was a new factory in town, the Bendix Aviation Company, making aircraft carburetors. Since it was wartime, labor was at a premium. Roger spoke to Dr. Smith, a dentist who was their very good friend and who belonged to the Rotary Club, and the doctor spoke to the personnel manager of the plant, not once but persistently. Finally Roger was called for an interview and, to his delighted amazement, hired. He began work in August.

One of his duties was to keep track of the labor needs of the plant and to screen prospective employees. If he thought an applicant could be used, he would send him to the employment manager, Glenn Wilson. Occasionally he was able to break down a little of the prejudice by getting another handicapped man employed, such as Arlo Parkinson, who suffered from severe curvature of the spine and whose wife Roger had known in school. Arlo had made a poor living by doing watch repairing. Knowing his mechanical ability, Roger sent him in to Mr. Wilson, and he was hired. Twenty years later Arlo was still voicing his gratitude.

It was also Roger's duty to take charge of all the factory equipment and keep records of it. Because his work involved traveling great distances about the plant, he was furnished an electric wheel chair. Now, for the first time since his accident, his handicap proved an advantage. He could travel twice as fast as the fleetest man on foot!

And for the first time also he had realized his goal of a salary commensurate with his ability and education. He was no longer dependent on his wife for help in supporting the family! It was a major triumph.

But the success, sweet as it was, had a bitter flavor. He dared not trust in its security, for he feared the job was only temporary. The glad business, if he could only develop it sufficiently, would be permanent.

And, come wars or new babies or new jobs, the glads bloomed. In 1943 Roger grew them on a farm outside of town owned by Dr. Arnold. It was heavy soil and weedy, and the season was extremely hot. But somehow he and Dick produced a fair crop and dug a vast number of bulbs.

He must have more land to grow them. And, with a family of four, the house was becoming too small. The next spring they began looking for a larger place and found it in Corunna, three miles away. It seemed ideal: a big square house, six acres of land, a large barn for bulb storage, yet right in town, only three blocks from the county courthouse, and on sale for just a little more than they could get for their house in Owosso. They put the latter up for sale and sold it in a week, moving into the new house in May, just in time to get the glads into the ground. Roger's father plowed and prepared the land. The place soon became home for everybody but Ronnie, who, every time he saw someone put on his wraps, would run and get his, crying, "Go home, let's go home!"

The new house had two floors and a basement. This time an electric elevator was installed. Roger's uncle Irving, his mother's brother, who had just lost his wife, came to live with them that summer and did the carpenter work, constructing a square shaft on one side of the house. Friends from the Bendix plant did the installing. Uncle Irving also planted a vegetable garden, helped with the glads, and assisted with the building of a new garage and ramp.

To their amazement Ronnie, now age two, was soon contributing his share of labor. One day in May he stood watching, fascinated, while Roger and Dick planted, Roger making the stake, Dick placing it in the ground, and then planting the bulbs just the right distance apart. All at once Ronnie picked up a stake and a sack of bulbs, walked to a new row, set the stake at the right place, and planted the bulbs with meticulous accuracy. His elders were astonished.

He displayed other aptitudes. One was an uncanny sense of direction.

"Come here, Mom," he called soon after they moved. "Look out the south window and see a fire."

LaVerna had to stop and decide which was south. When she did, and looked out the window sure enough, there was the fire. But how did that two-year-old know? After that Roger deliberately tested the child, taking him in the car and making many turns, then asking him in which direction they were going. Ronnie could always tell. Like some animals, he seemed to have a built-in compass.

His talents were not always so constructive. One morning when LaVerna was upstairs making beds, she heard him screaming. Rushing down, she found the toaster on the floor belching smoke, Ronnie jumping up and down beside it. Hastily she unplugged it. Then he led her to the stove. There in a small frying pan was an egg, yolk unbroken, no sign of a shell fragment, but no grease in the pan and, fortunately, no fire under it.

His genius for imitation was for a time a source of sore distress to LaVerna. Roger came in one day to find her in tears. She was sure Ronnie had been imitating her ungainly walk. Suppose it developed into a habit!

"Don't worry," he comforted. "He imitates me, too, tries to walk on one leg. And he's always wanting to ride around in my wheel chair. It's just a phase. It will pass." And of course it did.

With the end of the war in 1945 Roger's fears took tangible shape. There was talk of the Bendix plant shutting down. His father, who had been working there for more than two years, had already been laid off. Roger felt a surge of panic. Even able-bodied men were finding it hard to secure employment. What to do when the inevitable happened? Go back and beg for his miserable stipend from the welfare office? Pride forbid! He dreaded yet welcomed the necessity of making a major decision.

The idea long in the back of his mind now suddenly came to the fore. He had had long experience now in raising glads. Together he and his father had nearly four acres for cut flowers. Dick, with one year left in high school, was of invaluable help. Finally, after long debate and struggle with ominous misgivings, he decided to take the plunge, knowing that it might well be the end of his precious and hard-won independence. He would raise glads as his main occupation.

The first setback came when Dick chose to leave school and enter the service. Not yet eighteen, with no high-school diploma, he encountered strong opposition from parents and teachers, but his mind was made up. Regretfully Roger signed his papers. Dick went into the Navy just two weeks before the war ended.

That first glad season had to be one of major expansion. New markets must be found for cut flowers. One Saturday Roger took his mother to Flint, twenty-five miles away, and they rented a stall. To their surprise and delight their stock was sold out by noon, and they came home with ninety dollars. Then Roger determined to try the Lansing market. They sold out there. After that the older Arnetts, who were now in partnership with Roger and LaVerna, went to the Flint market, Roger and LaVerna to Lansing. They had a special trailer made which would hold a couple of hundred dozen glads. Since many of the varieties were from Roger's own crossings and different from any others, they had special appeal.

But Roger's ambition had expanded along with the glad business. He dared not trust to it entirely for the financial independence which had now become his chief goal. And it was a seasonal occupation. That fall he and two Bendix associates, Floyd Sawyer and Leonard Nogash, decided to go into business together. They pooled resources, borrowed money, and made a down payment on a machine shop in Owosso, with the intention of making toys. Floyd had much experience, Leonard was an engineer, and, thanks to the glads, Roger had his share of the cash. He also was secretary-treasurer, ran the office, and did the accounting. They started to manufacture toy refrigerators and stoves—too late for that year's Christmas season. And they soon ran into other difficulties. It was hard to get steel and other supplies. Although they had the punch press and machinery, all the dies had to be made. Troubles multiplied, and cash ran out. Roger emerged from the venture a sadder, wiser, and much poorer man, but fiercely determined to make the next glad season an even greater success.

More expansion was necessary. Now he really *had* to make money. He invested in an Allis Chalmers Model C tractor, similar to his father's, which could be used for plowing, cultivating, and in the fall for loosening the bulbs. Again he had to design his own hand controls, taking the ideas to a blacksmith for execution. Then he had to devise some way of getting on and off the tractor. Again he solved the problem with gadgets of his own device. Two cables were strung across the shed above the tractor seat; a block and tackle were swung from the top cable. He had a sort of boatswain's sling made, consisting of an iron frame covered with canvas. He would lift himself in the wheel chair, then somebody would slip the sling under him. Attaching a hook from the tackle, he could then hoist himself to a level just above the seat and, after locking the block, swing himself along the crossline to a point just above the seat, and lower himself into it. The seat was an old car bucket seat fitted with a cushion. Except for the necessity of assistance in getting into the sling, he was completely independent.

It was a terribly wet spring, which meant that they were late getting the land plowed and were unable to get early cut flowers. Roger and his father finally decided to plow at the same time in the same field. Then if one got stuck, the other could haul him out. In order to plant more bulbs, and faster, Roger designed a two-row planter out of an old tub with a chute down to the furrows. Then, when the shovels on the cultivator bar underneath the tractor plowed out the furrow, the man sitting on a special seat at the front of the tractor could drop the bulbs into the furrow the right distances apart, after which the shovels on the back end of the tractor would come along and cover them up.

Roger also had to find a more efficient way of getting around the fields after the planting was done. The wheel chair was much too slow, the earth too soft. He went over to the Cushman Scooter Bike Company in Lansing, and there he found just what he needed, a scooter bike with wheels six inches in diameter, eighteen inches high, designed to be dropped with paratroopers and usable on rough terrain. It had a side car low to the ground. He was exultant. Removing the frame of the side car, he took the top part of his old wooden wheel chair and welded it to the frame. Then he had hand controls attached to the cycle on the side next to the car. Sitting in the side car, he could easily operate the controls.

To accommodate the scooter they planted bulbs and bulblets in alternate rows, so the scooter could straddle the rows of bulblets, which did not grow tall. Roger could pass up and down the rows, doing all the weeding, hoeing, hybridizing, cutting, spraying, even the digging in the fall, almost without assistance. He often worked twelve or fourteen hours a day, sometimes long after dark by the lights on the tractor. During some fourteen-hour days he would not leave the tractor, and LaVerna would bring him his meals.

The season continued to be wet. He would go out in the field with the scooter bike, Ronnie usually with him, sun shining, then all at once—wham! A deluge of drenching rain! Flowers had to be cut on Monday, Wednesday, and Friday to prepare for marketing on the following days. One Friday when he was cutting, Ronnie was with him on the scooter bike. Roger could see the storm coming.

"Ron," he ordered, "run to the garage and get in the dry. Run quick!"

Ron ran a few steps, then turned back. "But, Daddy, Daddy, what are you going to do?" The answer was obvious: get soaked.

There were some setbacks that season. In the spring Roger started with a fine stock of about two thousand bulbs of a beautiful red variety, a cross out of Azalea by Picardy. They were big, tall, well-placed flowers, and he anticipated a heavy sale. But during the summer they fell victim to a new kind of plant disease, which killed every bulb and bulblet. However, there was triumph to balance this defeat. One crossing came this year to full fruition. It came from Euides out of Picardy and was a heavy-textured white blossom with a very light rose-pink blush and a faint rose feathering in its throat. It seemed to glow in the sunlight. Some of the stalks had as many as fourteen open blossoms at one time on a twenty-three-bud spike. Roger was intensely proud of it. It was his own creation, his gift of beauty to the world.

One Friday he took three perfect spikes of it and entered them in the Southeastern Michigan Glad Show at Detroit. The next day he received a telephone call saying that it had won the American Home Achievement Award, given for the best new variety, the most-coveted award any glad could receive in America. But he had entered it by number. It must have a name.

"What shall we call it?" he demanded of LaVerna excitedly.

They settled on the name White Challenge.

By working furiously, Roger in the field, LaVerna making hundreds of baskets, trays, sprays, bouquets; by taking hundreds of dozens of glads to market three times a week; by selling bulbs, bulblets, seedlings, they managed to meet their bills for all the new equipment. There was a new car, too, for the old one had been falling to pieces, and this also created a problem, for the new Olds had no running board on which to set a wheel chair. What to do? Then, wonder of wonders, they learned that the Everest-Jennings Company had just manufactured a folding wheel chair! Blessed coincidence that the collapsible wheel chair should come in just when the running board went out!

Successful though the season had been, the family still needed more income. So after the bulbs were dug, dried, and stored, Roger took a job as a bookkeeper. It lasted all winter and paid fifty dollars a week.

Not that the glad season ever really ended! In the fall there was the catalog to formulate and print, advertising the "Friendly Glad

Gardens" and describing all the varieties he had for sale. This year he sent out a mailing list of 900. And through the winter there were frequent meetings of the Michigan Gladiolus Society. With his father Roger attended most of them, not only in Michigan but in Chicago, Milwaukee, and other centers, where growers from all over the country would come to discuss new varieties, the trading of stocks, growing techniques, fertilizers, and other professional subjects. Roger soon became a popular man at these gatherings.

"The smilingest man at many gladiolus conferences, banquets, and shows," wrote Russell Everhart, a prominent glad grower of Ann Arbor in an article published in *The Gladiolus*, "is the handsome gentleman in the wheel chair, Roger P. Arnett of 220 Comstock, Corunna, Michigan. If you haven't met him personally and felt the warm cordiality of his handshake, let me introduce him to you. I know that your life will be much fuller for having known him."

That winter Roger, Russell Everhart, and Dr. Paul Krone, extension specialist in floriculture at Michigan State University, planned a lecture tour to interest different groups in the state in organizing local branches of the society. Each weekend they traveled to a different section of the state, starting in the early afternoon, holding their meeting, then returning late at night. Each would lecture on a different subject, Roger's being the crossing of varieties. Usually they would meet at Professor Krone's house in East Lansing, and he would do the driving.

His associates found Roger a jolly companion. He was always good-natured, never talked about himself, but chiefly about glads, which were his prime interest. At first they were a bit awkward in the presence of his handicap, questioning what to say or do, but they soon learned that, although he disliked being pushed or coddled, he welcomed help when necessary, which was often on these trips, since few public buildings were constructed without steps.

In Benton Harbor the meeting was held on the second floor of an old building used as a fire hall. It had very high stairs. Russ and Paul decided the only way to get him up was to carry him in his chair, so they puffed and struggled, finally setting him down to rest on the halfway landing. All at once somebody down below yelled up at them, "Why don't you use the elevator?"

On one occasion the handicap proved an asset. They were returning from Port Huron on a bitterly cold night. About midnight on the other side of Lapeer the car stopped dead. They tried to flag other cars, but all refused to stop. There had been a banditry on this same road recently. Cars became less and less frequent.

"Get me out in my wheel chair," suggested Roger. "Somebody will stop for me."

The next car stopped. A wrecker was routed out and the car hauled into Lapeer. But at two in the morning no mechanic could be found. The three sat in a hotel lobby all night. In the morning it took a mechanic scarcely ten minutes to remedy the trouble.

Roger and Russell Everhart remained closely associated through their work in this and other gladiolus organizations. Twice they attended national conventions together, Roger often driving all the way. Like most others who rode with him, Everhart was at first a bit nervous but soon completely confident. He derived great amusement from Roger's use of a stove poker to manipulate the accelerator when he got tired of driving with the hand control. He was less amused when at a meeting of the Michigan Gladiolus Society Roger played a trick on him. Both men were tied for the presidency. There was a commotion at the banquet table where they were sitting. "You'll take it, won't you?" gestured Roger from his end of the table. Everhart had a way of nodding when confused. Not understanding the gesture, he nodded now, and found himself president. Roger continued as secretary.

At the end of the article he wrote for *The Gladiolus* Russell Everhart summed up his admiration and affection:

"I can think of nothing finer to say of Roger than that he is running way out front in a perfect four-minute mile, which is the dream of every great miler."

But raising glads by no means monopolized all of Roger's energy and enthusiasm. His interest flowed through two other major outlets. One was the church.

He and LaVerna soon joined the Methodist Church after moving to Corunna. The minister, Harold Dakin, and his wife Margaret, with their four children, soon became their close friends. Faith, their daughter, used to help with the glads and often baby-sat with Ronnie.

Like most churches, this one presented difficulties for the handicapped. It had steps. Once Roger was being carried up by some of the older men of the church, and they almost dropped him. He was afraid one of the men was going to have a heart attack. This was always a worry, that a man with a bad back or a bad heart might insist on helping him. If one suffered an injury, he would never have forgiven himself. The experience kept him from services for some time. But both he and LaVerna soon became deeply involved in church work. There was a class of junior high boys which no one would teach. Roger took it. For some reason they were always attentive when he taught, partly because he talked on their level, perhaps more because he took such a personal interest in each boy. His handicap challenged them, made them both proud and protective. In fact, they wanted to do too much for him, push him around instead of letting him be independent. The Sunday-evening service was dying. Roger dusted off his violin and suggested hesitantly that he would play if it would help. It did. Then he was elected president of the Men's Club, and things started to happen. Suddenly his two major community interests—church and the handicapped—were flowing together.

It was in that same year, 1946, that Robert Cox came to see him. The change in the former bed patient was fantastic. Though still thin as a rail, a mere torso now that his legs had been amputated at the hips, he had turned into a human dynamo. He had left his bed for a wheel chair, learned to drive a car, worked for the Ford Motor Company during the war and traveled all over the country. Bob had designed and secured a folding wheel chair which would go inside a car, forerunner of the modern collapsible variety.

"You came to see me once," he said, "and look what you did for me. Now I've come to see you. Let's see if together we can do as much for some other people as you did for me."

Cox had gotten interested in the American Federation of the Physically Handicapped, headed by a remarkable man, Paul Strachan, in Washington. It was an organization of handicapped people banded together to work for one another and for all the handicapped. Its purpose was to act at both national and local levels, influencing legislation, promoting community activities, uniting for mutual helpfulness. He wanted Roger to help organize a chapter in Corunna. Roger was enthusiastic.

They made inquiries, advertised in the papers, and it was amazing how many physically handicapped people they discovered in the area. Organized into the Shiawassee County American Federation of the Physically Handicapped, a group of up to twenty-five met monthly with Roger and LaVerna. They came in wheel chairs, on crutches, hobbling with canes, led by friends or seeing-eye dogs.

There was Paul Olson, a blind man who had worked with Roger at Bendix, a fellow chess enthusiast, who with his wife had spent many previous evenings with the Arnetts. Because of him LaVerna had learned never to move the furniture around before a blind person came, and not to refill his cup with hot coffee without telling him. There were Raymond Dickinson, a watch repairman, and Marie Ebe, both severely handicapped by polio. Meeting here at the AFPH, they fell in love, were married, and adopted two children, besides having two of their own.

LaVerna always served refreshments. Although she prepared things which were simple and easy to eat, there was one blind young man who always refused. She decided finally that he was afraid of appearing awkward. The next time she put a plate on his lap, put his hand on it, and said, "Look, here is a sandwich." He ate ravenously. After that she made sure he knew just what was served.

"Would you like to help me pass things?" she asked another guest who had lost an arm and was obviously used to being waited on.

"Oh!" The reply was a little shocked. "Don't you see? I couldn't."

"Why not?" she replied. "You've got one hand, haven't you?" And the self-pitying one was soon busily involved in serving.

Roger soon developed mutual interest between his two groups, the church and the handicapped. He interested the Men's Club in projects which would make it easier for the handicapped to come to church. They devised plans for an S-shaped ramp to be built over one side of the two-way steps leading to a side door of the church. Then, working together on Saturdays, they scoured the community with tractors, picking up earth and stones; built forms, made a gently sloping ramp of cement, and enclosed it in an attractive railing. A big dedication service was held to which all members of the Federation branch were invited. Some came in wheel chairs, many on crutches. Aged church members who had found the steps difficult turned out in large numbers. Roger was one of the first to mount the ramp under his own power. Movies were taken of the ceremonies, and the publicity inspired some other churches to provide similar facilities for the disabled.

The success of the project aroused in Roger a crusading purpose which was to be lifelong: to educate churches in building ramps or constructing entrances without steps. He was amazed to find how many public buildings, even the newest, were planned with total disregard for the needs of the disabled and elderly.

So concerned did he become about this problem that a bit later he advertised in the Michigan *Christian Advocate*, offering to supply interested churches with free glad bulbs which could be sold for this purpose. Three churches answered the ad, one in Marshall, Michigan, with the idea of installing an elevator. Two interested members of the Corunna church, Bob and Leona Vincent, offered to prepare the bulbs. One night, working until early morning, they put up one thousand dozen for the church in Owosso, packing them in dozen lots in paper sacks.

But generally Roger discovered little interest. The average able-bodied church member seemed obtusely blind to such needs.

"Oh, well, that's O.K.," a group of men would assure him cheerfully when awkwardly manipulating him and his wheel chair up and down long flights of stairs to sanctuary, basement, or parish house. "We don't mind." They would, Roger could have told them grimly, if they were in his place!

But being handicapped, he had long since discovered, was by no means confined to physical disability. A man could be handicapped by narrow vision as seriously as by paralyzed legs. This was poignantly demonstrated the year he attended the state convention of the American Federation of the Physically Handicapped in Saginaw. On Sunday morning all the delegates attended church in a body. Because the building was close by and on the ground level, they chose the Salvation Army. The captain asked two men to take the offering. One of them, after taking it, turned to the congregation, weeping.

"You folks aren't so much handicapped," he told the visitors. "Just yesterday I got out of jail. I know what being handicapped really is!"

In fact, Roger's definition of the disabled who might need his help became more and more inclusive. For instance, there was Jim, who had lost his mother and, after taking magazine subscriptions, had spent the money and forged checks. After a ninety-day jail sentence, he was handicapped indeed and very much in need of a friend. There was even Roger's own minister, Harold Dakin. Often, perplexed by problems and discouraged by the myopia of parishioners, he would see a light burning in Roger's house and, even if it was after midnight, go in for both physical and spiritual refreshment.

"I could always tell when he had been there," his wife commented long afterward. "I could tell just by looking at his face."

9

When Ronnie was preschool age he was not allowed to cross the road alone to play with friends, and his playmates were few. Roger used to watch him standing beside the road looking wistfully down the street to where other children were playing.

"We shouldn't bring him up alone," he said one day. "Why don't you go down and tell Judge Matthews that we want another one?"

Busy though she was with one child and all her other duties, LaVerna could see the wisdom of the suggestion. She took Ronnie and paid a visit to the judge of probate.

"Oh, yes," he recalled when she introduced herself. "I remember this case. You know, I never had an adoption broken, but this had me scared for a while."

LaVerna was startled but, since the judge was very hard of hearing, asked no questions, merely told him that they would like a child old enough to be a playmate for Ronnie, that they would prefer a girl but would take a boy. He promised to see what he could do. Curious and concerned, LaVerna went downstairs to the welfare office and asked the social worker if she knew what the judge had meant.

"You mean you didn't know?" she returned in surprise.

Horrified, LaVerna learned that after Ronnie's blood mother had come to visit the baby with her brother, he had pressed her to take measures to reclaim the child. They had gone to the state welfare department and complained that she had been forced to give up her child because she could not maintain his support. The state social

143

worker descended with blistering censure on Judge Matthews. "Since when in America has a woman had to give up her baby because she couldn't pay its keep?" Such a tumult was raised that the judge feared the adoption would be nullified. But soon afterward the social worker suffered injury in an accident and never worked again, so the case was dropped.

LaVerna left the office weak and trembling. She clutched Ronnie's hand so tightly that he cried out, "Hey, Mom, let go! You hurt!"

It was months later, on May 1, 1947, that Judge Matthews called. "How would you like a girl?" he said. "She's just ten months younger than your boy. She has to be taken away from the home where she is, and we have to find another immediately. So if you won't take her, she'll have to go to the orphanage."

"Of course we'll take her," agreed LaVerna promptly. She called Roger at his work. "How would you like a daughter for a birthday present?"

"Sure," he replied with gusto. "Better than a million dollars."

They went immediately to see the child at her grandmother's in Owosso. "Surely this will be a blonde," thought LaVerna, with whose blonde heritage the brown eyes and hair of both Dick and Ronnie had seemed oddly at variance. "The third time shouldn't fail." What was her surprise, then, to find a tiny slip of a girl, black eyes as brightly wary as a frightened animal's, black hair forming a wild but not unattractive halo! The name Faye fitted well. There was an elfin, spritelike elusiveness in the dark, thin little face.

No wonder she looked frightened! The story the grandmother told held more pathos even than Dick's. Her son had lived up in northern Michigan with his wife and five children, the oldest about six. When he had joined the Army, the mother had tired of caring for the children and left them, arriving finally at the grandmother's home in Owosso. "But where are your children?" "Oh, back home." "You mean you left those five children up in that place alone?" "Why, yes, I couldn't very well bring them."

That night the grandmother with her husband had driven 400 miles to the cabin, found the children half starving, the tiny baby very sick, and had started back with them. Other sons and daughters had taken the children into their homes. Faye had gone to the home of a daughter who worked days while her husband worked nights.

He had locked the child in a bedroom by herself all day. Some children reported to the grandmother that they had heard Faye pounding on the window and crying. She had rushed over and taken her away. This very morning she had taken her to the judge's office, saying, "You'll have to find another home for her."

Roger and LaVerna went immediately to Judge Matthews and said they would take the child.

"Go to a lawyer this time and get the papers made out," he told them. "We're not going through another such experience as we did with Ronnie."

The papers were signed, and the next day, thirty hours after the first telephone call, they had a daughter.

It was Ronnie who adjusted most easily to the new relationship. To his five-year-old intelligence the acquisition of a full-grown sister was a *fait accompli* fully as natural and understandable as the usual method of sibling arrival, and far more desirable. His pride was belligerently possessive. The first Sunday Faye attended church with the family he stood in front of her with hands outstretched and warned away all trespassers. "You keep away from her. She's my sister."

For the new parents adjustments presented more baffling problems. Faye's education in the most mundane elementals had been incredibly meager. She did not know the meaning of a "front room" or the "back seat" of a car. She could not speak plainly. The first night they took her to church, as they came out and she happened to look up at the sky, she stopped dead and said, "What's that?"

"Why, those are stars," Ronnie told her. "Don't you know *stars?*"

She refused to move. People were unable to get by. Finally LaVerna said, "Faye, we have stars at home. Let's go home and look at them there." All that evening she could not get enough of looking at them.

But there was an excess of knowledge as well as ignorance. The first Saturday night she asked, "Aren't you going to dance?" Receiving a negative response, she continued, "Why, we always go to the dance every Saturday night. I sit and watch 'em."

However, she learned fast, for the elfin-bright eyes held intelligence as well as wariness. By the end of summer she had become as conversant with the vocabulary of the church service as of the dance hall. One day after the Vacation Church School LaVerna was amazed to hear her repeating the Lord's Prayer, which she had just learned, with a slight variation.

"Give us this day our daily bread," the child intoned solemnly, then after a pause, "and cookies."

But many problems persisted. The child would say bitter, spiteful things which LaVerna knew no normal five- or six-year-old would think of saying, born of resentment, not against her, she was sure, but against the previous rejection by two mothers. For some reason, too, whenever they were in the room together, the child would always watch her. This habit persisted for years. If she was wiping dishes Faye would look, not where she was putting the dish, but at LaVerna. Why? Was it insecurity, suspicion, or some more complex emotion which prompted the eternal watchfulness?

LaVerna tried in every way possible to make her feel loved and secure. People were coming to the house constantly to buy flowers. Inevitably someone would say teasingly to Faye, "Now your mother has two children, and I haven't any little girl. Why don't you come home with me?" Always LaVerna would interpose quickly, "Oh, we couldn't get along without Faye!" After the departure of one woman who had elaborated at length about her loneliness, Faye said seriously, "Mother, maybe I should have gone with her. She really needs me."

Would they ever be able to make her feel, LaVerna wondered, that this was her home, that at last she had a place where she belonged?

The glad business continued to be a source of triumphs, of fair but uncertain income, of grueling and backbreaking labor. During 1947 and 1948 in the Michigan glad shows Arnett glads won nine different grand championships. In most of them the winner was White Challenge, but Nancy, a beautiful red seedling from Picardy out of Rewi Fallu, brought a happy surprise by winning the American Home Achievement Award. It was a top scorer in both the Michigan Gladiolus Society's and the University of Massachusetts' Trial Garden Contests. The publicity, of course, boosted glad bulb sales, and soon orders were coming from all over the country and from as far away as Australia and China. They would start arriving by January and February, and from then until spring hundreds of boxes of bulbs and bulblets must be packed and mailed. LaVerna, of course, shared the task with Roger. Yet, onerous though it was, she found it preferable to the summer drudgery of making hundreds of sprays and baskets and bouquets.

Roger, she was determined, must not suspect how fiercely she hated the glads. For years she had felt their beautiful frail tentacles closing, tightening about her, like a jeweled golden trap. She liked flowers but detested the slavery they entailed. It was making the arrangements that she hated most, worse even than the sorting, packing, marketing, the constant dealing with customers. Always the perfectionist, she knew her bouquets lacked the florist's touch. They were too symmetrical, creations of a mathematician, not an artist. She would think one of her sprays looked wonderful, then, seeing it beside a professional arrangement, would know herself to be a raw amateur. Even a week's training at a florist school in Chicago in 1947 added little to her self-confidence.

If Roger failed to sense her intense distaste for the glad business, he was by no means insensitive to the drudgery it caused her. Constantly he smarted under the frustration of seeing her perform labor a man should be doing. That winter of 1947–1948 they were buried in snow, and, with Dick away, LaVerna had to do all the shoveling. After each storm the walk must be cleared so he could get out to the storage building. He would have done it from his wheel chair if it had been humanly possible. Then on the first of March came a heavy storm. It was night and freezing cold when LaVerna finished shoveling the path. He insisted that she go into the house instead of accompanying him on his evening trip to the bulb storage house. When he started to enter, the sliding door caught on his wheel chair, and over he went into a snowbank. He called and called, but nobody could hear. All his strugglings only thrust him deeper in the soft new snow.

"At least I won't know it when most of my body freezes," he told himself grimly, feeling the chill creeping up arms and shoulders, tingling cheeks and ears, crusting hair, for even in the coldest weather he never wore a cap.

Finally, after about a half hour, LaVerna wondered why he had been gone so long and came to the door and called. Seldom had her voice sounded more welcome.

That winter, as the result of the tour by Roger with Russell Everhart and Professor Krone, there were regional glad society meetings all over the state. Roger attended most of them with his father, usually doing the driving. On March 8 there was a meeting in Bay City, seventy miles away; on March 10 in Detroit, ninety miles. Roger would never forget the latter trip, for his catheter became plugged. After the meeting he was in a genuine hurry to get home, well knowing the hazard of such a condition in causing pressure sores. Coming through Bloomfield Hills he was going about sixty miles an hour in a forty-mile zone, with no traffic, but of course he got a ticket! It cost him a precious twenty-dollar fine.

Again for the third year planting was delayed because of rains. May came, and it was still too wet for plowing. The frustration which had long been nagging Roger grew into a gnawing canker. He was running a treadmill, working furiously but making little progress. His driving impulse to assume full support of his family had long since backfired. Watching LaVerna struggle through long hours of sorting, packing, marketing—work which he knew was a far greater burden than the teaching he had wanted to spare her—he felt trapped.

A suspicion which he had long been nursing sprang to full conviction: Michigan was no place to raise glads for a living. A farm three or four hundred miles south would offer big advantages.

"Why, I can plow in February!" boasted George Lash, a glad-growing friend in New Albany, on the Ohio River. Some spot between Cincinnati and Louisville, say southern Indiana, decided Roger, would be ideal. Fearfully, knowing how she hated new adjustments, Roger broached the idea to LaVerna. Her reaction was what he expected.

"Move! To another state? Oh—no!"

But Roger patiently detailed the advantages. There would be no retailing, he promised, the part of the business she hated most, only wholesaling. And as time passed, other inducements appeared. They would not be alone in the new enterprise. John Grayson, a laborer with the county road commission, wanted to go into partnership with them. He and his wife Pauline, with their four children, would join the Arnetts in whatever community they might choose.

LaVerna was not too hard to persuade. The Graysons were good friends, and the prospect of giving up the retail business was tempting. Besides, Roger and his well-being had long since become the most important values in her life.

At one in the morning on May 10 Roger and LaVerna left on a reconnoitering trip to Indiana, leaving the two children with the Graysons. At three they had a flat tire, so they slept until five thirty; then LaVerna walked to a gas station, where they bought a new tire. At two in the afternoon they arrived in Columbus, Indiana, where they talked with representatives of the Chamber of Commerce, a real-estate man, and an agricultural agent. All were considerate and helpful. Roger beamed with enthusiasm. "Ideal for glads," he pronounced the climate. Corn was planted. Iris, poppies, spirea were all in full bloom. They arrived home at midnight after a trip of nearly seven hundred miles.

During the summer plans developed swiftly. After another trip to Columbus with the Graysons they bought a house with an acre of land and put their property in Corunna on the market. The newly purchased house was big and old and had been unoccupied for three years, but it had an attached garage with an entrance on the same level, so no ramp or enclosure would be necessary. And it was cheap.

Roger's father and mother were stricken at the news. In spite of his vigorous denials they blamed themselves for having taken away his glad business. Then, too, since his accident he had never lived more than a quarter hour's driving distance from their home. Columbus seemed a thousand miles away. But they rallied helpfully, even made trips with them to Indiana to measure the rooms of the new house for curtains and wallpaper.

Meanwhile the glad season progressed at a terrific pace. Some days Roger was on the tractor from seven in the morning until nine at night. Either he or LaVerna took stock to market three days a week: to Royal Oak, to Lansing, to Pontiac. He entered innumerable glad shows. It was a minor tragedy when in July the scooter kept breaking down, for Roger was doing practically all the cutting. One rainy day LaVerna towed him in it for thirteen miles to Carland, where Eldred Waters was a garage mechanic, a grueling experience, for the route ran straight through Owosso and demanded expert driving. But Eldred repaired the scooter, and Roger drove it home.

Realizing the need for increased funds, Roger and LaVerna explored every sales possibility. Each Friday LaVerna took a load of bouquets and went over to the backdoor of Redmond's, an Owosso factory, selling to the employees as they came out of work. One day she took in twenty-nine dollars. Also on Fridays they made up dozen lots of 500 dozen mixed glads for a Lansing man who sold them on a street corner. A handicapped man in Pontiac, housebound, wanted to sell glads from his home, and Roger traveled sixty miles to take him a load; then on the same day took another load to the Everharts in Ann Arbor.

By late August the terrific pace was beginning to take its toll of Roger. One day he and a man from Flint took glads for the show at Battle Creek. He returned home at three in the morning. At five he got up and went to market, starting home at one thirty, planning to leave directly with his parents and John Grayson for another visit to the Battle Creek show. But on the way home he topped a rise in the road to come suddenly upon a tractor pulling two wagonloads of baled straw, with another car approaching. He ran into the rear wagon, wrecking it, bending the tongue of the other, and smashing the front end of his Oldsmobile. LaVerna wrote in her diary the following day, Sunday: "The sheriff brought Roger home yesterday. The car was towed in. All in church seemed to know about it."

The accident should have been a warning. He had become too fatigued to react normally in a crisis. While the car was being repaired he had to depend on friends to take his glads to market in their cars, so he had a slight respite from driving. But there were still the thousands of glads to cut each day, the cultivation, the bunching, so the grueling pace continued to take its toll.

The car came back, repaired, the middle of September, and again Roger could go to market. After his first trip he collapsed. He was in bed for a week with a huge pressure sore, near delirium, and three hundred thousand units of penicillin.

But there was no time for anybody to remain sick long. There were still hundreds of dozens of glads to be sold, many of them the inimitable White Challenge; a big old house 300 miles away to be made ready for occupancy and another house disposed of; 900 catalogs to be mailed out; ten acres of bulbs to be dug and cured; a houseful of furniture and thirty tons of bulbs to move. Roger had to be cured, and quickly.

John Grayson helped dig the bulbs. They worked for days from dawn to dark. Finding that it would cost $10,000 to hire the bulbs moved, Roger bought a truck and designed hand controls for it. They were able to move only about five tons at one trip.

To Roger's dismay it was LaVerna who bore the brunt of preparing the Indiana house for occupancy. Alvah Knight, a cousin of Roger's, was hired to do the repair work. Early in October La-

Verna, Alvah, Roger's Aunt Nattie, and his father went down to Columbus for a week of painting and papering. They arrived in the rain at about five in the afternoon. LaVerna was prepared for discouragement. The house was dirty, some of the floors warped, the paint smoked and dingy, the old paper hanging from the walls. But she was not prepared for calamity. The furnace man met them with a dubious face.

"Can't build a fire. Too dangerous. Got to have a new furnace."

The plumber was also at the house. "Sorry, madam. Both the pipes and the hot-water tank have burst. New ones must be installed. You must also have a new well and electric pump."

They went back to town, two and a half miles away. LaVerna was as angry as she was discouraged. Of course Roger had been unable to go down cellar when they had examined the house. She, who knew nothing about heating systems, had gone down in the dark, only to discover now that the electricity had been connected all the time. Naturally trusting, she had taken the word of the agent that all was in apple-pie order. She felt they had been cheated, and told him so.

"But I knew none of these things was wrong," he protested vehemently.

There were a few comforting developments. The rolls of wallpaper ordered were waiting in the post office, and the new kitchen cabinets had arrived by freight. But it was a hectic week. Contacted by telephone, Roger agreed that the improvements must be made. Plumbers, electricians, carpenters created a flurry of activity. Aunt Nattie and Cousin Alvah papered and painted, while LaVerna scrubbed and ran errands, found a carpenter to install cupboards, enrolled Ronnie in the first grade and Faye in kindergarten. One day when the plumber came to work he brought in a warm pumpkin pie. It was a small oasis of friendliness in a desert.

She returned to Corunna with the relatives, to pack, mail the catalogs, and get ready for the next trip. This time Roger went with her, and John Grayson followed with the first load of bulbs. Then both returned to Corunna in the truck, and she was left alone for the longest ten days she had ever spent. Days were busy enough. It was the nights which set her nerves on edge. Once she was wakened by a loud noise, but, knowing she would be frightened if she tried to decide what it was, forced herself back to sleep. In the morning she found that the pipes had burst in the upstairs bathroom, buckled the floor, and sent pieces of it flying across the room. Another expensive repair job!

The second load of bulbs arrived, and she returned with Roger to Corunna. That night a farewell party was given for both them and the Graysons at the church. The next day another bomb exploded. The Graysons had decided not to move to Indiana! It was a stunning blow, especially for Roger, for he could not possibly carry on the expanded business alone. At first the promising new road seemed to have come abruptly to a dead end. But he could not turn back now. He had already committed himself to the change. He must simply move forward on faith, trusting that at the seeming end of the road there would appear a turning.

It was the last of November before the family finally got moved, December before Roger brought the fifth and last load of bulbs. By Christmas LaVerna had all the painting, varnishing, and paperhanging done, the curtains hung. At last the big white colonial house with its six bedrooms, its circular stairway, its fireplace with solid walnut mantel, its huge dining room with an expanse of sunlit window seats, began to seem like home. Not, of course, that it was really theirs! The extra expenses had drained their finances to rock bottom. The house in Corunna had been rented but not sold. The sale of the small barn and of two building lots from its acreage had helped finance the new equipment, but a large mortgage had been necessary.

It was a happy Christmas, and the children seemed not to notice that their gifts had been purchased at Woolworth's. But troubles were not yet over, even temporarily. They were having Christmas breakfast in front of the fireplace when suddenly they smelled smoke. When they opened the basement door, smoke came rolling up. The basement was filled with trays of bulbs piled to the ceiling. A couple of trays had been pushed back against the smokestack of the furnace and were smoldering. Many more piles must be moved to reach them. Roger was unable yet to get into the basement. LaVerna could not lift the trays. She ran across the road to their nearest neighbors, who came rushing to the rescue. By the time they had taken down rows and rows of full trays, the smoking ones were already ablaze.

"What next!" thought LaVerna. Surely this eventful year could now ebb away in eventless tranquility!

She was wrong. Two days later the children came down with chicken pox.

For months their income would depend solely on bulb sales, and few orders would come in before March. They were down to their last dollar, with monthly payments due on truck and house. It was a lean winter. Roger tried to get a loan on his tractor, his sole debt-clear asset.

"What would we do with a tractor?" asked the bank officials skeptically.

One day LaVerna went to the supermarket with only three dollars in her purse. She felt she could spend only two and had to choose between margarine and sugar. As she went out to her car, she saw a policeman putting a ticket on it. Appeals were of no avail. Was she trying to get out of paying a fine? There went her last dollar. There was a family of woodchucks living near the house. Roger borrowed a rifle and shot a young one. It furnished one of their few meat dinners. But eventually the bulb orders began to come in, and they managed.

Roger found a helper in young Joe Sexton, son of the cabinet-maker who had worked on their house. When a warm spell came in February, he set out for the fields with high hopes. Besides the acreage going with the house, he had rented ten acres which adjoined his property. By planting two acres for an early crop he expected to get top prices. He began plowing, using the same technique as in Michigan, not realizing that it was a different type of soil. The ground looked sandy but did not loosen as it should. The more he harrowed, the harder it seemed to get. Finally he put the planters on, but the shovels would not stay in the ground and the bulbs were not well covered. One day a neighbor, Mr. Hormann, came over and educated him in the proper treatment of the soil. After that Roger had no difficulties. The early season was still all he had hoped it would be. The glads flourished and blossomed like plants in a hothouse. White Challenge was magnificent, and florists could not get enough of it. Roger was jubilant.

One incident brought him special satisfaction. He had a glad-growing friend, Claude Enslem, up in Marion, Indiana. Claude was blind. That spring Roger sent him a dozen bulbs of White Challenge. They happened to be in bloom at the right time for the Indiana State Gladiolus Society show in Wabash. The night after the judging Claude called Roger long distance.

"We won, we won!" he shouted in great excitement.

He had won the grand championship of the show with a spike of White Challenge. A real handicap triumph, Roger exulted. A variety developed by a man in a wheel chair and grown by a blind man, winning top prize over thousands and thousands of the very best spikes in the whole state!

But success was hard won, at a cost of backbreaking labor and innumerable difficulties. The season was dry, and it took weeks to procure a good irrigation system. The scooter bike kept breaking down, but fortunately there was a repairman in Columbus. He would drop every other job to come to Roger's rescue. The weeding of the six-acre farm—Happy Glad Acres, they named it—was too much for Roger and Joe, so three high-school boys were hired to work for the summer. Each evening Joe would load the truck with cut flowers, packing them in ice, and the next morning Roger would drive them to the wholesale market in Indianapolis, starting at five in the morning and traveling eighty miles before returning to work the rest of the day in the fields. He did most of the cutting, La-Verna the bunching and grading.

While she found the work easier than the floral arrangements, it was long and taxing. The flowers were picked in the bud, bunched a dozen to the bunch, all of equal length. The longer the stems, the better the price. On some days she worked eight hours, bunching and sorting up to five hundred dozen.

Roger's success was a marvel to his many colleagues in this glad-growing area.

"Growing glads is hard work," commented George Lasch, who operated a farm at Clarksville. "Many a man without physical handicap has tried it and given up. But not Roger. His amazing success in the field is a tribute to his ingenuity, determination, and spirit."

That fall they dug a marvelous crop of bulbs, about three hundred thousand of them, with close to three million bulblets. White Challenge, both the old and young bulbs, looked especially promising. But to Roger's amazement and dismay when they planted them the following year very few of them bloomed. It was evidently not the right climate for White Challenge. Bulbs of this particular variety brought from Michigan and planted in Indiana would flower beautifully, but bulbs grown in Indiana refused to blossom. Another one of the hazards of the glad business!

That first summer a division of the National Guard was posted in Columbus in an Air Force camp adjoining the Arnett property. One afternoon a lieutenant came down their River Road stopping at each house to locate lodging facilities for the men's families. In the big Arnett house he was sure he had struck a gold mine.

"Just let me look at it!" he begged. At sight of the six big bedrooms he became persuasively eloquent. It was ideal for his family and a friend's with their three children. The Arnetts simply must take them in. The other families along the road were cooperating. And the expense of making the rooms into two apartments would be small!

Roger and LaVerna felt they had to agree. The rooms were there, unused. There were people needing them. But when they came to transform them into apartments, it took all the money saved from their flower sales for the entire summer. With the government rent allowance of only forty-four dollars a month, the two years' rental would barely cover the expense.

By February they were again out of money. Orders for bulbs were slow in coming in. LaVerna decided she must try to find work. Seeing an advertisement placed by the Arvin Company in the local paper one morning, she went that same afternoon and applied for a job as secretary. She was given a test, most of it in mathematics, which was of course her specialty. So surprised was the company executive by the excellence of her score that he offered her a choice of eight positions. She accepted one in the Automotive Engineering Department because it had never before had a secretary, and somehow she always enjoyed the challenge of a brand-new enterprise.

It was fascinating but demanding work. She was secretary to the nine men in the department. Since she had taken dictation from Roger and typed all his business letters for many years, she had little trouble with the shorthand once she had become accustomed to the specialized vocabulary. Only one of the men, Mr. Danner, caused difficulty with his rapid dictation.

"Get your pad, LaVerna," he would order as she came in the door, and before she could get in her seat he would be dictating, punctuating the rapid flow of words with quick staccato pacing of the floor. She often longed for the telephone to ring so she could catch up, and fortunately it usually did. He would often be out of the door and halfway down the hall when he finished the dictation. But she learned to keep up with him.

Many of the secretaries brought bouquets to their various offices. "When are you going to bring some glads?" they kept pressing

LaVerna. One morning as she came through the garage where the bunching was done, she noticed a beautiful bouquet saved out for an order but never called for. "Here's my chance," she thought, for the glads were usually picked in bud, seldom in flower. She put the bouquet in a big white vase and, taking it to the office, looked for a place to put it. The office of Mr. Ludlow, the department head, offered the best vantage point with its big glass window, visible from all over the department.

"What! Flowers in Ed's office!" exclaimed one after the other of the men as they came in. "He's had that office for twenty-five years and never had flowers before. He's not going to like it, LaVerna."

The repeated warnings aroused her stubbornness. Why not share their glads? She would leave them there if it meant losing her job. At last the chief came in. They watched him, all nine of them, through the glass. He stopped stock-still, fairly choking, and they saw him looking through and around and under the bouquet, searching for a card. He came to the door and threw it open.

"Did you bring these flowers, LaVerna?" he demanded.

"Yes," she replied meekly.

His austere face broke into a broad smile. "How did you know it was my birthday?"

Her absence from home made complications. In the summer Roger had to hire the bunching done. One day LaVerna came home to find that the girl had facilitated her task by cutting off all the stems the same length, without sorting! All, of course, were the length of the shortest, which had to be thrown out as unsuitable for the wholesale market. The whole five hundred dozen were a total loss!

In school periods the children left before she did in the morning, and Roger was usually at home when they returned. On a day when it was necessary for him to be gone, LaVerna reflected, "Oh, well, they'll be all right. The women will be upstairs." Arriving home, she found a fire in the fireplace, the house littered with ashes, a hole burned in the rug. The next time it was necessary for them to be left alone she told them to stay out-of-doors.

"May we rake leaves?" inquired Ronnie with an unusual relish for industry. She gladly gave permission. What was her amazement when she drove into the yard to see several piles of leaves on the outskirts of the big lawn, all merrily ablaze! The tenants had remonstrated with Ronnie, but he had responded with blithe assurance,

"It's all right. I asked my mother, and she said I could." Usually one step behind her energetic son, it had never occurred to LaVerna that in his experience burning had always been a part of the raking process.

By the third glad season in Indiana some of this disturbing energy could be utilized for constructive labor in the fields. Roger was a less lenient and permissive parent than LaVerna, and by the time they were eight and nine respectively Faye and Ronnie were planting, weeding, cutting, digging with a skill superior to that of many others Roger was forced to employ. The children were occasionally rebellious, especially Faye, who had a quick temper and an allergy to work.

"No!" she refused once audaciously when Roger asked her to do something when company was present, and she thought she had gotten away with it. She was wrong. When the company was gone, her mouth was gently but firmly washed out with soap. It was Dad who usually administered the punishments. Mother's disciplinary measures were largely confined to such female areas as washing dishes.

But Roger's happy exuberance lent an air of jollity to what might have been sterile drudgery. And after the work there was always playtime, not mild, sedentary play such as might be expected with a wheel chair victim, but rough games such as tag and baseball and wrestling. Dad's leg potential might be nil, but his arms could have belonged to Superman. He could do almost anything except play football and run bases. The rough house tactics often disturbed LaVerna, especially when they resulted in tipping over Roger's wheel chair.

For Roger also her absence at work all day created problems. During digging season in the fall he would take Ronnie out early in the morning and use the tractor; then after the boy left for school he would use the scooter bike and dig with his trays. One cold day when he was digging alone the motor chair broke down in midmorning in a remote corner of the field, and he had to sit there all day, motionless, idle, slowly congealing with the cold, until some of his family returned home and found him. Another hazard, this time neither of glads nor of paraplegia, but of the machine age!

Four glad seasons passed in Indiana, each one with its peculiar satisfactions and problems. One of the latter was thrips, which descended like a plague in 1950. This tiny insect, no more than a sixteenth of an inch long, yellow in youth and black with an orange belt when old, was the bane of glad growers, tainting leaves with silverish spots and petals with discoloration. The recommended antidotes: spray and pray. Roger was equally at home with both. He hired a plane that year to spray the field, a method less expensive and more effective than hand spraying. Another season brought serious drought.

"If we don't get rain soon," said Roger to the former owner of the house, from whom he rented the adjoining ten acres. "I don't know what we're going to do for money."

"I don't know, either," replied their well-to-do landlord dubiously, obviously more concerned for his rent than for the welfare of his tenants.

Another problem was securing adequate help. Whenever possible, Roger tried always to employ the handicapped. After Joe Sexton left for a better job in 1950, Roger hired a young man of seventeen with a severe nervous ailment. With careful supervision he did a creditable job, particularly with the cleaning and grading of bulbs in winter. For short periods also Roger hired a young man who was deaf, another mentally retarded.

The handicaps were not always physical. In the summer of 1951 he gave work to an alcoholic and three of his twelve children. All proved good workers, even the oldest boy, who was a mischievous young rebel. Once when moving the irrigation system Roger found big clods of earth in the pipes. The boy had put them in just to see what would happen. But even when he had to bail the father out of jail for drinking, Roger did not regret hiring them. They had needed the employment.

It was some of the non-handicapped who gave the most trouble. One morning a man came with his two daughters, all huskily healthy, requesting work. Roger was digging bulbs. Yes, he could give them work, and stated a moderate wage. They seemed agreeable. After a day's work he paid them the agreed amount. Was that all? Unable to cajole him into paying more, they went away, disgusted. That night when he went into the fields to pick up the trays, he found that the girls had gone back and tipped over every tray they had dug.

But all such frustrations were trivial beside the satisfaction of turning a barren field into an infinity of color, especially of watching bulbs of one's own crossings bloom into unexpected miracles. He had been far more fortunate than most glad growers. Sometimes a man could work a lifetime and have only one flower that he developed become well known. Bulbs from his seedlings had traveled to many parts of the world. His 1952 catalog listed fourteen varieties as Arnett creations. It had probably taken a million seeds to bring them to fruition. Not all, of course, were as consistent champions as White Challenge and Nancy. But all had their own special qualities of beauty.

Roger labored over the wording of his catalogs. It was hard giving names to the new varieties, putting into words the results of long years of patient and agonizing labor. "*Cascade Splendor,* a ribbon of smooth satiny color . . . *Chapel Bells,* rich salmon with snow-white throat. . . . *Polar Queen,* sixty-two inch willowy spikes. . . , *Remembrance,* ravishing tint of pure clear salmon blending to a waxy white throat. . . . *Candlelight,* planted in the cold ground of April, will bloom in June. . . . *Dancing Flame.* . . . *Dark Melody,* silky deep wine red. . . . *Embers.* Florists have taken to Embers like an elephant to peanuts! . . ."

But he had no trouble finding words in his numerous lectures, such as the one he gave to an annual meeting of the Southeast District of Indiana Garden Clubs. Like most of his talks, this one was about hybridizing, and he called it "Adventure." Hybridizing, he told them, was "working with God." It took time, study, and a vast amount of patience. Weeks and months must go into the planning stage when the proper "parents" were chosen. Then after the cross was made it would be three years before color would show in the first plant. It had taken him ten years to perfect his first new variety.

He gave ten hints to his listeners: Have faith in God, pick one flower to work with, study it thoroughly, do lots of crossings (out of a thousand there might be only one good result!), *work,* have patience, join societies pertaining to your chosen flower, never fear to try something new, never give up hope, and be prepared for disappointment.

"But there's a heap of satisfaction in it," he told his enthralled listeners.

He was often enlisted as a judge at glad shows. One such occasion at Bardston, Kentucky, kept him chuckling for many years. He was busily examining entries when he was approached by another judge.

The arbiters for an adjacent table, it seemed, needed some help in deciding the winner of the entries over which they were presiding.

Competition was narrowed to two entries. There was long discussion, each of the judges pointing out the superlative qualities of both. They seemed to be reaching agreement on one of the entries when Roger declared he believed the other to be the better. He won them to his point of view and smiled gleefully as he rolled away.

"Wait till they see the name on the one that takes second," he chuckled to a bystander.

The judges looked both sheepish and chagrined when they read the tags and saw the names of the winners. The tag on the entry against which Roger had argued and to which he had persuaded them to give the second award bore the words: "Roger Arnett, Columbus, Indiana."

10

The crack opened by Bob Cox and others in the hard shell of Roger's self-concern had long been growing wider.

"I wish growing glads could be my hobby," Roger said once to a reporter for the Columbus *Evening Republican*, "and helping the handicapped be my job. But one must eat."

However, raising glads for a living need not keep help to the handicapped from being a major interest. And he managed to find an increasing amount of time for the "hobby."

In 1949 he was appointed to the President's Committee on Employment of the Physically Handicapped and made the first of numerous trips to Washington.

"Roger Arnett of Columbus, Indiana," wrote a Washington reporter, "came to Washington yesterday. He got here at 2 A.M. He spent the day attending the President's National Conference on Employment of the Physically Handicapped. Then with his son Ronnie, seven years old, he started for home at 5 P.M. He said he had to get back so he could keep a date with a doctor at Ann Arbor, Michigan, today. . . .When he wheeled himself, with Ronnie helping, into the departmental auditorium of the Department of Labor, he was one person attending the session who knew what helping the unfortunate get a new start really means."

Many of his subsequent trips to Washington were in his capacity as a vice president of the American Federation of the Physically Handicapped. Soon after arriving in Indiana he received a letter from Paul Strachan, founder and president of the organization, suggesting that he organize chapters in Indiana. Roger seized on the suggestion with his usual energetic enthusiasm and proceeded to organize eight chapters.

Strachan was one of the most inspiring personalities Roger had ever encountered. He was deaf, read lips, walked with a cane, had at one time suffered a broken back, but his six feet three inches of bone and sinew were pure fire and dynamo. He had but a single purpose in life, embodied in the organization he had founded, and his primary technique in attaining it was through legislation. He had been one of the three originators of the act establishing Vocational Rehabilitation after World War I. In that era he had been at least a quarter century ahead of his time. After World War II he had been instrumental in introducing into Congress a bill to establish a National Employ the Handicapped Week. It had passed, and the week was celebrated all over the United States the first of October. The board of his AFPH (*his*, for he was inclined to be a dictator) was weighted with important names: educators, doctors, union officials. But, to Roger's disappointment, no ministers. Strachan had found little interest and less cooperation in his crusade for the handicapped within the church.

Roger went to Washington for meetings with the board, to attend hearings, to testify before committees of both the Senate and the House. He went in different ways: driving, flying, by train, by bus. And the experiences he encountered in travel were often more relevant to the problems of the handicapped than the issues discussed at the meetings. At least they highlighted the attitudes of the general public.

There were the children on the platform when he waited for the train who were anxious to satisfy their natural curiosity about the man in the wheel chair but prevented by the well-meaning but mistaken aunt who blocked their vision and "shushed" their healthy interest with a "mustn't stare." There was the smartly dressed young woman who boarded the train a few stations beyond Columbus and sat down in the seat which he had thoughtfully left beside him. He would never forget the look of shock and astonishment that crossed her face when she looked down and saw that his leg was amputated. Soon afterward she left and found another seat. Then there was always the too sympathetic fellow traveler, such as the man in Roger's coach who had overly imbibed. Face distorted with concern, he requested the full sad story. Oh, yes, he had seen many such unfortunates. He had been in the war. He was so sorry. Finally he offered the choicest palliative he could think of. "Here, friend, have a drink."

In those days railroads were as ill equipped to deal with the handicapped as their passengers. One time when he was coming into Indianapolis the trainmen were puzzled. How to get him off? They decided finally to leave the platform up. Then two men would get hold of the front wheels when he rode to the edge of the platform, and two others at the back end would hold the handles, letting his wheel chair down gently. But the plan misfired. The two in front pulled the chair out too far, so the men behind could not hold on, and when the chair had descended three of the four feet, the back ones had to let go. Roger fell solidly on his back, hitting his head. They were four startled and frightened trainmen. Fortunately Roger was not hurt badly and, understanding the men's predicament, would not press charges.

Washington itself was equally illuminating in human attitudes. On one cold, snowy night Roger left his hotel with barely enough time to get to the station. He got out into the street and tried to hail a taxi. One pulled up, and he wheeled toward it. But an able-bodied man and his wife, dressed in expensive, formal clothes, pushed their way ahead of him. As traintime came nearer, he became more concerned. Finally a policeman saw his predicament. When a taxi came along, far out in the middle of the street, he hailed it, stopped all the traffic, pulled it to the curb, and helped Roger and his wheel chair inside. "I sure didn't know what I'd done!" exclaimed the driver in relief. Equally relieved and eternally grateful to the policeman, Roger caught his train.

The mistaken attitudes of people could sometimes be as difficult for his friends as for the handicapped person himself. Norman Hagen discovered that when he went with Roger on a visit to the National Flower Show. As he strolled along beside his friend, Roger insisted, as always, that he needed no help manipulating his wheel chair. They came to a big exhibit where there was matting on the floor, and the wheels met with more resistance, but, disdaining help, Roger pushed stubbornly ahead, powerful arms pumping, head slightly thrust forward, obviously struggling against difficulties. Person after person stopped to offer help, but on each Roger would bestow his big beaming smile and a happy "No, thanks." Then each would turn and glare at the husky blond giant strolling beside him. Norm felt his stature steadily shrinking as the evening wore on.

But on another occasion Roger was on the receiving end of such embarrassment. He drove himself to many of these meetings in Washington, often making the 650-mile trip after a hard day's work. On one such trip he took Paul Schmitt, a muscular dystrophy victim who worked for the Good Will Industries in Indianapolis. Although both were in wheel chairs, they encountered no difficulties either on the trip or at the hotel. Paul, however, required more help than Roger and found it hard to wheel himself up an incline. As they approached a building with a rather steep ramp one of the delegates offered to wheel him. Accepting, Paul made no effort to help. Only when the chair swerved to one side and tipped him over did he realize that his assistant had only one arm. Roger, who had tipped over himself so many times that he knew no harm was done, could not help laughing at the plight of his embarrassed friends. "Ho, ho, the blind leading—" He stopped short, merriment quelled by the glances of shocked amazement from the passers-by rushing to the rescue.

On at least one of his Washington trips it was a member of Roger's family who suffered all the hardship involved. Soon after Roger left by plane, Ronnie became violently sick, with nausea and soaring temperature. LaVerna called the doctor, and that evening he drove the two-and-a-half miles from town to see the child. He was concerned. The next morning he called up to see if the patient had improved. No, LaVerna told him, he was still vomiting and running a high temperature. The doctor said, "Come into the drugstore, and I'll phone him a prescription."

When LaVerna came back with the medicine, Roger had already returned by plane. She was amazed to see the child playing friskily with his father, apparently in the pink of condition.

"But—Ronnie's been sick!" she exclaimed. "What's happened?"

"Sick!" Roger was equally surprised. "Why, there's nothing wrong with Ron!"

And there wasn't. Nothing, that is, which his father's safe arrival had been unable to cure. Ronnie, who had been reading the newspapers since prekindergarten days, had come across an item reporting the crash of a Washington-bound plane into the Potomac, with all passengers killed. He had literally been worried sick all the time Roger was gone.

Roger was a valued and articulate member of boards and committees meeting in Washington. In 1949 he made an eloquent appeal before the House Committee on Education and Labor in behalf of a bill to establish a Federal Commission on Services for the Physically Handicapped.

"As I see it," he said in part, "H. R. 3095 doesn't bring charity to the disabled. Thank God for that. Above all, we don't want charity. This bill will give the physically handicapped a far better chance to earn his way through life. Untold millions of tax eaters will become taxpayers."

He told of Robert Cox who, with both legs amputated at the hips, had supported himself decently and *paid taxes,* but had died the preceding week because he could not afford an operation and H. R. 3095 was not a law; and of Orville Mitchell who, though paralyzed from the neck down, after twelve years in the hospital now owned his own home and ran a thriving little business which enabled him to *pay taxes.*

He went on, "Rehabilitation said when I went to them for help eighteen years ago that I was not feasible for rehabilitation; I was too seriously disabled." Then he told simply and modestly what he had been able to accomplish because of the interest of one man, Mr. Whitehead. "With that little start and the help of God, I have been able to marry, adopt three wonderful children, own my own home, and conduct a ten-acre gladiolus business. Above all, I am proud to *pay taxes.*"

He ended, "But for every Robert Cox or Orville Mitchell or myself, I know of at least ten physically handicapped individuals who are a burden to society. Present agencies have failed them. Gentlemen, it is that other 90 per cent for whom I am speaking."

The chairman of the committee was obviously impressed. "Mr. Arnett, you say that you do most of your work yourself. Do you do it from that chair?"

"I have a tractor that I fixed up, and I have a motor truck that I get around through the field in, and I do my own cutting and plowing."

"Do you move yourself from your chair to the tractor?"

"Yes. I have a hoist designed so that I can get on the tractor myself. I drive my own car and my own truck."

"That is a remarkable presentation and demonstration," remarked another member of the committee. "It is very effective."

Roger's promotion of the AFPH took him all over Indiana, from South Bend to Evansville. He made speeches to local chapters, service clubs, church groups, testified at a state senate hearing, where he fearlessly lashed out at the state vocational division and accused the agency of "intimidating" handicapped citizens.

"There are 7 million severely handicapped persons in the United States, of whom less than 10 per cent are gainfully employed," he told one Lions Club. "Fifty per cent of the total number could do gainful work if others would only give them employment."

In churches he stressed his growing concern over the lack of proper access facilities to church buildings.

"What problems do the handicapped have here in your church and parish?" he asked one prominent minister in Bloomington, after being carried up a steep flight of steps to the sanctuary.

"Why, they don't have any problems here," assured the cleric heartily. "Everything is just fine for all of them."

No handicapped, either, reflected Roger, noting the complete absence of wheel chair occupants in the large congregation.

He found one eager listener, however, among the clergy. Father Schneider was an old acquaintance. When a Catholic missionary in China he had written to Roger asking for a shipment of glad bulbs for his parish. Earlier, at home in East Lansing, he had met Roger at glad shows, visited him at Corunna. Now occasionally he stopped off overnight in Columbus, on his way to his church in Memphis, Tennessee, keeping the children enthralled with stories of his missionary years in China and teaching them to eat with chopsticks.

"Every church should have some means for a handicapped person to get in without help," Roger asserted more than once to his friend.

The priest nodded in serious agreement. Like the crossing of glads, it would take some years for the concept thus created to come to fruition, but Roger was to see it bloom in a remarkable way.

While the work with organizations was important and rewarding, it was his contacts with handicapped individuals which Roger found most satisfying. And in Indiana he came to know dozens of them personally. There was Paul Alden, president of the Indiana AFPH, a prominent Baptist minister and former student pastor at the University of Illinois, who had suffered a stroke in his forties and had never been able to adjust to his handicap. Although he could drive a car, walk with a cane, and his speech and marvelous memory were unaffected, the church had denied him all further opportunities for active service, and he was extremely bitter. "But your disability is far greater than mine," he admitted to Roger with humility, "and look what you have done!"

There was Ada Marie Yeoman, who had become deaf and blind when she was twelve. She wore an alphabetic glove with the letters all printed on it, four letters to each finger and thumb and six in the palm of the hand. An upward motion of the hand was "Yes," a sideward, "No." By spelling out the words one could communicate with her. When a word was barely started, she could often guess what it was and speak it. Once she came and spent a week with the Arnetts. When Sunday came they supposed, of course, she would not want to go to church, so LaVerna decided to stay at home and talk with her, a diversion of which she could never get enough.

"Why, I love to go to church!" she said to their surprise. "Do you know what I do? I ask God to bless this one and that one through all my friends, until sometimes I get as many as 400 God Blesses. But the time goes so fast I can never get through."

She even gave a talk to Roger's Sunday-school class. He had learned to use her alphabet without recourse to the glove, so he sat beside her while she talked. Being deaf, she was sometimes hard to understand, and when he saw that her message was not getting across, he would press her hand and she would stop while he interpreted. Once when he did so she was so interested that she failed to stop. He pressed a little harder. Still she kept on speaking. Then he gave her hand a vigorous squeeze. "Ouch!" she exclaimed. Then she laughed. "What a good joke on me!"

Ada Marie loved to ride. So did the blind glad grower, Claude Enslem. One February Roger drove them both to the winter glad meeting in East Lansing. Leaving at nine in the evening, he picked up Claude and his wife in Marion, then drove across to Galveston, where Ada Marie joined them, then on to Chicago. They arrived just in time for the "Welcome Travelers" program, where Roger was invited to participate. It was an interesting experience, a man in a wheel chair taking a blind man and his wife and a woman both deaf and blind on such a long expedition. But, curiously enough, it was Mrs. Enslem, the only able-bodied member of the party, who suffered the most embarrassment. In the Chicago hotel she was guiding Ada Marie downstairs from the rest room. Coming to the long flight of steps to the lower level, she indicated their presence by the use of the alphabet glove. "Oh, pshaw!" exclaimed Ada Marie.

Whereupon she took the easiest way down, seating herself and sliding. Mrs. Enslem was both shocked and scared, but even more amused by the bewilderment on upraised faces at sight of an elderly woman using the stairs to a huge hotel lobby as a toboggan slide.

It was soon after his arrival in Indiana that Roger became deeply involved in the case of Carl Dean Selby, a seven-year-old child born a spastic, oddly enough the same age to the day as Ronnie. The father had abandoned the family at the boy's birth, and the poor mother could not cope with the situation alone. When Roger became interested in the case, the child was a charge of the Department of Public Welfare, which boarded him in a foster home, where he was sometimes tied in bed so he would not injure himself or become a nuisance to the family. Roger indignantly protested that he should be in school. After one hasty and shockingly inconclusive test he was committed to the State School for the Feeble-minded at Muscatatuck.

"This is the type of treatment I am fighting against," Roger exploded in an article published in the Columbus *Evening Republican*. "Wherever possible spastics must be provided the care and training which will enable them to become useful and self-supporting rather than a lifetime charge of the taxpayer. In the case of Carl Dean, he is at the end of the line in a school for the feeble-minded.

"What this child needs is care and proper training. I know of dozens of cases comparable to Carl Dean's where the proper training has enabled them to become self-sustaining and successful businessmen. Many have college degrees and are authorities in their fields.

"I know this child," Roger continued. "I have held him on my lap and talked to him. He is like many who, with a chance, have freed th'mselves from the public-welfare rolls."

Here also he tried to discover some support in his tremendous concern for such problems from church leaders. He took a district superintendent of his denomination with him to Muscatatuck to see Carl Dean Selby and to talk with a psychiatrist about the boy's case. While there they met a deaf boy who, although not a mental case, had been consigned to this institution for the feeble-minded merely because of his deafness.

"Now what can the church do about this problem?" Roger inquired of the superintendent.

The church official merely threw up his hands.

The changes for which Roger crusaded would be slow in coming, but in subsequent years he would see them come. It was no mere coincidence that six years later another article in the same newspaper quoted extensively from Roger's critical statements and conceded that he had been right. It was called "Boy 'Who Shouldn't Have Been at Muscatatuck' Has a Future Now." After two years in the institution Carl Dean's intelligence quotient had dropped to thirty-eight. But "more recently," the article stated, "since expansion of rehabilitation facilities at Muscatatuck, Carl has begun once again to develop the mental ability which he always had, so that present tests reveal his I.Q. at eighty-three. From all present indications Carl should continue his upward growth. We would say further that in general he should develop into a normal self-sustaining adult.

"Mr. Arnett was last reported in Michigan after leaving the Columbus area," the article concluded, "Perhaps someone will tell him about Carl."

And to Roger's satisfaction someone did. He would have been more gratified, however, if the organization featured in the article as cooperating with the new state program of rehabilitation at Muscatatuck had been the church. Instead it was the Lions Club.

It was the constant impact of such experiences that slowly led Roger to a strong conviction. Much as he loved glads and the creation of new forms of enriching beauty, there must be some more important way to earn a living. *He wanted to work with people.*

"Things have been changing," he said to LaVerna as each grueling glad season seemed to leave him with less and less time and energy for these more important activities. "Since I graduated from college, schools have been making lots of advances for the handicapped. Who knows? Maybe I could get a job now teaching, perhaps in some college in Michigan."

The thought was tantalizing, for he had never given up the dream of teaching. LaVerna, never enamored with the glad business, gave eager encouragement. She knew, too, that he could not possibly maintain the fiercely competitive pace of such an enterprise for many years, plus the many other obligations he insisted on assuming. The long hours and backbreaking labor would have drained the resources of an able-bodied man. It was a miracle that he had avoided hospital experience during these Indiana years. When she

169

had dreaded leaving Michigan and their beloved Dr. Arnold, he had promised her that if she ever needed him he would fly down to Columbus in his small private plane. But it had not been necessary. Roger had had minor illnesses, but they had found adequate medical service nearby. However, if he kept on at the present pace, some crisis was certain to develop. She welcomed the prospect of a return to Michigan.

Hopefully Roger wrote to his alma mater, now Eastern Michigan University, and asked them about the possibility of a teaching position. Although he still had his life certificate, he indicated a willingness to make any other preparation necessary, even to go back to college for a year and get a master's degree. When the reply came in the spring of 1951 both Roger and LaVerna were transported to the seventh heaven. *The university was awarding him an honorary master's degree!*

"It's a college job," exulted Roger. "It must be. And who knows? Maybe right there in the old alma mater!"

Immediately they started making plans, put the house on the market, and prepared to make the coming glad season their last. Then on May 1, Roger's birthday, there came a telephone call.

"Mr. Roger Arnett? Western Union calling. We have a telegram from Ypsilanti, Michigan."

"Yes, yes. Arnett speaking."

"One moment, please."

He turned from the telephone, smiling from ear to ear, eyes two blue scintillating sparks. "It's come, darling. This is it. Wire from Ypsilanti—the college!"

It was the college indeed, but not the announcement of a teaching job. It was a stereotyped wish for a "happy birthday." It tore La-Verna's heart to see Roger's face fall.

Later came another call. Another Western Union voice. Another burst of excitement. Another false alarm. "Happy birthday!"

Yet these were not really disappointments, merely postponements of an anticipated but sure development. It was curiosity that Roger felt rather than uncertainty. What sort of job was in store for him? Not that it mattered too much! He would gladly take a humble assistantship in science to start with, as long as it was teaching.

Graduation time approached, and still there was no word of confirmation. O.K. Then it would all come at once, the honor and far more cherished guerdon for which it was being given. They left for the exercises in Michigan in June with every confidence that the reason he was being given the degree was to make him more eligible for a teaching position.

The university outdid itself in paying him honor. The citation was a lengthy "This Is Your Life" eulogy, dripping with honeyed phrases.

". . . one of the best distance men the college ever produced . . . returned to college in a wheel chair . . . planned to teach mathematics and science . . . unable to get a position because he could not walk . . . worked up to head of accounting department . . . raising of gladiolus became a full-time occupation . . . pushed himself into the front rank of American hybrid flower growers and turned a $300 investment into a $6,500-a-year business . . . motto is 'nothing is impossible' . . . has turned his own troubles toward helping others. . . ."

The citation concluded: "Because of his conspicuous endeavors in the service of those who suffer, and his bold and fearless determination to face the vicissitudes of life with courage and fortitude, I recommend on behalf of the faculty that Roger Arnett be awarded the honorary degree of master of education."

During the festivities that followed Roger waited in vain for the subject of his future employment to be broached. Finally he said to one of his former teachers, "Well, how about it? Did you find a job for me?"

She gave him a startled look. "A job? Were you looking for a job?" Then, regaining her composure, after a pause she added kindly, "Well, we might be able to find a part-time one some place."

Roger's lips felt stiff as he smilingly endured the long succession of congratulatory—what? Requiems, could they be called? At least this was the way a death's head must feel!

Later, after probable consultation with some of her colleagues, the teacher came back to speak to him. "I was wondering. How— how much would you expect to be paid if we should hire you?"

Listen, sister, he wanted to say, *it's a job I want, not charity.* Instead, he replied with what charm he could muster, "Please, Professor, don't give it another thought. I can see it wouldn't work out."

To add to his chagrin, he discovered that they had given an extra degree this year—*his.* A generous gesture, tacked on as an afterthought. Not since the months following his accident had he felt so bitter and disillusioned. They considered him capable of riding ten or twelve hours day after day on a tractor seat, a job that demanded little of a well-trained mind. That was wonderful. He had earned his maybe $6,500 a year. But to pay him half that amount for sitting four or five hours a day in a classroom doing the work they had trained him to do—that would be charity! Well, that was that. He had asked for bread and been given a—stone? No. A soft sop for his vanity.

All right, he must think of something else. For some time his mind had toyed with a daring possibility. The church for years had been a major interest. He had taught Sunday-school classes, headed men's groups, been a lay leader, worked on official boards, called on the sick—done almost everything a minister did except preach. Was it possible that he could do that also? And if so, how about the ministry? A daring idea, indeed, but lack of courage had never been one of Roger's weaknesses. He wrote to Harold Dakin, now pastor in a rural church near Midland, Michigan, and asked him for a chance to supply his pulpit some Sunday. Dakin was glad to give him the opportunity. Roger and LaVerna drove up one Saturday night, and he preached the next morning. The attempt was neither a great success nor a total failure. Many people commented kindly, and at least Dakin was not discouraging. But Roger knew as well as he the long preliminary training and many difficulties involved in entering the ministry. While the door had certainly not been opened, at least it had been set ajar.

The furious pace of the summer glad season confirmed their wisdom in making a change. The house was sold, possession of the new owners to await the digging of bulbs in the fall. Then began the frustrating hunt for a place to live back in Michigan. Roger and LaVerna would leave Indiana when she got out of work on Friday evening, drive all night, and look for houses all day Saturday. The first weekend they hunted in Ann Arbor. There was nothing they could afford. On the second weekend in Ypsilanti they found a house, old but redecorated, which they thought could be remodeled to suit Roger's needs. They made a small down payment and returned to Indiana well satisfied. But the next day the real-estate agent called with the news that another buyer had come who agreed to pay cash, and the owner had accepted. Again they took the harrowing weekend trip and spent another fruitless day in Ypsilanti.

At five o'clock they were desperate. They could not go back without finding *something*.

"I'm going over to Belleville," decided Roger.

They drove the ten miles, saw a real-estate sign. The agent was in. LaVerna told him what they wanted. "I think I've got just the place for you." He beamed. "A new house, completed only six weeks, all on one floor for your husband, and with nine acres of land for your glad bulbs."

It seemed too good to be true, and it was. The house was new, yes, but it had only two bedrooms, no garage, not a blade of grass or a tree, no paint inside. But the cleanness after all the old dingy places they had seen! And the nine acres of land! For Roger had been unable to sell his bulbs in Indiana. And, best of all, the price was no more than that of a small prefabricated unit in Ypsilanti. They took it.

It was November before they could move, for again the bulbs must be dug. This time the family stayed together until the end. Dick, now home from the Navy and married, lived just over the border in Michigan, so Roger would drive a truckload of bulbs to Dick's place, pick up his son, drive on to Belleville, where Dick could help him unload the bulbs in a rented barn, then drive Dick home. In this way two round trips could be made in one weekend, 1,300 miles traveled in three days. It was the middle of November before the many trips with more than six hundred thousand bulbs were completed.

Of course none of their furnishings fitted the new house. It was like moving from a mansion to a trailer. Neither of their big rugs would fit the living room, which was only twelve feet wide. When LaVerna found one that would do, Roger's wheel chair refused to surmount it, pushing its edges ahead on the smooth tile floor, so she had to remove it. The bare white walls reminded her of a hospital. Her cherished dining-room set, an elephant in the pony stall of the living-room end, had to be discarded. And the two small bedrooms made life unbelievably cramped. Even when they were finally settled, it did not seem like home.

Immediately Roger began searching for a job, any job. He was a good accountant with eight years of experience. He had two college degrees. The area was full of factories, and he visited all within a radius of twenty miles, not once but many times, offering to serve in any capacity. But none would hire him. They were sorry, but

173

their insurance rules would not cover his handicap. He came home each night more and more discouraged.

After six weeks their finances were again at rock bottom. LaVerna knew she must do something. Someone had suggested that an employee was needed at the bank. She jumped in the car and started for the center of town. But only two blocks from the house she saw a little manufacturing plant, and on an impulse she decided to go in. No, she thought, on her way up the walk, it was too small. They could not need more than one girl. Opening the door, she saw a young lady at a desk and almost backed out. But it was too late. The girl had already asked her business. At that moment the office manager walked in.

"I was just looking for a job," said LaVerna, "and I thought I would see if you needed a secretary, but I see you have one." She turned to leave.

"Just a minute," interposed the manager, "not so fast. We need another one."

Then the owner appeared. "How did you know we were looking for a secretary?" he asked. When they learned her qualifications and experience, they hired her on the spot.

LaVerna started work the following Monday, but not as an assistant. The secretary had scheduled her wedding for the preceding day without informing her employer. That Monday she was on her honeymoon. Returning on Wednesday, she was promptly fired. The occasional overtime LaVerna had been promised soon turned into several hours each evening and all day Saturday. With two children nine and ten the work was exhausting, and she gave notice in June.

For Roger had finally been able to secure a well-paying full-time job. It was Paul Alden, his friend from Indiana days, who performed the miracle. Dr. John Brown, head of the Department of Mathematics at the University of Illinois when Alden had been student pastor there, was now at the University of Michigan's Research Center at Willow Run airport. Paul advised Roger to consult him. Roger went immediately to the Center, only four miles from home. Dr. Brown recommended him to the employment manager, who referred him to the Data Processing Group which was building an electronic digital computer. Roger's science training equipped him with just the qualifications needed, and he was hired immediately. It was a university position with academic standing on the level of a research assistant, with all promotion opportunities and attendant benefits. For the first time in more than twenty years Roger felt like a free man, living in a free country where men were considered equal and not treated with discrimination because of a physical handicap.

Certainly he encountered none in his relationship with fellow workers. If they thought of him as "different," it was because he was more genial, more friendly than most, and took a personal interest in each one of his associates, even the maintenance men who did the lawn and carpentry work about the plant, such as Harvey Dicks, a carpenter. Roger learned that Harvey had boys who liked to fish. "Harve, you take 'em up there to the lake. Take time off to go fishin'." He heard that one of Harvey's friends had a retarded child and kept encouraging the parents until they got the child in school.

"The men at the office don't think of Roger as handicapped." Harvey voiced the opinion of all Roger's fellow workers. "They don't waste any sympathy on him. Heck, he's just an ordinary guy like the rest of us."

But he changed his mind the first time he saw Roger hoeing glads with one hand while guiding the motor scooter with the other. He stared in amazement. No ordinary man would ever be so crazy smart as to do a thing like that!

LaVerna had worked too hard and too long to be content to stay at home while the rest of the family left each morning for work and school. In August she decided she wanted to teach. Then she could be at home when the children were. But high-school teachers in Belleville, the superintendent told her, were hired as promotions from the grades. She would have to start in junior high. And there were no openings in math, her favorite subject. He finally persuaded her, against her better judgment, to accept a fifth grade. After a year this would make her eligible for teaching senior high. But she was never to fulfill the agreement.

She went from the superintendent's office to Susterka Lake, where she had previously taken the children to swim. On this hot afternoon Faye came running to meet her, shaking with chills. That night LaVerna heard the child constantly turning. Perhaps it was her own vivid childhood experience which sounded a warning bell. In the morning she said, "Faye, put your chin down on your chest."

"I can't," the child replied. "It hurts."

"Oh, dear God, not again!" LaVerna prayed. But already the

warning bell had become a knell. She knew as well as if a doctor had spoken the word. *Polio!*

She took Faye to the doctor that morning, but there was no paralysis, and he did not confirm her fear. "Watch her closely and keep me posted."

The child slept much that day, slept well that night and into the next morning. At noon LaVerna wakened her. "Aren't you about ready for some lunch?" "Yes."

LaVerna poached an egg, sat down on the side of her bed, and started to feed her. The child's lip seemed to disappear into her mouth with the spoon. "I—I can't swallow."

The following hours were a succession of horrors: Trying vainly to reach the doctor, locating him finally. "Take her to Ann Arbor immediately. I'll phone ahead." Driving the car frantically to where Roger and Ronnie were working in the fields. Another frantic drive home, with them following on the scooter bike. The relief when Faye found she could walk into the contagion ward, a little wooden shack behind the hospital. The doctors laying her on the table to examine her, then leaving. The terrible choking, while she looked frantically to LaVerna for help. Rushing to the door and screaming, no one coming. Screaming again, "She's choking to death!" All of them trying to rush in at once. The conversation with the doctor: "You don't need to tell me. I know it's polio."

"Yes, her throat is completely closed. Before the night is over we may have to perform a tracheotomy, perhaps something more drastic."

"You mean her life is in danger?"

"Yes."

LaVerna sat stunned, numb. "Am I an unnatural mother," she thought, "to feel nothing?" Then she remembered with relief an article she had just read, explaining how the body takes care of shock with a feeling of temporary numbness. Still calm, she drove home with Roger, to discover that Ronnie was running a temperature and complaining of headache.

"Very likely he has it, too," the doctor in Ann Arbor told her when she reported it. "But that doesn't mean it's the paralytic kind. Watch him."

This was Saturday. Sunday there was no change in Faye's condition. On Monday LaVerna spent all day at the hospital; then in the evening she stayed with Ronnie, who still showed disturbing symptoms, and Roger went to be with Faye. She had hardly lain down to rest when he called her. "The nurse says for you to come at once. The crisis is about here. And—they don't think she'll make it."

Frantically LaVerna searched for someone to stay with Ronnie. Finally she found a woman with her family grown who was willing to expose herself. There was no car. Her neighbor across the road agreed to drive her to the hospital. The twenty miles seemed interminable. When she entered the hospital room and looked from the motionless figure to Roger's stricken face, she thought she was too late. But no, the nurse told her, Faye was still alive, barely. There was no blood pressure, little hope. This time LaVerna felt no numbness. Emotion came with a rush, stabbing all her senses. No guilty suspicion now that she might be an unnatural mother! As they sat waiting the doctor came in and ordered them out on the porch. "Suppose she became conscious and saw the look on your faces!"

The miracle happened. After an eternity of waiting the nurse came and said, "The crisis is over. Her blood pressure is up, pulse is up, and she is breathing normally." They drove home offering silent prayers of thanksgiving.

Ronnie was sick for a week, while LaVerna watched him in an agony of suspense, expecting him to choke at any minute. But no paralysis appeared. Nine-year-old Faye was in the hospital a month, for more than half the time her throat completely paralyzed, a nurse in attendance around the clock.

"She may still feel she doesn't belong to us," thought LaVerna. "Perhaps now she'll be worried about becoming permanently crippled and will feel we don't want her." The idea became an obsession, so every day she drove to the hospital and spent the afternoon with her. Long before the month was over she was in a state of nervous exhaustion. She traveled the twenty miles like an automaton. Once, turning a corner into an expressway, she suddenly skidded as on loose gravel, and veered almost into the path of an oncoming vehicle. Thinking there was something wrong with the car, she took it to a garage.

"You must have had a muscle spasm that whirled it," said the mechanic, finding nothing wrong. "You shouldn't be driving." Still she persisted in going every day.

Faye returned home at last, her round little face pared to a pathetic knife edge, cutting at their heartstrings. The muscles in her neck were too weak to support her head, so she had to wear a collar for six months. The left side of her face was completely paralyzed and all the muscles on that side of her body very weak. Twice a day LaVerna would place her on the kitchen table and put her through a regimen of exercises, going back to the hospital at intervals to learn new ones. When the exertion became too great for her frail strength, she taught the exercises to Roger and Ronnie, then stood by while they performed them. Later they would give Faye two years of acrobatic dancing lessons which limbered her stiffened body in a remarkable way.

They tried to prepare the child for her return to school. Who could know better than LaVerna the hurts in store for a sensitive child of nine bearing the ravages of polio? Even adults found the sight of the twisted little face above the grotesque collar, the pitiful first attempts at speech and laughter, a distressing shock. What indignities must she suffer from the brutal candor of children!

LaVerna went to see the school principal and explained the situation. The principal assigned Faye to the fifth-grade teacher who she thought would be most understanding.

"Of course," said Muriel Bearance, smiling out of her long experience. "I know just how to prepare my children for her coming. We'll discuss ways we can help. And since she can come only a half day, I'll plan to put the most important classes into those periods."

It was not Miss Bearance's class who made faces at the child at recess and dubbed her "Horse Collar." But even these jibes Faye accepted philosophically and with a surprising aptitude for tart rejoinder. She had not lived five years with Roger and LaVerna Arnett to be cowed by a physical handicap. The real test, however, as LaVerna well knew, would come later. The pain of boys' taunts at nine was nothing compared with that of their averted faces at sixteen!

Those first years in Belleville were for Roger an aggravated repetition of the nerve-racking pace in Indiana. For, full-time job or no, the bulbs were there and must be planted. He rented three acres out on the Ridge Road which had good sandy soil, besides using the large tract of land behind the house. Again the summer passed in a hectic round of cultivating, picking, sorting, bunching, selling, all done after work and on weekends. But LaVerna felt less inward rebellion, for this time she could see the end. And in spite of her dislike of the drudgery involved, she still dearly loved the flowers.

They sold many from the house. And, since they were no longer dependent on them for a living, they could be more generous with them. Occasionally, if there were cut flowers left over on a Sunday, when they did no picking, they would put them beside the road in pails with signs attached: "HELP YOURSELF. FREE." The result was an interesting study in human nature. Some people would stare unbelievingly, then drive on. Some would stop, then, thinking there must be a catch to the invitation, would gingerly take some and look around suspiciously, as if expecting a trap. Some people would take a few, others whole bucketfuls. A tiny minority would leave a scribbled note saying, "Thank you."

But the end of an era was approaching. The *Gladiolus* of 1953 held the following advertisement:

HAVE YOU WANTED TO START YOUR OWN GLADIOLUS BUSINESS?

That Old Wheel Chair Has Got Me
I am selling out my glads and going into other work.
This gives you the chance of a lifetime.
Over 600,000 bulbs, with trays, etc., all for sale!
Orders taken 100 to 100,000 bulbs.

But Roger's exit from this stage of his career was attended by a bang rather than a whimper, for the same issue of the *Gladiolus* listed 311 varieties each of which, according to the New England Gladiolus Society, the parent organization, took three or more blue ribbons. White Challenge had sixteen top awards to its credit.

And in 1953 Roger received a gold medal from the New England Gladiolus Society: "For his fine work in hybridizing; for his ingenuity in devising farm machinery for gladiolus growing adapted to paraplegics' use; for his cheerful, smiling, industrious pursuit of a livelihood in gladiolus culture in the face of terrific adversities that would have defeated all but the very bravest. He has demonstrated that you may be 'down' but you are never 'out' until you quit. He is a *man*."

11

The dream of the ministry persisted. It was by no means a new impulse. Back in high-school days, when Roger had joined the church, he had sometimes felt the urge to become a foreign missionary but had considered himself incapable of meeting the challenge. Later, whenever he had heard a minister give an appeal for full-time Christian workers, he had responded silently, "I should, but I can't." Now, as he became increasingly conscious of the spiritual needs of handicapped people and of the failure of the church, not merely to meet but even to recognize such needs, the urge became imperative. "We have no problem with handicapped people," the minister in Bloomington had said. The very denial had been an acknowledgment of the serious nature of the problem. Somehow church people must be alerted to these needs.

But even more compulsive was his own desire to minister with greater efficacy to the handicapped. He longed to have every one of them experience the same blessings which he himself enjoyed. A man's spirit needed nurture just as his body needed food and his mind education and training. Words from Paul's letter to the Corinthians kept burning into his consciousness: "Blessed be the Father of mercies and God of all comfort, who comforts us in all our affliction, so that we may be able to comfort those who are in any affliction, with the comfort with which we ourselves are comforted by God. . . . If we are afflicted, it is for your comfort and salvation; and if we are comforted, it is for your comfort, which you experience when you patiently endure the same sufferings that we suffer."

But he had no illusions as to the cost of such a ministry to himself. It would mean years of special training, all secured at a sacrifice of precious leisure time and with incalculable strain on an already overtaxed body. If he managed to attain full-time status, it would mean giving up the first job he had ever had commensurate with his ability and training, with financial security for his family, for he knew the ministry he contemplated could never be a lucrative one. If, as he suspected, he should not attain full-time status, it would mean forfeiting all opportunities for promotion at the university, which would demand undivided ambition and energy. For the first time in his life he was able to support his family like a *whole man*, without dependence on his wife. Give up both the security and the satisfaction for a purpose which many of his scoffing friends, such as Paul Strachan, would term a "nebulous pipe dream?"

"The church! Those pious Job's friends?" He could imagine Paul's reaction. "What in heaven's name do you think *they* could do for the handicapped even if they wanted to? Get them jobs? Pass rehabilitation laws? It's here and now the handicapped need help, not some 'pie in the sky' day when they can leave their wheel chairs behind and go bouncing into heaven!"

Roger agreed. And it was here and now, after counting all the costs, that he was stubbornly determined to help them.

While still in Indiana he had made inquiries of leaders of his denomination—bishops, district superintendents, pastors—but had received no encouragement. The idea of a specialized ministry to the handicapped was outside their realm of thinking. How could he perform the stereotyped duties of a pastor, how get around his parish, how get up into his pulpit? One man even said to him, "How could you stand up to preach?" and Roger felt like retorting, "Was Jesus a less effective preacher because he did it sitting down?" The ministry seemed as much a closed occupation to a man in a wheel chair as had teaching.

But now in Michigan he met with mild encouragement. Bishop Reed, formerly a pastor in Ypsilanti, remembered Roger from college days and referred him to Dr. Fitch, the district superintendent of the Ann Arbor District, who was immediately sympathetic and explained the steps a man with Roger's education must take to enter the ministry. Feeling, however, that the conference course of study would be insufficient to prepare him for the sort of work he wanted to do, Roger started evening classes in the Graduate School of Wayne State University in Detroit, choosing courses leading to a master's degree in Special Education. He studied techniques of dealing with the blind, the deaf, the emotionally disturbed, the mentally retarded, the epileptic, the brain damaged—in short, almost every kind of physically disabled persons.

In April, 1953, the Official Board of the Belleville Methodist Church recommended him for a local preacher's license, a first step in the long trek toward qualification for the ministry. In June, at the Annual Conference in Albion, he appeared before the Board of Ministerial Training and Qualifications, which approved the granting of the license and agreed that he could proceed to take the conference course of study, which for a man with his educational background might be an alternative to seminary training. But Roger left the session more disillusioned than encouraged. There had been little interest expressed in his crusade for a specialized ministry to the handicapped. The idea was good if unlimited funds were available, but a half-dozen other special ministries should have advanced priority. They had been willing to give him permission to take the studies, since no commitment of a job or of financial obligation was involved.

He felt like an outsider at the conference, timid, fearful, bewildered, as much an oddity among the smooth-functioning, tight-knit ministerial brotherhood as was his wheel chair among their efficient, bustling, rapidly striding lower limbs. The church and its surrounding area seemed all steps and curbs. He was balancing hesitantly on the edge of an unusually steep descent when an energetic, pleasant-faced man hurried up.

"Hello there! Need a little help?"

"Thanks. I could use it."

The stranger lowered the chair to street level, then with unusual thoughtfulness did not offer to push it but walked along beside it.

"My name's Hartoog. Al. Pastor at Glenwood Church, Wyandotte. You here for the conference?"

"Yes." Roger introduced himself. "Maybe you won't believe it, but I'm presumptuous enough to think I might sometime make a minister. The committee just gave me the go-ahead."

Instead of the anticipated skepticism, the frank, friendly eyes revealed only an alert interest. "Good!" Hartoog nodded approvingly. "We're always in need of new men. Want to tell me about yourself?"

Briefly Roger told something of his purpose. Hartoog was enthusiastic. "Wonderful idea, a minister to the handicapped! I can think of a dozen people in my parish who need such a ministry. And most of us have neither the time nor the qualifications to give such service. More power to you! If there's anything I can do to help—I say! Belleville's only about twenty miles from Wyandotte. How about coming over to preach for me next month when I'm on vacation? I'll call you."

Surely it could not have been mere chance, marveled Roger later, that of all the 350 ministers attending conference, it was Al Hartoog whom he met that day on the street corner!

Heartened by the encouragement of this one man, Roger returned to his work at Willow Run, his evenings at Wayne State University, and somewhere in the extra hours his conference course of study. True to his promise, Hartoog called and invited him to preach on a Sunday in July. Roger accepted with alacrity. Too inexperienced to realize his deficiencies as a beginner, he fulfilled the assignment with his usual outward bravado. But Glenwood Church would have inspired confidence in the most timid novice. It was a new small structure, seating barely two hundred, as yet without pews. And, wonder of wonders, it had no steps on either the outside or the inside, leading to the sanctuary! For almost the first time since his accident he felt like exulting as he wheeled himself easily through the door, "I was glad when they said unto me, let us go into the house of the Lord."

It was LaVerna who worried and agonized in her obscure corner of the congregation. She was nervous for both of them, and still frightened at the prospect of becoming a minister's wife. At first the very idea had appalled her. Active though she had been in church work, even in the big city church in Indiana, she shied from the conspicuous and demanding role of minister's wife like a frightened rabbit. In spite of Roger's assurance that he would probably never assume the responsibilities of a church, she was overpowered by a sense of inadequacy. Yet standing beside him after the service, seeing the strange faces light into friendliness under the spell of his glowing eyes and irresistible smile, she realized that all their years together had been preparing her for this new role. Ever since she had known him he had been helping people, especially the handicapped. Now the circle of his concern had merely widened, his definition of "handicapped" stretched to include every kind of human need he might encounter.

"We're all handicapped some way or other," he was fond of reminding his able-bodied friends. "There isn't a soul living who's not blind or deaf or lame or paralyzed in some vital function of body or spirit. And some of the worst handicapped people I know have the strongest eyes and ears and arms and legs."

Her role in years to come, LaVerna suddenly discerned, was exactly what it had been in the past, serving as a gentle foil for his spring-wound, contagious exuberance in public; patiently rewinding the springs when they ran down, as they often did, in private; performing the innumerable behind-the-scenes chores which were the inevitable lot of a paraplegic's wife and which were bound to increase in volume and intensity—the extra washing and ironing, the remodeling of clothes to fit both the wearer of a brace and an amputee, the medication of the frequent infections and pressure sores, the cleaning up after bladder and bowel accidents; and loving him with all the intensity and devotion of which her sensitive being was capable.

"I hope he appreciates all you do for him," the irrepressible Treva remarked tartly some time after Roger became a minister. "Does he ever say so?"

"Oh, yes," came the cheerful if somewhat cryptic reply. "Often. In his sermons."

Now during this period of accelerated preparation for the ministry, she gladly assumed the additional duty of typing the papers required both for his conference course of study and for his graduate work in special education.

Roger was deeply and sensitively aware of all these quiet and uncomplaining services, especially those which a wife would not normally have to discharge. If he appeared sometimes to take them for granted, it was because he found the very acknowledgment of his masculine deficiencies humiliating and repugnant. He spared her wherever possible, performing every personal service he could, transferring himself from bed to wheel chair to car, then, if LaVerna was with him, after he had jerked himself into the driver's seat, letting her do no more than straighten the rubber rings under him, fold the chair, and tilt its big forward wheels to car level; always giving it the final strong pull himself, then folding back the seat behind him. Otherwise he did all these things for himself. A wheel chair occupant could observe many masculine amenities, such as rolling on the curb side of the street or opening a door to let a lady pass through first, but one courtesy was forever denied: handing the lady passenger you were driving in and out of your car!

Yet, considerate though he tried to be, by temperament he was a "now" person, and when his "LaVerna!" rang through the house, it usually held a note of immediate expectancy. If her reply, "Yes, dear, I hear. I'm coming," sometimes bore a hint of patient resignation, it was born, not of reluctance, but of a sense of inadequacy.

Would she have married him if she had known all the labor, worry, heartache, increasingly difficult problems the relationship would entail? The question which once so haunted Roger's moments of despondency had long since become as defunct as his amputated right leg. He knew very well that to both him and La-Verna any life worth living would be inconceivable without the other. Yet, just as he felt twinges of pain which he could have sworn came from the lost limb, so the tiny nagging doubt frequently stabbed at his nerve ends, a not unhealthy antidote for the vanity of any husband, handicapped or otherwise.

His ego suffered another slight jolt when months passed and he heard nothing more from Al Hartoog. Not that he expected or wanted commendation for his amateurish performance in the pulpit! He knew he must have been pretty terrible. But Hartoog's kindling of interest in the idea of a ministry to the handicapped had seemed more than a transient flare, and Roger coveted not only his cooperation but his friendship. Then in October the telephone rang. It was a long-distance call.

"Arnett? Al Hartoog speaking. I want you to come over and meet with my Official Board next Wednesday evening. Suppose you can make it?"

Roger found difficulty keeping his voice steady. "Yes. Of course. But—what—"

"Can't tell you now. Just want you to come. O.K., then. See you Wednesday."

During the following days Roger was alternately excited and uncertain. He hoped, yet dared not believe, that the meeting presaged some development affecting his future. At least Hartoog must have sparked some interest in his people. If he had merely wanted Roger to make a speech on the subject of ministering to the handicapped, surely he would have told him. But conjectures were futile. He waited impatiently for Wednesday to arrive.

It might have been a homecoming instead of a second visit. Men crowded around his chair to shake his hand. "Glad to see you again, Arnett." . . . "People are still talking about that service last summer." . . . "Understand you think our church is pretty nice, all on one floor and few steps. Only one like it in the district." Some of them he recalled from his previous visit and was able to greet them by name. Many whose faces he did not remember flashed him cordial smiles.

The meeting opened, and Hartoog formally introduced him. "I've been telling our people, Roger, about this vision, and they're just as enthused about it as I am. But I want you to tell them about it yourself. We think it's a great idea, and we'd like to have a part in it."

When Roger entered the house that night, his wheels were almost riding on air. They fairly bounded up the ramp. Seldom had LaVerna seen him so happy and excited. His blue eyes shone like polished cobalt.

"What do you think? It's come, darling, the chance I've been waiting for! Al Hartoog wants me to be his assistant, with special responsibility as minister to the handicapped in his area, church members and non-church alike! It's practically settled now, but the board will give its final O.K. next month. Isn't it wonderful?"

His new relationship with Glenwood Church in Wyandotte began the following month. Of course it was only a part-time responsibility and brought no remuneration except a small amount for expenses. At the Annual Conference the following June his appointment as assistant minister was made official. A humble beginning, to be sure, but to Roger a God-sent opportunity for service!

Each Sunday he left early, driving the twenty miles to Wyandotte and participating in the two church services and the Church School. Occasionally Hartoog invited him to preach, and slowly Roger became more expert in this department, although with his excess of enthusiasm and abundance of ideas he was inclined to be a bit too lengthy. Not too long-winded, however! Forced to speak from his lungs since his diaphragm functioned imperfectly, he frequently ran out of breath and announced a hymn midway of the sermon, an innovation that proved popular with the congregation.

Finally this difficulty was obviated when an anplifying system furnished a microphone, plugged into an outlet beside his chair. With a pulpit gown slit down the back for easy donning and a lectern built by one of the carpenters at the Research Center which slid neatly over the arms of his wheel chair, Roger could perform his duties as assistant pastor with both ease and dignity. Even the two steps to the platform were not a major obstacle, with a half-dozen teenagers usually vying to display both strength and chivalry. Or, if they were not around, he could depend on the strong arms of Al Hartoog. Later, when an addition was built on the church, it was constructed with the needs of the handicapped in mind, with two spaces left in the back of the room for wheel chairs.

For Roger the high point of the morning came after the services, when he sat at the 21st Street entrance and greeted the children as they came out of the Church School. As weeks passed and he saw the children's expressions change from fear to curiosity to acceptance to confidence to radiant affection, he felt a satisfaction which no adult accolade of "Good sermon today, Roger," could ever arouse.

But the Sunday services were secondary to his real ministry in Glenwood Church. It was understood that he was there to help the handicapped, not only of the church or even of the community, but wherever the need might be discovered. There was no dearth of opportunities. Roger was soon spending not only his Sunday afternoons calling but most of his free evenings after leaving the Research Center at four fifteen. Al Hartoog seldom had to suggest names. Once started, the project moved by chain reaction. One call would inevitably lead to another.

"Have you seen Jim H———? I hear he's got arthritis again, bad." . . . "There's a woman over on the next street I wish you'd call on. She's been flat on her back for six months." . . . "I have a friend in a wheel chair like me. He doesn't go to our church, but I sure wish you'd see him." . . .

His ministry soon came to involve far more than making calls. Not long after he began work at Glenwood a trust fund was established to provide means for assistance to people who came to Roger with special needs. Inspired by his enthusiasm, many people in the parish contributed to it generously. It was used in various ways to help people with many diverse problems.

For instance, there was Chris, the Danish man who had had both legs broken and who lived alone with his two big dogs in a garage home with outdoor plumbing. After visiting him over a long period Roger was able to help him get indoor plumbing installed. There was Eddie, who had been stricken with polio at age ten. His father had died, leaving his wife with six children to care for. Severely disabled and confined to a wheel chair, Eddie was unable to get out of the house except when his mother carried him, for there were many steps and no ramp. In fact, Roger had to take Ronnie along when he went to visit Eddie, to help him get up the steps. But from the trust fund lumber was provided to build a ramp, and under Roger's guidance Ronnie, who was becoming adept at tools, helped to build it. It was a proud day when Eddie made his way down and up the ramp for the first time, slowly and with grim, laborious persistence, for the muscles of his arms had been badly weakened, but triumphantly. The comprehensive nature of the church's concern was well demonstrated in the case of Eddie, for the family were Catholics.

Roger soon found a loyal core of supporters for his work in both the Glenwood and the Belleville churches. There were the Hopemans, who had moved to Belleville at about the same time as the Arnetts. They had three sons, two of them near Ronnie's age. One summer Roger took the three boys vacationing at a camp site owned by his parents on the Shiawassee River. The association sparked an intimate friendship between the parents, and Victor Hopeman, an executive with the Ford Motor Company, and his wife became generous contributors to the project, in both funds and service.

There was Doris Ritter, the faithful church secretary at Glenwood, who cheerfully assumed the extra burden of all his records and reports. There were the Miles family, the Touses, the Shepherds, and many others.

Some of the handicapped people Roger visited were old acquaintances, such as Walter Roth and Joe McIntyre. Walter, who had been in college with Roger, had been stricken with arthritis in the early 1940s and was a single amputee confined to a wheel chair. His wife Alice was a teacher, and Walter contributed to their support by making leather goods. One day when Roger visited him he found Walter the proud possessor of an old Packard car. "I made up my mind that if you could drive one of these things, Roger, I could, too."

Joe also was an acquaintance of college days who lived in Ypsilanti. Afflicted with cerebral palsy from birth, he had taken a vicarious interest in Roger's athletic career and witnessed most of his racing triumphs from the sidelines. Now he welcomed Roger's visits with pathetic eagerness. Unable to speak plainly, he had his own method of communication, a talking board with letters arranged as on a typewriter. He would point out the letters with his one functioning though poorly coordinated hand or, occasionally, try to spell them out in the air. Roger spent hours playing checkers with him. Often Joe would telephone him, using a pencil for dialing the numbers, and make pathetic attempts to talk but communicating nothing except the fact that he wanted to see him.

"All right. I'll be over, Joe," Roger would assure him.

Here also example and not words bore fruit, for, watching Roger's dexterity, Joe was stimulated toward independence. By the use of ropes, pulleys, and other gadgets he learned to move himself between chair and bed and bathtub and, after his parents died, take care of himself with the aid of a housekeeper.

But most of Roger's contacts came as the result of others' suggestions. For example, there was Stefan Florescu.

Someone in Glenwood told Roger about him. He lived four miles away in Lincoln Park. Roger visited him first in the summer of 1954 just two years after Stef had broken his neck in a diving accident. He found a young man, perhaps in his middle twenties, helpless, disheartened, frustrated, with little to do, little to look forward to. His experience was a striking parallel to Roger's. Both had been college athletes. Stefan also had been a trackman as well as a swimmer. He had graduated from college the spring before his diving accident, which had left him a quadriplegic (paralyzed in both arms and legs), although with a limited use of his arms. He had just returned home from two years in the hospital, eight months of them in the Detroit Rehabilitation Institute. But he had not been considered an acceptable candidate for vocational training. He was being cared for by his parents, a couple of Romanian background.

"He's like a lost soul on a desert island," thought Roger, studying the dark, moody features, the slumped shoulders, the once muscular arms now pitifully flaccid. "How can I possibly build a bridge to him!" But it became suddenly of the utmost importance that he should do so.

"What you need, Stef, is a ramp," he suggested cheerfully. "Ever thought of getting yourself one?"

189

"Yah," said Stefan indifferently. "I tried once to get one, but my father tore it up."

"So? I suppose he had a good reason?"

"Just thought it wasn't any use, I guess. Or maybe he thinks I'm better off where they can keep me out of any more trouble."

"I know." Roger grinned. "My father was like that, protective." Telling Stef about the shotgun episode, he was encouraged to see lines of amusement crinkle beneath the moody black eyes.

A ramp is a bridge, decided Roger, knowing that the simplest and most obvious answer to a problem was sometimes the best. Again he and Ronnie built it together, Stef ordering the boards from a lumber company, his brother giving eager cooperation, his father silent and grudging tolerance. At least he did not tear it up.

And—*a bridge is a bridge is a bridge,* Roger was to discover delightedly in the months and years that followed. For the simple wooden ramp opened up for Stefan Florescu a succession of new and exciting worlds. Soon he was not only speeding full tilt across the bridge himself but building endless spans to occupants of other desert islands.

There were not enough hours in the days and nights. Roger begrudged the time spent in making a living. Returning to his computers, records, figures on a Monday morning was like manipulating dead robots after helping to mold images of God in flesh and blood. For the first time since his accident the pattern of his life had taken on shape and meaning. It was as if he had been weaving more or less blindly for years on a dark tapestry, then suddenly turned it over to find the whole piece glowing with color. His only regret was that he had waited so long before making the discovery, spent so many years of his life helping to create beauty in mere flowers instead of in human life. He felt a tremendous compulsion to make up for lost time.

His energy seemed boundless. He could hardly wait to get out of work each night, eat a hurried supper, then either travel off for some evening appointment or spend the hours until midnight or after in study. He did not begrudge the evenings at graduate school or those spent on his ministerial courses. They were as necessary as the weeks and months when he had pored over glad catalogs and studied mountains of books on gardening. For the bodies and souls of human beings were infinitely more complicated than gladiolus, and the crossing of life-giving substances from one to the other a far more delicate process. He needed all the knowledge and skill that were available.

Every new contact was an adventure.

"You must see Faye Sloan," someone told him soon after he started work at Glenwood in 1953. "She's not only as badly handicapped as you are, but just as bugged on helping others."

Roger called her, told her about the work he was starting.

"Come and see me," she said promptly.

Roger suggested that very evening, then posed the usual question: "Are there any steps?"

"Yes," she replied ruefully. "But my uncle will help you in."

He found a wonderful little woman bundled into a wheel chair, disabled by childhood polio, but wired with electric energy. She wanted no comfort or sympathy and wasted no time talking about herself.

"I've been waiting for someone like you," she greeted joyously. "We must organize a handicapped club here in Wyandotte. What do you say?"

It was from others that Roger learned Faye's story. Fired by a passion for service and needing money to finance her ideas, she had recently traveled to New York, appeared on the "Strike It Rich" show, and won $500. With this small nestegg, reinforced by the resulting publicity, she had established the Faye Sloan Foundation designed to provide unique services for the handicapped. The development of these projects was to become increasingly dramatic in the next dozen years.

Roger worked closely with her in the beginning. "He's my greatest inspiration," she insisted. "I knew whenever I called, any hour, any day or night, he would be here helping. And, oh, that beautiful, beautiful smile!"

Together, assisted by Marjorie Campbell, a beautiful young woman afflicted with partial paralysis and occasional seizures, they launched the Downriver Handicapped League, containing members from Wyandotte, Lincoln Park, Southgate, Taylor, Ecorse, and other towns. Stefan Florescu was one of its most enthusiastic supporters. And in time others of Faye's dreams for service came to fulfillment. After finishing eight years of work at Wyandotte's General Hospital, she rented a small place to be known as the "House of Talent," becoming, reluctantly, its manager. Here craft work made by the handicapped, donated clothing, furniture, and other articles repaired and refurbished by the handicapped were marketed. Outgrowing this small shop, the foundation purchased a building, starting the new venture with a capital of only $300. This "House of Talent," however, was only one of the many projects to which she lent her energy. "Little Jim" was another, a midget whom she adopted and with whom she shared her home, like herself a small bundle of vivid, dynamic personality.

It was through Faye that Roger met Clara Kelley, badly crippled by polio, very hard of hearing, and a patient for twelve years in the tuberculosis sanatorium at Howell. Roger drove the thirty-five miles to call on her. Finding that she could make beautiful jewelry, he suggested to the women of the church that they sell some for her in their fall bazaar. This gave her a bit of spending money. Sometimes he and LaVerna would take her for a ride, and even in winter she reveled in the outing. "How beautiful it is!" she would breathe ecstatically.

One year, just before Christmas, she called long distance. "Do you suppose," her voice was wistful, "I could come to your house for Christmas? I would like so much to see little children!"

That year they were to have with them their three very small grandchildren. LaVerna hastily considered. Would it be dangerous to expose them to tuberculosis? But surely the authorities wouldn't let her come if they considered her contagious!

"Yes," she replied as cordially as possible. "We'll be up and get you."

It was one of the happiest Christmases Roger and LaVerna had ever spent. Eyes beaming, completely enthralled, Clara sat on the divan watching the three little tots open their gifts. Her own were piled beside her, unopened. It was the first time for twelve years that she had been in a home for Christmas.

Roger's first call on Vivian Wakeford was a visit to a new world, a grim, macabre world. Wayne County General Hospital at Eloise was forbidding enough on the outside, a vast, impersonal city of cold brick façades, rows and rows of walls staring like blank faces, with who knew what fierce angles and projections behind! Even the buildings were nameless, bearing such labels as A, B, C, D. Roger's destination was one of the psychopathic wards in D.

"City of lost identities," he thought as he wheeled through a labyrinth of rooms and corridors, an aseptic figure in white unlocking doors before him, locking them again behind. "A limbo of forgotten souls."

Passing through a huge crowded ward with endless rows of beds, he was conscious of waves of troubled faces, advancing, receding, parting like the Red Sea to let him through. Then finally came the last locked door. When it opened, he entered bravely but with a peculiar ferment in the pit of his stomach, heard it closed behind him. It was his first experience in an institution for mental patients, and he felt nervous, inadequate. What should he say? A flash of blue-green feathers followed by a raucous chattering did nothing to allay his nervousness.

"Chico, quiet! Can't you see we have company? Please excuse him, Reverend Arnett. That is, you *are* Mr. Arnett, aren't you? A friend wrote me that you might be coming."

Roger looked from the gay parakeet now perched on the head of the bed to the face outlined by the white pillow. They belonged together, the bright bird and this girl with the arrestingly vivid features, the black hair springing up like glossy wings, the clear but restless eyes. Roger felt like laughing aloud but settled for one of his broadest smiles. Afraid of finding some point of contact with this alert young spirit? Never had he seen eyes more brightly sane.

"Yes. I'm Roger Arnett, and I've been looking forward to meeting you. You and I must have a lot in common, with the same old problems of paraplegia and, I can see, the same zest for life in spite of everything."

"Yes," agreed Vivian, still smiling but with a forced automation which suggested a grimace. "There's one thing we don't have in common, though. Freedom."

Roger followed her gaze to the parakeet's cage with its open door, returning quickly to her face. The black eyes were all restlessness now, the vividness gone, leaving the girlish features plain, almost ugly. How long had she been confined here, he wondered, within these four stifling walls, an outcast from a society which had chosen to interpret a fairly normal reaction as a mental aberration? He strongly suspected that she was no more a mental case than he was, perhaps less so. Heaven knew he had been tempted in those hopeless days after his accident to take his own life, and with far less reason than this vivid young creature may have had, finding herself an impossible burden for a large family of low income! He reckoned hastily. She had been fourteen when the accident occurred, in 1941. A good thirteen years ago. How many of them had she spent here in this sterile cage within these locked doors, with its deadening insistence on abnormality? And how in heaven's name had she managed to keep herself sane!

Vivian lifted her hand, and the bird left its perch, cavorted about her head with a gleaming swirl of wings, and settled gently on her outstretched finger. The black eyes kindled again into bright candle flames. The smile became warm and genuine.

"Chico!" she said gaily. "Know what it means? 'Little boy.' "

And suddenly Roger understood. This bright bird of motion and color *was* her invincible spirit, her means of release from the two prisons which bound her. By unhooking the door of its cage, she broke the barrier of her own locked door. Its soaring wings became the vicarious liberation of her own inert body.

Vivian's problem became an obsession with him. Like Carl Dean Selby, whose cause he had championed in Indiana, she was the victim of a society which, with all its psychological and social insights, had not yet learned to distinguish between the physically and mentally handicapped. The fact that a person under great stress had once tried to take her own life was no reason for her permanent interment in a stultifying cell behind locked doors. Roger was determined to correct society's mistake.

He explored many avenues. He tried to interest her family in securing her release, but her father was unable to assume the responsibility of her support, and her stepmother, with the burden of seven other children, was understandably cool to the prospect of caring for a helpless invalid. Roger turned to other possibilities. He contacted many officials, the doctor who had been her psychiatrist, the judge who had committed her. He was both elated and appalled to find that she had an I.Q. of 164. "Why," he kept asking one person after another, "*why* are you still holding her?" One of the psychologists connected with the hospital gave great help and encouragement. Meanwhile Vivian responded to the new climate of hope like a glad bulb to warm earth and rain and sunshine. The mere fact of another human being's concern banished bitterness and discouragement. The restlessness left her eyes. The gay smile became spontaneous. When Roger wheeled himself into the room, her face lighted like a neon sign.

"What a man!" she was heard to comment. "It's put spunk into me just knowing him."

Roger felt that she should be receiving vocational training, but the hospital was equipped to give instruction in nothing but crafts. He encouraged her to do creative writing, knowing that she had real talent, but she lacked confidence. He went to the vocational training center.

"Get her out of the hospital for six months," they said. "Then we'll consider giving her some training."

Get her out! That was exactly what Roger intended to do. But it was more easily said than done. He soon discovered that it would be a long and tedious process, involving endless red tape and court procedure. It had taken less than two weeks to put her in. It would take five years to get her out.

Meanwhile Roger's own luck in keeping clear of hospitalization had run out. In March, 1954, he was taken suddenly ill and after a serious crisis when he found it almost impossible to get his breath, frightening LaVerna almost out of her wits, he was rushed to the urology ward of University Hospital. He was there for five days, an investment of time yielding doubtful dividends, for the doctors were unable to find anything the matter with him.

But to another the dividends were of bank-breaking value. He was placed in a bed next to a young man named Sam, another paraplegic who had been in the hospital three years. Medically Sam's condition differed little from Roger's. He had the same problems, the same potentials, but hardly the same disposition toward either. He welcomed Roger with the grim satisfaction of the "misery loves company" addict.

"So you got it, too! What happened?"

"Automobile accident." Roger willingly supplied the details. "What happened to you?"

The cynical lips twisted. "Wife shot me. I was in bed asleep. No accident. She wanted me out. Just my luck. A damned bad break."

Roger proffered the dose of expected sympathy, followed by a shot of optimism. "A good thing, though, it happened while you were still so young. You'll find it much easier to adjust. I suppose you'll be getting out of here soon."

The young man scowled. "What do you mean, getting out! I know when I'm licked. And, anyway, what's the use of leaving? I know other guys that have gone out, and they just keep coming back again, like you." The dull eyes showed a spark of curiosity. "How long are you in for this time?"

"Not long, I hope. I can't spare the time. There's too much to do."

The curiosity flared into interest. "What sort of things?"

Roger told him. Before long Sam was firing questions, and Roger was giving him straight answers. Most of the questions ended in a single word.

"You get up in the morning, dress yourself, do all those disgusting chores on yourself—*how!* . . . "You're telling me you have a good job, support your family, drive your own car to work, then go and take classes at night—heavens above, man—*how!*"

All through the five days they went on, the questions and answers. And when Roger got ready to go home, the curtain had to be drawn around both their beds so Sam could see the dressing process. His eyes followed each step with an intense, almost fevered concentration, and when it was finished they were popping with excitement.

"Well, by God," he swore softly, "if you can do it, I can do it, too!"

When Roger went back to the hospital ten days later for a checkup, he inquired for Sam.

"He's gone home," was the amazing reply.

This time Roger's own respite from hospital was brief. He was back in August with a deep and painful pressure sore, probably the result of neglect because of overwork. Besides his regular job at the Research Center, and his usual calls on the handicapped, he had not only supplied the pulpit at Glenwood all through July, but attended sessions of summer school at Wayne State University, to say nothing of raising and marketing a fair crop of glads. It was a flare-up of his old trouble, decubitus on the right hip.

This time the condition was serious. But in recent years medical knowledge of paraplegia had been increasing, and a new operation had been devised.

"A fairly simple procedure," explained the surgeon to Roger and LaVerna. "Unless we run into complications, it shouldn't take too long."

But there were complications, and it was not at all simple. Roger went into the operating room early one morning. The surgeon found a vast amount of scar tissue, remnants of the extensive decubitus suffered in 1940. Once inside the area the surgeon was forced to keep going and going and going.

"You mean to say they haven't ever operated on this before?" he demanded of Roger.

It wasn't enough for him to reply "No." As if finding the answer impossible to believe, the surgeon kept repeating the question.

As time passed and the operation dragged on, Roger endured torments, not for his own sake, but for LaVerna's. Why hadn't he insisted that she go home! But he dared not send word for her not to wait. It might make her worry even more. And who knew? Perhaps this time she had cause to worry. Perhaps this was *it*. But, no. It couldn't end now, just when his life was beginning to find fulfillment. He wouldn't let it!

Expecting Roger to be in the operating room no more than an hour, LaVerna waited . . . and waited. Six hours passed. She was nearly beside herself with worry. She knew, of course, that the operation had not gone as planned. They must have discovered something fatal, perhaps a malignancy. She could eat no lunch. Afternoon passed, and still she was unable to get a report.

"I'm sorry. I can't tell you anything yet. He's still in the recovery room."

At least he was alive! She waited, sitting, walking, standing, until eight o'clock that evening. With two children at home aged eleven and twelve, she could not wait any longer. She sent a message begging the surgeon to come. He did so. But neither his manner nor his words were reassuring. A former army surgeon, he was accustomed to stating facts with bald clarity.

"You really don't expect him to live, do you?" he asked abruptly.

She gasped. Shock and outrage at the severity of the question kept her voice steady. "Why—yes, Doctor, I certainly do."

He shook his head. "I'm sorry." His voice softened. She saw that beneath the gruffness he was deeply concerned. "He has too many strikes against him. I don't see how he can possibly live through this one."

LaVerna drove home. She made the proper turns, came to a halt at "Stop" signs, avoided oncoming lights, put on the brake when necessary, all with a mechanical and unconscious proficiency. She put the children to bed. She finished preparing the glads which must be sent to market the next day. But when she finally lay down to spend the night staring sleeplessly into the dark, she could not have told a single motion she had made.

As had often happened before, Roger fooled the doctors and

lived. But the postoperative period was not at all satisfactory. Within a week's time infection had entered the hip, and practically all its remaining flesh was affected. Dr. Berry, the head surgeon, stopped finally beside his bed.

"Well," he said reluctantly, "we're going to have to do something here. It looks like a colostomy."

Roger had a fierce desire to protest. He had fought this development ever since his accident. But he was doing no fighting now. Knowing that it was a choice between possible life and certain death, he nodded weakly. This time Dr. Berry himself performed the operation, and there followed long days of treatment with soaks and irrigations. After two weeks the area began to show signs of normal functioning, and Dr. Berry decided that he was ready for further surgery, this time a rotary flap operation. It was his third major surgery in a month, and he was on the operating table six hours.

LaVerna did no more waiting at the hospital. Never again! Always after that long, unforgettable day she remained at home, calling the hospital at intervals and leaving only when informed that he was ready to come out of the recovery room.

The success of this third operation was for a long time problematic. As with a delicate gladiolus crossing, it required much time and patience, much agonizing suspense, to discover whether the complex grafting of flesh was going to "take." There was one stubborn area that refused to heal. But that he had survived the operation at all was a miracle, as Dr. Berry, a humble as well as an extremely skillful surgeon, was willing to admit.

"God had his arm around us, Roger," he commented more than once.

The creeping days of waiting seemed interminable. Week after week Roger lay, trying vainly to be patient, waiting for the infinitesimally slow process of healing. Hours, days, weeks crept past at a snail's pace. September crawled relentlessly into October. The children were in school. His desk at the Research Center was empty. No money was coming in. How long would they hold his job? How long would LaVerna be able to carry on alone, having all the care of the children, substituting occasionally in school, driving over to visit him, in spite of his protests, nearly every day. And now the additional burden of Dick and his family. . . .

For in September Dick and his wife Val and their three children came up from Indiana to spend a week, primarily to visit Roger in the hospital. Returning to Indiana, they found that Dick's job had been given to a relative of his employer. Unable to find work, Dick called LaVerna asking if they could come back for a short period, since he believed jobs to be more available in Michigan. Of course she agreed.

"Oh, we're getting along fine," she assured Roger. But he could imagine the pressures on her high-strung nerves, the tensions created by eight people crowded together in the little two-bedroom house, the youngest of them a baby only a few weeks old. How long before she would break under the pressure? How long . . . the words became the pulse beat of each dragging hour, day, week . . . *how long!*

Finally in desperation he called for Dr. Berry. "I've got to get up." He fixed his stubborn gaze on the surgeon's equally stubborn face.

The doctor shook his head vehemently. For a full minute the two men glowered at each other, each trying to outgaze the other.

"O.K." The surgeon threw up his hands in disgust. "You win. I'll let you get up for ten minutes a day." He stomped away, muttering, "For goodness' sake!"

But it was three days before he came back to give the order. Then Roger was permitted to sit up for ten minutes. The next day the interns expressed surprise that the affected area looked so much better. After three more days Dr. Berry came himself to check on the reported improvement. He could not believe his eyes.

"Well," he admitted with good-humored grace. "You learn something new every day."

Roger called LaVerna one day in November. "I'm coming home," he announced jubilantly.

"That's—wonderful," she responded faintly.

Happiness was mingled with dismay. Roger, of course, must have a full bedroom to himself. That meant crowding eight other people into the second small bedroom and the living room. With the three children inevitably crying, it created an impossible situation. It was Val, quiet, competent, even-tempered, who solved the problem. "I'll go to my folks in Indiana. When Dick gets a job and a place for us to stay, we'll come back."

"But—that long trip, with three babies!"

"It's all right. Don't worry."

LaVerna drove her to the bus station in Ypsilanti and saw her on board with her big suitcase, two small children, and a tiny crying baby. As the bus pulled out for its long trek, she waved cheerfully from a window.

"Convalescence" was a word unknown to Roger's vocabulary. Urging him to "take it easy" was like telling a bird not to fly. LaVerna did not even try. Within days of his returning home after the near-killing operation he was back in the routine, acting on the cheerful assumption that the best way to heal an obstinate trouble spot was to forget it.

12

"There's a family I wish you would see," said Al Hartoog one day in 1956. "You both have a handicap problem. Maybe you can help them."

This was Roger's introduction to the Mente family. His first visit was not propitious. First he went to the wrong house, which meant a double sequence of folding and unfolding chair, rearranging cushions, sliding from car to chair, from chair to car, and back again. Then when he finally arrived at the right house, he could see from the faint expression of distaste which crossed Bud Mente's face that he was not too welcome. Later he found that "Bud," seeing him at church, had been made uncomfortable by the sight of the wheel chair and wanted to keep as far from it as possible.

Bud and Dolores Mente had a severely handicapped baby. Joyce was their fifth child. Having already lost two children out of the five, their concern over this little one, afflicted from birth with congenital amyonotia, lack of muscle control, was tinged with bitterness as well as frustration.

"Oh! It's you, Mr. Arnett. Will you—come in?"

"Thanks," he responded cheerfully." "If you'll just give me a boost up those steps." A good thing, he reflected, that Ronnie didn't happen to be with him. There was nothing better than tugging and bumping a wheel chair up and down steps to break down the restraint between people. Besides, he was beginning to suspect that Bud's aversion to a wheel chair was associated with an unwillingness to accept the fact of their child's handicap. "That is, if I'm not too heavy for you," Roger added with apparent innocence.

"Heavy! Of course not!" After a slight hesitation Bud seized the handles of the chair with all his young and energetic vigor and pushed it up the steps like a toy. Already Roger could feel the barrier of ice melting.

Before the evening was over the Mentes were talking of little Joyce and her handicap as if it were the most natural thing in the world. Realistic acceptance was beginning to replace rebellion, hope to glimmer faintly through despair. Here also Roger did no preaching. None was necessary. It was amazing what advantage you had, being in a wheel chair! You could show a person, not simply tell him, that having a handicap didn't mean the end of the world.

It was the first of many visits. Roger often held the child. There was a natural bond between them, the big man with over half his body powerless and the frail little creature, limp as a rag doll. Sometimes he helped exercise the flabby muscles. The child died soon after, but not before her father and mother had learned to accept the tragedy with faith as well as resignation.

The relationship between Roger and the Mentes developed into more than friendship. Bud and Dolores became ardent supporters of his work. They contribute a large amount each month to the trust fund. Bud often accompanied Roger on his calling missions. His first experience as a passenger, however, was unsettling. He had always thought of a handicapped person as being unusually cautious. Not Roger! He drove as confidently, as fast, perhaps a little faster, than most people with four, instead of two, muscular extremities. And these were the days before he acquired an automatic shift. To see one pair of hands, however competent, manipulate a hand brake, a hand accelerator, a hand clutch, to say nothing of hand steering apparatus, was both novel and startling. But Bud was soon more at ease with Roger at the wheel than with many of his able-bodied acquaintances. For Roger had long since learned to compensate for lack of feet with extra arm strength and lightning-swift coordination.

In his wheel chair he was a notorious speeder. "Have you got your license?" his associates at work would ask when he came whooshing through corridors, tearing around corners, once almost getting a cup of coffee full in the face.

Roger liked to take Bud with him on his calls. Although somewhat slight, the young man was strong and wiry, better than two of most men in helping him up and down steps. Others were often too careful, and Roger was afraid they would tip him sideways. Not Bud. He always preferred to do the job alone. He would get behind the chair and lift with precision and confidence . . . bounce, bounce, bounce. At first these visits were something of an ordeal for Bud. Although Roger would accept help when necessary, he prided himself on his independence. If there was only one step to be descended, he would wave help aside, take it by himself—slap, dash, plunk! Watching him career around corners, roll in high gear, full tilt, down ramps, such a contrast to the slow, cautious wheel chair patients they visited, Bud at first exclaimed in alarm, then whistled in admiration, finally chortled with amusement.

"You're nothing but a big playboy at heart, Roger," he accused him. "Just a show-off!"

Results of such nonchalance were not always happy. Traveling with a companion, Roger would depend on him to hold the chair tightly at right angles against the side of the car while he slipped between it and the front seat. Alone, he found it more complicated. Getting out, he had to fold forward the seat beside him, slide the chair out, fold the seat back, lift himself into it, unfold the chair, arrange the cushion and rubber rings, then rely on the chair to remain firm while by sheer strength of arm motion he jerked himself across the intervening space. Once after visiting Vivian Wakeford he failed to make the proper transition. The chair pulled away from the car, and he fell between them, badly wrenching his right shoulder. Something, he knew, must be done. There were no brakes on chairs then, and even with a brake the chair might not be too stable. Again necessity prodded his inventive skill. He designed a metal rod hooked at both ends which would fasten on the wheel of the chair and into the opening of the door hinge to hold the chair firmly to the car. It was perfect, like a third arm! But the damage had been done. The wrenched shoulder would trouble him all the rest of his life.

Other improvements made the burden of travel less harassing. After living in the small house for four years, they still had no garage. Roger drew careful sketches, took them to the Center, and gave them to Harvey Dicks. "Look, Harve, know anybody who could build this for me?" Harvey, who had built three houses for himself, agreed to do the job. But he found himself working for a hard taskmaster. If they disagreed about plans, it was Roger who had his way, not Harvey. Once started, a job was not likely to be interrupted or postponed. It must be done "right now." But Roger was always partner rather than boss. He expected no more of the workers than he was willing to do himself. He handed boards, made trips to the lumberyard for more materials, shouted approving and encouraging comments. After putting in three wells for him, building the garage, and doing a variety of other odd jobs on the place, Harvey was dumfounded to discover that Roger was a minister. "But he never talked religion to me, never preached!" In fact, it was only from newspaper articles about him that Harvey learned the extent of his friend's accomplishments.

"I'd sure like to write him up in those 'Unforgettable Characters'!" he summed up his estimate simply.

The garage simplified travel amazingly. Its most helpful feature was a mechanism smoothly raising or lowering the door by means of a marvelous electric eye, which set the eyes of grandchildren popping. Later Harvey connected the garage with the house by a beautiful sun parlor in the shape of a ramp, which Roger could traverse at high, low, or medium, depending on his object: watering the plants which lined its low shelves, enjoying the sunlight pouring through its windows, or, most often, getting to and from the car with all possible speed.

It was the Mentes who made another invaluable contribution to Roger's ministry.

"You should have a film made," said Al Hartoog, "a colored movie showing some of your work. And I think I know just the one to do it."

Bud Mente was a skilled amateur photographer, and he had the necessary equipment. The film he and Roger made together in 1956 was a graphic commentary on both the needs of the handicapped and the work already accomplished. They spent four months taking the shots. It was a simple, unglamorous chronicle of life situations. It showed Eddie laboring doggedly but triumphantly up his new ramp; Joe McIntyre eagerly pointing out letters on his talking board; Walter Roth displaying his leather handicrafts and sitting at the wheel of his old Packard; and many others.

And the sequence which required the most elaborate preparation and preliminary red tape, an intimate little communion service in Vivian Wakeford's room in Wayne County General Hospital, was the most beautifully unposed and natural of them all. The sunburst of a smile as Roger came wheeling into the room, the sweet reverence of the closed eyes and bowed head as she partook of the bread and wine—these were just Vivian. And the one feature which was pure Hollywood was an unexpected bonus. As Roger opened his small communion set and started the brief service, Chico flashed in a blue-green arc from the head of Vivian's bed and perched on his shoulder.

"A highly dramatic and successful ministry," was the approving comment of many who saw the picture. But Roger was far from satisfied. And as the months passed, he became more and more conscious of his mistakes and shortcomings as a minister to the handicapped.

His mistakes were many and easily documented. Some were owing to ignorance, some to inadequacy, some to overzealousness, many to errors of judgment. And most of them bore the names of individuals whom he had somehow failed.

One of the errors in judgment was named Paul. He was a muscular dystrophy victim, perhaps twenty-five years old. Having known many others with this disability who became progressively worse, Roger did not encourage him in his ambition for economic independence. Even though Paul had managed to get a high-school education, Roger felt that his chances for getting out were negligible. During three visits he administered comforting sedatives rather than stimulants; then, pressured by other duties, as in all too many other cases, he let the relationship slide. What was his amazement six months later to find that Paul was gainfully employed in an office half of each day!

He made equally serious errors in expecting too much. At first he felt that anyone with a broken back should be able to conquer his disability as well as he had, if not better. Raymond was one of these mistakes, a boy of twenty-one, who had suffered an accident two years before.

"You should get out more, try to learn a trade, maybe get yourself an office job," he urged the boy. And while not actually saying, "and be more like me," his own blatant evidence of success spoke more loudly than words. But Raymond did not respond. And when he died of an infection two years later, Roger knew that somehow he had failed him.

It was the same way with John, a young paraplegic of twenty-five with a college education, an engaging personality, and everything but the desire to be independent. It should be a simple problem, Roger thought, for him to get a job, and told him so. After repeated failures John lost confidence in Roger as well as himself. Apparently simple problems, Roger learned after sad experience, were in reality very complex, and with passing years he became less naïve, more and more hesitant about telling people what they ought to do.

And, though usually an inspiration, his own conquest of a handicap was sometimes a deterrent. At the request of a niece Roger visited Kenneth, a patient in the psychopathic ward at Wayne County General Hospital, suffering from deep depression. On the first visit Kenneth seemed friendly and mildly interested. On the second he seemed resentful. "Please don't visit me any more," he said finally. Later Roger learned from his niece that it pained him to see a man who was in so much worse physical condition appearing so cheerful and active while he was confined.

At first Roger often made the mistake of talking and giving advice rather than listening. There was Jane, a wheel-chair victim of *spina bifida* who wanted desperately to find some way to earn money. While she tried to communicate her needs, Roger worried about how he could help solve her problem. All the suggestions he made failed to suit her. After giving considerable time to an attempt to help her, he gave up. Later she solved her own problem by starting a phone-answering service. What she had needed was sympathetic attention, not advice.

But perhaps his greatest sin was overzealousness. He was so anxious to make as many contacts as possible both for his own satisfaction and to impress his friends at Glenwood that his intimate relationship with individuals suffered. They became "cases" rather than persons. It was so with Laura, a twenty-year-old sufferer from cerebral palsy. She never seemed to appreciate his visits, and not until long afterward did he understand why. He had gone to her as a professional visitor, not as a concerned friend.

His overzealousness extended to religion. At first he was so intent on acting the role of proper minister that he alienated some he was most anxious to help. Such as old Chris Thompson, a lonely bachelor of seventy-five, who eagerly welcomed Roger's visits until he was urged to go to church, when he began eying him with the cold suspicion he might have accorded a traveling salesman. Or Walter Roth. Once when Roger visited his old friend and they had been happily reminiscing about college days, he felt constrained to leave him some devotional literature. The warmth of friendliness instantly froze.

"Thanks. I'll choose my own reading matter."

But timidity was just as bad a sin. Never would Roger forgive himself for one grievous error of omission. Soon after entering the ministry he went to see his old friend, Orville Mitchell, now happily married to Marie and conducting a successful business from his bed and wheel chair. Should he mention religion to Mitch, now that he was a minister? No, Roger decided, Mitch was the last person in the world to be interested in religion. Mitch seemed glad to see him, and they talked of a dozen things, all of little consequence. A short time later Mitch died, and Roger attended his funeral.

"He knew he was going soon," Marie told him, "that day you called. For several months he had been deeply conscious of his spiritual need and had a burning desire to talk with some minister, but somehow he couldn't bring himself to let down the bars when you were there."

The knowledge that he had failed Orville in the hour of his greatest need would haunt Roger for the rest of his life.

It was many years before he solved to his own satisfaction this problem of how much to act the minister in such relationships. It was a book by Paul Tournier which finally clarified his thinking. The pastor's most effective witness, implied Tournier, is less in his conventional role as minister than in his life and action as a concerned human being. His religious faith is best transmitted, not through words, but through the love he bears his parishioners, by his personal commitment, by the radiation of his own personality. For Roger this came to mean whatever response to each individual need a warm, loving interest and deep concern might indicate; in other words, just being himself.

But perhaps his greatest sense of failure came in his relationship with the handicapped in his own household.

He came suddenly face to face with the issue in an assignment for one of his classes at Wayne State University: to write a paper developing the case history of a school pupil involving some of the problems in special education which they had been studying. At first he was at a loss. How could he, a nonteaching teacher, write about a classroom pupil when he had no classroom! Should he create a fictitious student? Or obtain facts from some teacher? No, there must be something unique which he alone could contribute to the class thinking. Surely he had had intimate contact with plenty of traumatic experiences, his own and many others! How could he best use this experience to help these teachers to a better understanding of their "disturbed" pupils?

And then light broke. Faye! A "disturbed child" if there ever was one, and heaven knew she had plenty of reason! Here he could not only present a firsthand observational study of "How a Person May Become Emotionally Disturbed," but in the process his own troubled thinking about the child's problems might be clarified.

"The wonderful thing about this venture," he wrote in his introduction to the paper, "is the fact that I shall love my child even more after this is written."

How true it proved to be! In reviewing the child's terrific load of traumatic experiences—rejected by father and mother, locked up in solitude for long periods, abandoned by grandmother, adopted by strangers, moved twice to new communities, stricken with killer-type polio, facially disfigured—and comparing them with his new knowledge of psychology, he entered into a state of empathy which was far more than a mere understanding of causes and effects. He not only understood *why*, he suffered *with*. For both him and La-Verna it was a therapeutic experience. Many of the child's irritating and baffling ways became comprehensible: the lack of security which made her hide sandwiches under the garments in her bedroom and then deny knowledge of them; the deliberate "slow-down strikes" with which she tantalized and annoyed her mother; the seemingly stubborn unwillingness to conform.

For Roger it was a sobering and soul-searching experience, for it showed him how often he must have failed his own handicapped child, especially in the period when Faye first came, at the age when a girl child is most in need of the assuring love and tenderness of a father. To have been deserted by her own father, then suddenly presented with a new father in a wheel chair, much too concerned with his own problems and the burden of making a living to cope intelligently with her needs. . . . No wonder she had reacted with weapons of jealousy, antagonism, non-cooperation!

And now to add to the child's problems the major trauma of physical disability! "How well she is!" people often commented, noting her ability to walk. Her parents knew better. They had seen the shock and horror on her face when she brought home her first school pictures after suffering the facial paralysis.

"Mother!" The wailing treble had torn LaVerna's heart. "I didn't know I looked like that!"

The study helped both parents to understand Faye better. For LaVerna especially, who bore the brunt of the defensive slowness, the non-cooperation, all the annoying, seemingly spiteful little habits, it had cathartic as well as therapeutic value. It relieved her of some feelings of guilt. At least the resentment was directed, not toward her, but toward some obscure mother figure who had neglected, repelled, deserted. But it did not relieve the yearning for a closer intimacy and understanding with her only daughter.

"An *excellent* analysis, description, and anecdotal record of an extremely well-documented study," commented the professor at the end of Roger's paper. But its value could not be measured in terms of a college grade or an intellectual achievement, nor even of increased understanding and love toward a member of his own family. The soul searching it had involved had been a cleansing, humbling experience, worth far more than all the facts gleaned from his voluminous reading. Because of it none of the hundreds of handicapped people he would visit in years to come would ever be a "patient," a "case," an "inmate" of an institution. Every one would be a *person*.

He wrote his thesis for the master's degree in Special Education on a sociometric study of the School for the Deaf at Flint. He and LaVerna spent a whole day visiting the school, observing the program, studying records, and talking with students from preschool to high-school age. He found the children surprisingly alert and curious, crowding around his wheel chair and making full use of eyes and sense of touch to compensate for lack of hearing. One five-year-old boy was especially interested in the fact that Roger's leg was amputated. He kept staring, mouth wide open, then finally, touching Roger on the arm and pointing down to his leg, made a sawing motion, as if to ask, "Doctor took it off?" The high-school boys, equally interested and bright-eyed, were eager to help him up and down the stairs.

Yet Carl Dean Selby, consigned to a school for the feeble-minded, remembered Roger, had also been alert and curious. And deafness was considered by many a worse disability than cerebral palsy.

The comparative difficulties resulting from various physical disabilities had long been a matter of keen interest with Roger. Early in his graduate work at Wayne State he conducted a survey to determine which disability the average person considered the most difficult. About a hundred people were consulted and asked to list five disabilities in order. The results in percentages were amazing: blindness, 100; deafness, 69; cerebral palsy, 65; epilepsy, 59; heart defects, 35; mental defects, 34; quadruple amputees, 30; total paralysis, 26; and—*paraplegia, 25!* Only twenty-five people in a hundred considered paralysis from the waist down a major handicap! The truth was, of course, that the public scarcely knew what paraplegia was, to say nothing of its difficulties!

Because of them, plus his full-time job, his Sunday services at Glenwood, his evening and weekend calling on the disabled, it took Roger four years to complete his training as minister to the handicapped. He was ordained deacon in the Methodist Church in 1955, elder in 1957, when he also received his master's degree in Special Education from Wayne State University.

The difficulties were by no means trivial. In the fall of 1956, under stress of extra work, he developed a huge abscess, this time on his *left* hip. By the time necessity forced him into the hospital it was as big as a grapefruit. Fortunately the skilled Dr. Berry was again his surgeon.

"You know what makes ulcers come." He eyed his patient severely. "Either from giving up or overdoing. In your case it's *not* giving up."

"I know." For once Roger did not smile. "It's my fault. The trouble is, there's always so much that needs doing."

"Well," the doctor nodded grudging approval, "I shouldn't complain. Heaven knows I have plenty of paraplegic patients who get them from sitting still! O.K. Let's get going. It should be just a routine abscess operation."

Roger grinned. "That's what you said last time, remember?"

He was perfectly at ease on the table, lying on his face, talking and joking with the anesthetist, who took his blood pressure every five minutes. A needle inserted in his arm and a tube leading to a blood supply were in readiness in case he needed a transfusion. After about two hours Roger noticed on the chart that the pressure was starting to drop. His vision blurred, and he felt himself breaking into a cold sweat.

"Feel—cold," he managed to tell the anesthetist, who jumped up in alarm just as he passed out.

When he came to consciousness perhaps a half hour later all he could see, in every direction, were pairs upon pairs of feet. He tried to count them, catalog each pair according to its wearer—doctors, assistants, nurses, anesthetist—but they advanced, receded, danced up and down, went whirling through the air like the feet of dervishes. He heard voices, far away, muted, then jarringly close, and knew they were talking about him.

". . . thought sure he was gone . . . no pressure at all . . . coming up again . . . Look, opened his eyes . . . at least he's alive. . . ."

Roger tried to say something, to assure them that he was indeed alive and intended to remain so, but the effort was too great. He remained conscious but in a state of lethargy during the rest of the operation. There was no more light banter.

The next day he looked up to see Dr. Berry standing by his bed, shaking his head with a mingling of amazement, admiration, and—was it awe?

"Boy, Roger, you sure gave us a rough time there for half an hour yesterday! I still don't know how you made it. I believe you live in spite of us!"

"You think I'd let you get rid of me yet," returned Roger only half jokingly, "with all the work I have left to do?"

He was in the hospital for a month this time. The area of the operation did not heal properly, in fact, never did entirely. But he was back at his desk within days after his return home.

Fortunately LaVerna did not know until the danger was past how near she had come to losing him.

The next time she was not so fortunate. It was next to the last day of 1957, a pale, wan, gray day, well suited to a dying year. Roger had for some time been ailing, weak in energy, unable to digest food properly. But there seemed no reason for it. Lacking the blessed monitor of pain, he had faithfully practiced the paraplegic's eternal vigilance: the daily baths, the rubbing alcohol, the powder, the thorough examination of every inch of the body for reddened areas, using a hand mirror for back, hips, heel, elbows; the frequent changing of position; the rigidly controlled diet. But the absence of pain left many internal areas of danger without warning safeguards. It was purely by accident that he discovered what seemed to be a large hard growth on his right side.

"Yes," said Dr. Robb, their local physician. "I can feel it, back, front, and on the side. I'd say it was in the region of the kidney. Get in touch with University Hospital immediately."

Roger did not tell LaVerna what he suspected, that the growth was malignant and that at long last the extremity they had been fearing for nearly a quarter of a century was reached. This was *it!* He did not need to. Words Dr. Arnold had spoken long ago dinned in her ears. "It's the kidney, Roger, that's going to get you sometime. That's the Achilles heel of all paraplegics." And in spite of the usual broad smile and dogged optimism, she could tell they were surface deep. She saw his face when he thought she wasn't looking, lips grim, flesh sagging over the high cheekbones, eyes lusterless, their blueness dulled to a hard gray. And he was much more specific in the directions he gave "just in case," even telling her what arrangements he wanted made for his funeral.

The climax of her despair came on New Year's Day, the eve of his going into the hospital. She went out into the kitchen to get lunch but, suddenly overcome with a violence of emotion, was unable even to go through the motions. Instead, she went and stood in the kitchen window, facing west, and stared into the grayest, emptiest sky she had ever seen.

New Year's Day! Symbol of hope, of new life, new opportunity! What a mockery! It would certainly be a new life, but how could she possibly face it alone? No, not alone, of course. There would still be the children. But the thought brought panic, not comfort. Faye just starting high school, face grotesquely twisted, dark eyes growing more and more haunted and withdrawn! Ronnie, popular, handsome, easygoing, with his fine but careless mind ("Gosh, Mom, the crowd think you're a square if you study!"), knowing just how to take advantage of her loving permissiveness! Roger had always exercised the firm competence of discipline in the household. And she would have to get a job, of course.

Twenty-three years, almost, they had had together. No matter that she would once have thought it the most blessed good fortune if they could be given ten—or even five! Another two years and they would have celebrated their twenty-fifth wedding anniversary, once a seemingly impossible dream. The loss became somehow symbolic of all the empty future, just as the dull sky was an omen of the year just beginning. Clinging to the windowframe, she felt the gray landscape bounding her new world twist and reel about her. She closed her eyes and tried to pray, wordlessly, but with the despairing faith long ago given more perfect expression by Another. *Oh, God, let this cup pass from me. But if I must—help me!*

212

She opened her eyes. The world seemed suddenly alive with brightness. It streamed through the window, filling the room as if with sunlight. But the window faced west, and the sun was overhead. No matter where the light came from! It was astir with hope, ablaze with assurance.

"How's lunch coming, darling?" called Roger with his usual energizing vigor. "I don't hear you moving. Better get going."

"It's coming," she replied confidently. So was the future and whatever it might bring. She would not be timid or dismayed again.

Roger grinned up into the doctor's face. "Well, here I am again, Doctor. Bad penny, you know, and all that."

This time the smile felt more like a death grimace. He was rebellious through and through. He *couldn't* die now! He had just started learning how to live. Life, even with its grotesque accidents, was just becoming intelligible. Here for twenty-five years he had tried to be of some use in the world *in spite of* his handicap. And now, just when he had made the overwhelming discovery that he might be of even greater use *because* of it, here he wasn't going to have the chance even to try! The bitterness and frustration in the months after his accident had been nothing compared with this. To have found the "one pearl of great value," to have sold all he had to pay the price of it, and then, just as he reached out his hand for it, to have it snatched away!

There were several days of intensive tests, all of which seemed to verify his fears of malignancy. They only gave him time to brood more fruitlessly. What would happen to LaVerna and the children? They were just at the stage when they needed him most. And the seventy-five or more handicapped people who had become his special concern? Who would play checkers and listen patiently with the Joe McIntyres? or build ramps for the Eddies and the Stefan Florescus? or keep prodding to get Vivian Wakeford out of her horrible sterile cage? It wasn't that he believed himself to be indispensable. But nobody else seemed to care particularly about doing any of these things.

Roger went into surgery on January 6 convinced—far from resigned!—that this was really *it*. If he prayed, it was not in terms of "Thy will be done." He came out minus his right kidney and a stone which had grown around it, half as large as a regular-sized big-

213

league football. No wonder there had been little room for food properly to digest! There had been no malignancy. He came out also with a beaming smile, a glint in his eye as flashing bright as Vivian's parakeet, and a more compelling faith and purpose than he had yet known. Perhaps his tremendous will to live had been another way of praying, "Thy will be done."

He returned home on January 18. Recovery was rapid, and three days later he was back at work at the university.

During subsequent months the "ins and outs" continued with normal regularity but fewer elements of crisis. He was back in hospital for two weeks with a pressure sore in the fall of 1958; again for ten days in July, 1959.

"Do you suppose he'll come back?" wondered his colleagues at the office each time his desk became suddenly empty. Then presently the word would go around, "Roger's back!", the wheel chair would again be rolling at top speed through corridors and around corners, and the gears of routine would mesh a little more smoothly under the stimulus of the beaming smile.

He had been given a reprieve and he made full use of it. But, although he worked just as hard, made just as many calls, studied just as late at night, he felt a greater confidence, less of fevered tension. With his new discovery his handicap had suddenly become friend and ally instead of antagonist. It was to be *used* for the benefit of others, not fought against. And he was no longer driven by the necessity of accomplishment. His function as a minister lay not in doing or saying, but in *being*. And his handicap was a vital and integral part of that being. He was no longer divided, half dead and half alive.

"The eye cannot say to the hand, 'I have no need of you,' nor again the head to the feet—foot?—'I have no need of you.' On the contrary, the parts of the body which seem to be weaker—paralyzed?—are indispensable."

The words of the Apostle Paul came suddenly to have astonishing pertinence. For the first time in his life Roger felt himself to be a *whole man.*

13

It was in January, 1958, that Roger took a short journey which was to change the rest of his life.

"Would you go with us to visit the Coles?" asked Merle Touse, a member of the Belleville church. "They're over at the Eastlawn-Resthaven in Northville."

It was Roger's first trip to a nursing home. He traveled the twenty miles with the Touses, and they had a pleasant visit with their mutual friends, the Coles.

"Mr. Arnett," said Mrs. Cole wistfully when they were about to leave, "would you come and conduct a church service for us? We haven't had one for five weeks. None of the Northville ministers seems able to come."

"Why—yes," replied Roger, flattered by the invitation. "How about next Sunday afternoon at four o'clock?" He learned that there were about a hundred people in the home, that there were hymnbooks available, and that a woman would be present to play the piano.

He planned his short service carefully and, with LaVerna, arrived at the home a short time before four o'clock. In the meeting room, a large lounge off the dining room, were a dozen people: Mr. and Mrs. Cole, one other man, and nine women. They sat in chairs placed flat against the walls in groups of two or three, far removed from each other, two of them out of sight behind a partition. From his position in one corner of the room Roger was some fifteen feet from the nearest member of his congregation, at least thirty from the farthest. The rest intersected his vision at varying points, like distant planets long since grown cold. Only his two friends' faces showed sympathy. "For me" wondered Roger, "or for the congregation?"

It was one of the longest half hours he had ever spent. Long for LaVerna also, for, the piano player being ill, she was pressed into playing. "It was bad enough to play," she deplored later, "after not touching a piano for years. But—those stony faces!"

Roger could not help, for he was no singer. Perhaps four people made faint sounds, mostly drowned by the constant commotion of people coming and going. All through the service visitors kept entering, passing through the room to see relatives or, if they spied them in the congregation, removing them with audible whispers. In the kitchen the help were clattering dishes, banging pots and pans, laughing loudly as they prepared supper. Down the hall radios and TV's were going full blast. At least three times a telephone rang, and someone rushed through the room to answer it. An orderly passed through to click a Coke from the vending machine. "No wonder," thought Roger grimly, "no minister wanted to come and hold a service!"

The light was bad. His throat became dry, and his voice sounded like a croak. He felt as useless as a paperhanger without arms. His mind was a blank. But somehow he got through the service. He bowed his head and mumbled a benediction.

"Good!" Relief flooded his whole being. "I've done *that* for the last time. They'll never want to go through a farce like this again."

But to his shock and amazement three of those present came up and thanked him. "Will you please come back next Sunday?" they begged.

He was even more shocked and amazed to hear himself saying, "Why—yes, if you really want me."

LaVerna scarcely spoke during the long ride home. He knew she was too chagrined for words. During the following days he thought much, prayed much. Was it possible for him to take on this extra burden? Could he do it without neglecting the seventy-five handicapped people already on his list for calling? Could he stand the strain of both this and his work at the university? Was he really capable of making any contribution to these people?

Common sense answered "No" to all these questions. Yet some inner compulsion urged him on. Certainly if other ministers could not find the time for this work, there must be a genuine need. He wanted to be a minister to the handicapped. Heaven knew there were plenty of them in the nursing home! Some of the hundred residents were comparatively young. He had noticed one in particular, a man younger than himself who had suffered a broken back in his youth and was also paralyzed below the waist. Roger had been haunted ever since by the hopeless loneliness in his eyes.

"There," he had thought, "but for the grace of God and my wonderful parents might go I."

The week was a torment of struggle and indecision. He knew that it was a whole new area of ministry which was challenging him. Preaching was but a small part of the work of a pastor. If he accepted this new responsibility, it would mean becoming involved in the lives of a hundred people, sharing their pains, their joys, their despairs, their loneliness. How *could* he! Yet if they needed him and there was a service he could render, how *couldn't* he!

He spent nearly all of the next Saturday visiting the residents of the home, talking with them, but mostly listening. He felt like a stranger in a foreign land. They received him politely but were skeptical of his genuine interest. Other ministers had been there and had not returned. Many of the patients were too mentally ill to respond. But Roger sensed a genuine hunger for some personal and intimate fellowship. When he left that day he knew what his decision must be.

The second service was better. Fifteen people attended. He felt more relaxed. The people were more friendly. There were the same interruptions, but somehow they bothered him less. And the resident pianist was on hand. Her playing was firm, loud, and confident. More people came up to express gratitude, to ask him to return. It was the beginning of a long succession of such services in the Eastlawn.

Four months later the Coles and three other residents left the Eastlawn for the Bancroft, a newly opened nursing home on the west side of Detroit. When they asked Roger to visit them in their new residence, he could not refuse. As new people moved into the Bancroft he was asked to see them also. Soon he was visiting every resident in the building. Finally, after urgent and repeated requests from the people who had attended his services at the Eastlawn, he agreed to hold a service at the Bancroft every third Saturday evening.

But this also was only a beginning. Such a specialized ministry was an idea whose time had come. Homes for the aged, the handicapped, the convalescent were mushrooming all over the Detroit area. Hotels were being converted, new buildings erected, old ones luxuriously face-lifted. Yet usually little consideration was being given to the spiritual needs of the residents. Local pastors, already burdened beyond capacity, had little time for such visitation. Once Roger had started, one involvement led to another. Residents such as the Coles would move to another home, and he would call on them there. Relatives would ask him to make special visits. Inevitably these contacts would lead to others. Eventually the casual visit paid to the Coles at the Eastlawn in 1958 would lead to chaplaincy service with a circuit of eighteen nursing homes, plus several hospitals, involving monthly contacts with at least 2,500 people.

But in 1958 the possibility of such expansion was almost as remote as that of his walking again. The development of the idea was a slow and agonizing process, like the crossing of gladiolus, involving intense labor, vast patience, and months—years—of waiting, and before it was to come to full fruition he was to pass through a period of frustration and disillusionment almost comparable to the three years following his accident.

For in 1959 Al Hartoog left Glenwood Church. Roger was left as associate pastor with the new appointee, and the relationship was characterized by mounting tension. Perhaps the conflict was inherent in the situation. Hartoog had chosen Roger, given him training and opportunity. He was intensely interested in the ministry to the handicapped. Both selfless and dedicated, he was utterly immune to any thought of competition. He and Roger were like the head and hands of the same body working together. It was understandable that in the new relationship tensions between completely variant but equally positive personalities should arise. Roger was both popular and beloved by the people of Glenwood. Friendly, deeply interested in every individual, an object of both sympathy and interest because of his disability, he had been performing his own peculiar ministry among them for five years and was entrenched in their hearts. Lack of coordination between head and hands was bound to create nervous tension in the whole church body. The most tragic factor in the situation was the deep misunderstanding of the actual facts engendered in the minds of high church officials sensitive to only one prejudiced viewpoint. It was a tragedy which almost wrecked an imaginative and extremely dedicated ministry.

Too hurt and bewildered either to defend himself against untrue accusations or try to justify his mistakes, he endured the ordeal in silence. Not so his innumerable friends at Glenwood, who doubtless aggravated the tenseness of the situation by their unswerving and outspoken loyalty. Throughout the two-year period Roger quietly continued with his appointed tasks of assisting at morning services, making his rounds of visitation on the handicapped, and with the little time remaining on evenings, Saturdays, and Sundays developing a new type of ministry in an increasing number of homes and hospitals.

But beneath the quiet, smiling exterior raged a constant and bitter battle, fierce as any fought during the years after his accident. Then he had been tempted more than once to end his physical life. Now the temptation was even stronger to end his life as a Christian minister. He had been so sure that he was somehow called by God to turn the curse of his handicap into a blessing, that in spite of it he could use his peculiar experience and passion to help others in the service of the church! Had it all been a delusion? Easy enough to give up the whole dream, to work eight hours each day at his comfortable, well-paying job, then either stay at home or make a few calls on people he knew would appreciate his fellowship . . . far easier than to spend every waking moment, abuse and overtax his fragment of a body, in the service of an organization which seemed to consider his contribution worse than futile!

But when the temptation became almost too strong to resist, he would see the Coles, grateful for a chance to worship even under difficulties . . . or Eddie laboring doggedly but triumphantly up his new ramp . . . or Vivian Wakeford, bowing her head with sweet reverence over a communion cup, while Chico chattered on his shoulder and pecked at the bright stone in his tie clasp. Especially Vivian.

For Vivian was no longer in Wayne County General Hospital. The five years of constant negotiation, of red tape, of legal maneuvering, had finally availed, and she and Chico had been moved to one of the nursing homes near Detroit. Of course Roger visited her there, which led to the opening of another "home" to his ministry. Even in the stark confines of her room in the psychiatric ward she had been a joy to visit, her courage and vivacity unquenchable. Now in this freer atmosphere she was the epitome of radiance.

"What do you think?" she greeted him one day, her small dark gamin face bright as a sunburst. "There's a boy here in the home named Tommy. He's a ham radio fan. And he's going to teach me how it works. I'm going to be able to talk to people all over the world!"

No! As long as there were cases like Vivian in the desert of his disillusionment Roger had to push on, even while fearing his goal might be only a mirage.

And during this barren period there were areas of refreshing progress. One began with the meeting of Jim Alward.

Because of Vivian and other patients she had told him about, Roger had been visiting Wayne County General Hospital regularly for some time. Often, with the permission of the supervisors, he would wheel through some of the wards, stopping to talk with anyone willing to respond. In one of the wards on a certain day he heard the sound of a piano bravely tinkling its cadences through the confused blare of voices, TV sets, radios. Wheeling toward the sound, he found a resident named Jessie keeping a small coterie entertained with familiar tunes.

"Why, Jessie!" he exclaimed when his presence interrupted the flow of "Swanee River." "I didn't know you could play. And so well, too!"

Her wistful face crinkled joyfully. "You think so? Not so well as I used to."

"Could you play a hymn?"

As the plaintive refrain of "The Old Rugged Cross" crept through the huge room its confusion seemed to lessen. Figures drifted in its direction like floating leaves drawn into an eddy. Seeing the sudden interest, Roger tried to sing the words, and a few voices chimed in feebly. It was a sorry performance, but it gave him an inspiration.

"If we could have a hymn sing," he thought, "with someone to lead, someone to play well!"

It was soon after that, in September, 1959, that he met Jim Alward.

During lunch hour at the Research Center some of the men, including Roger, often enjoyed the game of Kriegspiel, a form of chess in which the opponents play blind, each seeing only his own board, while a referee, who can see both boards, has a third on which he keeps the set. Tournaments waxed hot, sometimes lasting for days, for it was the truest and most competitive form of chess, war in miniature. A great spectators' game, it drew observers from all over the building, men who came to watch while they ate their lunch. One of these was Jim Alward, who had come to work at Willow Run in June.

A tournament game between Roger and Dave went on for days. The two were skilled players and keen rivals. Finally Dave managed to get an advantage over Roger, forcing his king and pawns into a corner. Then Dave started coming down the board, his king in front. Excitement was at a white-hot pitch. As each man called his move, the referee would call out "Yes" or "No." Roger moved a pawn.

"Yes!" called the referee, adding with dramatic emphasis, "checkmate!"

It was the winning move. Dave's king had no place to go. After the excitement had subsided, Jim lingered to congratulate Roger.

"Good playing! I say, I just found out something. You're a minister!"

Roger looked sheepish. "How'd you know? Not because I act it, surely!"

"I was at Belleville church Sunday. Saw your name on the back of the program as an ordained minister."

Roger scanned the alert young face with interest. "You're interested in church work?"

"Some. But not your kind. My bent is music."

The blue eyes sparked. "What kind?"

"Oh—piano, organ—"

Roger could hardly contain his excitement. "I—don't suppose you'd be willing to go to a hospital and play the piano for a hymn sing?"

"Why—why, yes, I think I would."

This was the beginning of a relationship which was to last for seven years. Jim, a young man in his early twenties, a graduate of Purdue in electrical engineering, was an accomplished musician. He went with Roger to Wayne County General not once but many times. Then Glenwood Church was in need of an organist, and Roger suggested this to Jim. He began playing there regularly.

After some time Roger conceived the idea of using a tape recorder for his services in the homes. He purchased one. Then, with Jim playing, Roger leading, the Glenwood choir singing, and son Dick handling the machine, recordings were made of hymns, doxology, and Gloria Patri. But it soon developed that Jim was proficient also with recording. Now intensely interested, he bought a better microphone for the project.

At first Roger used the machine alone, transporting it on the footrest of his wheel chair. Then, as Jim became more interested and more involved, he began accompanying Roger to the services, running the recorder, doing all the taping. By use of a large external speaker along with the speaker in the recorder, the volume could be turned up so that the congregation had the feeling of singing with a large group. Unchurchlike though the surroundings often were in the homes where Roger held an increasing number of services—in dining rooms, therapy rooms, hallways, sitting rooms—an atmosphere of genuine worship was created.

"I felt just as if I were in church!" more than one resident exclaimed.

During these desert years even home was not always an oasis. Sometimes the children seemed to be maturing more like thorny cacti than symmetric palms. Ronnie, handsome, popular, happy-go-lucky, had breezed through high school with no great mental effort or achievement and graduated in 1959. In spite of his high potential he showed no desire to go on to college. He had little interest in religion, even seemed to resent the enforced habit of going to church all his life. Out of high school he exhibited no urge to settle down, and was unable to get a job because of his youth until he and some of his friends were old enough to join the Navy. He had a deep affection for his parents, thought Roger was "tops," a "great guy," his mother the "most patient woman he had ever met." But he considered them both too quiet and serious. There were inevitably many conflicts.

Where, wondered Roger, had he failed? In making him work too hard with the glads? By the time they had finally gone out of the business it had been too late for the boy to go out for the football he had always yearned for. By being too dependent on his help? Ronnie had accompanied him willingly enough on his calls, bumped him up and down steps, built ramps, but Roger knew much of the time he had been bored. By spending too many evenings and weekends away from home in his passion for helping others, when perhaps the members of his family needed it just as much? There was no way of knowing. With outward cheerfulness but inward disappointment they saw him off, handsome and debonair in his new Navy uniform, all three of them knowing that he was glad to get away.

It was LaVerna who bore the brunt of Faye's adolescent unhappiness and confusion. Through Faye she suffered the tortures of her own youth all over again, the constant gnawing awareness of a physical defect, the sense of being "different," of envying other girls the attention of their boy friends, of suspecting that all the boys who showed an interest in her must have an ulterior motive. Knowing well the reason, LaVerna was patient with her moodiness and irritation, even frequent rebellion. Seeing her pathetic attempts to hide her twisted little face, covering it with her hand when she spoke or laughed, LaVerna yearned over her daughter, longed for the closer understanding which never seemed to materialize, even though they had so much in common. Faye did not want pity. Perhaps Roger with his handicap had taught her that.

"I'm acting like a baby," she sometimes scolded herself, "side of what he's been through."

"Couldn't she be helped by plastic surgery?" they had often inquired of doctors.

The year Faye was sixteen they were told it was time. She had the operation. After that the facial disfigurement was far less noticeable, and she became a different person, happier, less moody. She no longer lifted her hand to cover her cheek when she smiled or talked. But she still held herself aloof, was wary of the opposite sex. When in her senior year in high school a boy named Ken wanted to date her, she refused him five times in order to test his sincerity, then accepted the sixth time.

"I wouldn't have asked you again," he told her frankly.

Except for Roger's discouragement and frustration, which she of course shared, LaVerna was finding life full and satisfying. In 1958 she accepted a position at the Willow Run Laboratories of the University of Michigan, where Roger worked. She fitted the requirement exactly, having both teacher's qualifications and office experience. It was fascinating work, far less taxing than grade or high-school teaching, and with much responsibility, for she was secretary to the head of publications, with sole access to records. She also tested all clerical applicants, gave instruction to new employees placed in her Typing Pool, gave them trial assignments in different locations when the regular girls were ill or on vacation, and prepared them for permanent jobs. Her salary was commensurate with the responsibility of the position. No longer the need to choose between oleo and sugar when one went to the store, to spend backbreaking hours sorting glads!

And on a day in February, 1960, she knew the joy of almost complete self-fulfillment.

"Mr. and Mrs. Roger Arnett of Belleville were the honored guests on Sunday afternoon when his parents, Mr. and Mrs. James Arnett, were hosts in their home at 220 North Comstock Street for an openhouse celebration of their twenty-fifth wedding anniversary. . . ."

Twenty-five! They had expected perhaps five years of married life together, hoped for ten; fifteen would have seemed a miracle; anything beyond, an inconceivable dream. For, after all, four years before his marriage some of the most eminent doctors of the period had given Roger Arnett less than a year to live!

The wedding picture topping the newspaper article was still a fair likeness. LaVerna's petite figure was almost as youthful, cheeks as freshly smooth, eyes still clear and serene, neat blond waves still framing a pleasantly rounded face. Roger's shoulders were a little less straight, perhaps from the constant dogged forward thrust of the wheel chair, his features were more sharply chiseled, but the deep-set eyes were the same intense, sparkling blue, the smile as wide and contagious, the upspringing wave of hair thinner but just as brown and vigorous. If the eyes looked somber at times, the features gaunt in repose, it took only the smile instantly to restore the sparkle, the virility.

"This is our life," thought LaVerna as the hundred or more guests from Corunna, Owosso, and surrounding towns poured through the house bringing gifts and congratulations, signing the guest book, sharing the huge four-tiered white-frosted, pink-and-silver decorated cake. They were a cross-section of the quarter century: relatives, fellow teachers, pupils, glad growers, church workers, business associates, blind friends, deaf friends, friends on crutches, friends in wheel chairs.

Perhaps in no time in all the twenty-five years had they known more reason for gratitude and satisfaction. They were economically secure. Roger's work at the university was mentally challenging, his salary adequate. The time had come now when they could take life more easily. LaVerna smiled to herself, ruefully, resignedly, but with full sympathy and understanding. Roger sit back and take it easy? Instead, deliberately and full tilt, he was heading into the most strenuous, most harassing, but most exciting period of his life.

It was no wonder that on August 28, immediately after helping to conduct the Sunday service at Glenwood, he was taken suddenly ill and rushed to University Hospital. Diagnosing the trouble as a red-hot infection of the epididymis, doctors placed him in the nineteen-bed ward of the Urology Service. As if the desert through which he was plowing were not enough, there had to be a sandstorm! But as he had often found to his amazement and awe, the ill wind which seemed to clog his pathway might be blowing the way clean for another.

During the days of his examination and treatment Roger became friendly with a young male nurse, Jim, who was studying to be a doctor. Wednesday evening, August 31, Jim came to his bedside looking worried.

"I know you're interested in the handicapped," he said. "There's a boy in a room down the hall that I wish you could talk with. He's only twenty-one, was in a horrible accident a few months ago. He and three other fellows were on their way home, lost control, and rammed—" Jim suddenly recalled his bedside training. "But maybe I'd better not tell you the details."

"Go ahead. I'm not squeamish."

Roger listened with profound sympathy. Frank, who lived in a small town in central Michigan, had gone with three friends to a drive-in theater in a nearby city. Following the show they had stopped to eat, starting home about two in the morning. Frank had curled up and gone to sleep, because he had to get to work early in the morning. A tire had blown out, and the car had rammed into a tree. The two in front had been killed. Frank's back was broken. Fortunately he had retained consciousness and had not permitted himself to be moved except by ambulance. But even after an operation there was no assurance that he would ever walk again. He had endured all the curses of a paraplegic—

"I know," said Roger grimly. "And now he's in a nadir of despair. I'd like to see him, Jim."

There was one difficulty, the nurse explained. Frank was harboring a staph germ and had been placed in isolation. No one was allowed to see him, certainly not another patient who might spread the dread germ through the hospital!

The next day it was decided that Roger could continue treatment at home until the infection subsided, but he was to return the following Wednesday for further tests. He went home, but did not forget Frank Aymer. How was the best way to reach him? After mulling over the problem for days, he suddenly knew the answer. But he did not tell LaVerna what he planned to do. He was afraid of worrying her. Checking in at the hospital on Wednesday, he asked to be put in the same room as the young man.

"I'm sorry. That's impossible. Mr. Aymer is in isolation."

"I know. I still want to be put there."

"But you don't understand. You'd run the risk of dangerous infection. I tell you, he's in *isolation*."

"Yes. I know."

The attendant, competent to handle all emergencies, looked dazed. "I—Permission would have to be granted by your doctor," she said finally.

"Then please let me see him."

Understanding Roger's purpose, the doctor gave permission.

That very afternoon Frank's mother drove a hundred miles to visit him. Putting on the special robe required for all visitors to "isolation" patients and entering the room, she was amazed to see a second bed and a smiling, strangely familiar face.

"Mrs. Aymer? I'm Roger Arnett. I hope you don't mind my joining your son. We're just beginning to get acquainted."

"Arnett!" She repeated the name wonderingly, her eyes darting from his face to the wheel chair, first incredulous, then tearfully radiant. "You're the gladiolus man! If you could only know how I've hoped and prayed to find you!"

The coincidence was awe-inspiring. Emily Aymer had been at the home of the Arnetts in Corunna on the Sunday before Labor Day, 1945, for a gladiolus show. She had been impressed because a man in a wheel chair could operate a business, marry, adopt children, appear happy in spite of all difficulties. When her only son's hopes and aspirations had been suddenly shattered by paralysis, she had remembered Roger. If only Frank could meet and talk with him! But Roger had moved out of the state, she could not find out where. And now to find him here in her son's room! Such an answer to her prayers was overwhelming.

The assistance Roger gave Frank was largely in the nature of friendship and encouragement, for in recent years knowledge of paraplegia and techniques of rehabilitation had developed at an astonishing pace, and the boy had come to one of the finest rehabilitation centers in the country. But braces and strengthening devices were as essential for the spirit as for the body. It was enough that when he left the boy could smile, if a bit crookedly, and wave him a game good-by.

"Hi ya, feller," Roger waved back. "See you at the race track!"

"Yeah. You've said it. At the race track."

The following year Roger learned that Frank had gone back to high school, which he had never finished, and planned to start junior college in Bay City the next fall. He was driving his own car, had on one occasion got underneath it and removed the transmission. There was even hope that he might someday walk again.

Give up the ministry? Let the criticism of a few vested officials oust him from the opportunity of being partner with God in his job of rehabilitating priceless human beings? Not on his life!

In the spring of 1961 he was offered the position of Minister to the Handicapped of the Ann Arbor District of the Methodist Church. He was jubilant. At last the church was recognizing the need and value of such work! . . . Jubilant, that is, until he found out the terms on which the job was offered.

His friends at Glenwood were both sad and happy. "So sorry to lose you." . . . "Won't seem the same." . . . "But what a fine opportunity for you!" . . . "We know it's just what you've been hoping for." . . . "But what will we do without you? . . ."

They supposed, of course, that it would be a full-time job, with appropriate financial recompense for time and services. He did not tell them the truth, that he would be receiving nothing except a title and the petty sum they themselves had been paying for his expenses, that it was merely a polite way of removing him from a troublesome situation. It was much better that they should not know.

14

Long ago Roger had devised a set of "Rules for the Handicapped," techniques by which, according to his own experience, a good life could be attained. There were eleven of them in all. Last but not least in importance was: "Have a sense of humor."

To this he might well have added, "Be able to laugh at your own handicap." Perhaps this was one of the hardest tests of adjustment, to take jibes with equanimity. And it was still harder for one's friends to give them. It was a long time before Russ Everhart was able to say with jocular ease after Roger had had a touch of pneumonia, "Well, half a man *ought* to get over it quicker!"

Al Hartoog was another who knew him well enough. One day, visiting Al's new church, Roger saw an undertaker riding up with a car full of flowers.

"He seems like a friendly man," he said to Al. "A perfect stranger, yet he waved to me."

"Probably thinks you're a potential customer," shot back Al without the slightest hesitation.

Roger never missed an opportunity to poke fun at himself, as when Tom, a fellow worker at the Research Center, inquired, "How are you today?"

"Not so good," replied Roger, pulling a long face.

"So? You look pretty good to me."

"How can I," shot back Roger, "when I've got my right foot in the grave?"

The other ten "Rules" had proved equally valid in Roger's own experience:

1. Engage in physical competition. But if you become engaged in competition with a non-handicapped person, expect him to win and be content. There is no necessity to "save face" in such an uneven contest.
2. Eat and drink whatever can be easily digested and assimilated, and in moderation. Overeating is the resort of the bored, the unhappy, the lonely, and the frustrated.
3. Dismiss business problems and worries upon going to bed. The purpose of going to bed is to sleep. Do it.
4. Be useful, be needed.
5. If you believe in eternal life, start living it now.
6. Have faith in God, in men, in yourself.
7. Love. The greater the handicap, the more love is needed to be given and received.
8. Accept discipline of some sort, if only self-discipline, in the wisdom and knowledge that the game of life must be played according to the rules.
9. Belong! A "lone wolf" may be romantic to contemplate or write about, but his true nature is to belong to the pack. Human beings must be integrated: in family ties, friendship, social environment.
10. Create. Ability to create is the one thing we are sure to have in common with Deity. There is no greater source of satisfaction than the capacity to bring something into being.

Now, as his work in nursing homes and hospitals mushroomed, he was faced with the need of a new set of techniques, this time for a *minister* to the handicapped. For it was a pioneer ministry, with few charts and guideposts. Books on pastoral visitation gave some scant assistance. His graduate work in Special Education was of considerable value in helping to understand the needs of various types of disability, and his own experience as a handicapped person was of inestimable help. But the techniques of visitation which he came to adopt were largely the result of many months and years of trial and error. Their guiding principle, however, was from the beginning very simple, the personal human touch: a friendly greeting, a kind word, a smile, a handclasp, and a listening ear.

It was also a peculiar and unorthodox ministry. On Saturday, a calling day, he often left the house at seven in the morning, in order to arrive in a home by eight o'clock. The residents would be eating breakfast or just finishing, and he often had a chance to visit with some of them in the dining room. Then came his round of the rooms. If a door was closed, he knocked before entering. Usually the call came, "Come in." But if the nurse was working with the occupant he would return later. Sometimes he helped severely disabled men to get dressed. If they were paralyzed in the arms or blind, he might help to feed them. He also played postman, carrying along paper, stamps, cards, and for many who could not use their arms he wrote letters at their dictation.

The first requisite, of course, was to care, to be concerned, about every person visited. He did not need to acquire this quality of empathy—more than sympathy. He had it in full measure. The next requisite, to know as much as possible about the people he wished to serve, was more difficult.

The residents of homes—he always called them *residents*, not patients, and never *inmates*—constituted a cross-section of society. There were the rich and the poor, elderly and young, teacher and student, doctor and patient, minister and layman, believer and unbeliever, American-born and foreign-born, happy and unhappy; persons with practically every type of disability, physical and mental. Most of them were lonely. After only a short experience he came to the conclusion that *every one* was lonely.

How establish contact with these hundreds of separate and diverse personalities, find the "open sesame" which might slowly break down the barriers to a friendly and helpful relationship? As time passed he found many ways. A woman might have flowers or plants in her room. She would always appreciate a compliment about them. If she had several plants, she was probably a lover of the soil, and they could immediately find a common interest in gardening. But by no means dwell on his own preoccupation with gladiolus! Let her talk about the gardens *she* used to have.

When entering a new room he would look for signs of handcrafts. Some women did sewing, made dolls or jewelry. Men did leatherwork or metalcraft. A simple but sincere compliment would often make dull eyes light, turn dour faces into friendliness. There was Joe, for instance, who with his right side paralyzed had learned to paint with his left hand, although he had never held a brush before. For eight hours each day he painted steadily, until his colorful dabblings lined the walls, overflowed the dresser, were piled high in every corner. Many of the pictures were religious, bearing unmistakable marks of his Catholic background. Meeting Joe early in his ministry, Roger visited him regularly for years.

"He's my inspiration," declared Joe, delightedly posing for a picture with his friend.

In one room in a convalescent home near Ann Arbor Roger saw three rather yellow and aged letters in a frame. Thinking they might be treasured mementos, he asked about them.

"Oh—yes!" James Barker's face immediately lighted. A slender, sensitive-faced man in his eighties, he had long been employed by the Argus Camera Company of Ann Arbor. "There's quite a story. Like to hear it?"

It *was* quite a story. Because of his reputation as a fine artist Mr. Barker had been engaged in 1925 by the Queen of England to paint a full-length portrait of the Prince of Wales in royal dress. Eagerly he described having tea with the queen, meeting the Prince. He had been given an option of three days as appointments for the sittings. One of the letters on the wall expressed the Queen's appreciation for his fine work. Hands trembling with excitement, he removed the treasures from the wall and placed them in Roger's hands. In the interest of another person he had recaptured this great moment of his life.

A man with gnarled but now empty and idle hands might like to be drawn into reminiscences about his work. Such was John, now ninety-four, who had been an engineer for many years and had a host of rich memories to share. One disabled woman, Mrs. Fraulein, always had a humorous story to tell him, and he invariably remembered to ask for it.

Always the "open sesame" was attentive listening, for the lonely were in desperate need of sharing. Many liked to talk about their children and grandchildren, or, if unmarried, nieces and nephews, to exhibit letters and photographs. The prayer which then followed could be more personal and meaningful. Others, having too much idle time to brood, wanted to talk about their troubles, and the experience of sharing could be cathartic, freeing them for a happier exchange before the call was over. Some wanted to talk about their church and the things they used to do as members. He found many who had been in a home for months without being visited by a minister or members of their churches. Some had come from other cities or states, and the local churches knew nothing about them. Neglect was often owing not to disinterest but to lack of communication. For this reason such a chaplaincy ministry was tremendously needed and appreciated.

Often the wheel chair was a means of making contacts. Homes and hospitals were full of wheel chairs. They sat idle in rooms, roamed corridors, were lined in rows before TV sets, hovered in lonely isolation in corners, against walls, any haven to escape the bustling tide of able-bodied moving figures. Another wheel chair introduced a common bond of interest. What happened to Roger? How did he get that way? So? Too bad. "Well, my case wasn't quite like that. Want to know what happened to me?" Sometimes Roger's wheel chair itself, an old-fashioned model, was a conversation piece, as to Mr. Gardner, a young man badly crippled by polio.

"I know," replied Roger. "It's an old model. I ought to turn it in. But it does have advantages for me, you know. After thirty years I'm used to it. Yours is easier to push."

The friendship thus begun was to last for many years.

But the wheel chair was far more than a conversation piece. Elderly people, sick people, disabled people, were almost always either sitting or lying down. Entering a room, he was immediately one with them, *on their level.* No need to treat him as guest, hunt with embarrassment for an extra chair, make an awkward seat for him on a bed! And no need for him to stoop to take their hands, to place an arm about a thin stooped shoulder, to look eye to eye, to speak so they could hear.

"A voice and a hand," said a nurse in one of the homes he visited, "they are the things these people know best."

For the deaf, one of the most lonely groups of all, there was not even the voice. Roger often blamed himself for not learning the sign language so he could talk with them. And there were other disabilities which prevented normal communication. For many of them he came in time to find ways of making intelligible contacts. Those who had suffered strokes or other ailments affecting speech often found it difficult to talk. He learned to ask questions which could be answered by "Yes" or "No," so they could reply by a slight movement of the head.

Visiting a patient on a rocking bed, able to talk only when the head of the bed goes down, expelling the air from the lungs, he learned to wait without interrupting until the person could fully express himself. In fact, this was a lesson which applied to all his visitations and which was one of the hardest to learn: not to interrupt with ideas of his own. Always the purpose must be to help the person find expression.

There were other barriers of communication, such as language. In one home he visited there were many residents born in Poland.

Some could not speak English. One day some of them asked Roger to get them a priest.

"But the Catholic priest comes here once a month!" he explained.

"No, no, not him! A Polish priest!" They were hungering for someone who could talk their language. By good fortune Roger knew just such a father, in a nearby parish. Called by phone, he agreed to call and soon was going to the home regularly.

But there was a language of the heart which helped dissolve such barriers. One day Roger found a man at the Dion Home looking like a desert island in a sea of humanity. Even in appearance he was a loner, his long, snow-white hair and beard looking as if they had never been cut. Something in his clear blue eyes told Roger that here was a great soul, now in agony.

"Where were you born?" he asked.

"Russia." The man articulated slowly. "English—hard for me to speak."

With much halting Ted told his story. He had come to America as a young man from the Ukraine and settled on a small farm near Plymouth, Michigan. He had belonged to the Eastern Orthodox Church. He had never married but had found happiness and satisfaction in truck farming and in giving lessons on the violin, piano, and accordion. Recently a stroke had left his left side paralyzed. All alone, ostracized because of his "difference," denied his beloved music, dependent on others even for getting in and out of bed, he welcomed Roger's interest and concern with pathetic eagerness. Wheeling to his dresser, he pulled from one of its drawers envelopes containing letters, clippings, and pictures of some of his pupils. A bridge, small though it was, had been built to the desert island.

At first Roger was terribly tense and ill at ease in making visits. He felt he had to make a good impression on every person visited, that it was some weakness on his part if he failed. He was self-conscious, timid about offering prayer. He felt that he should give everybody good advice, not realizing that people in nursing homes needed assurance of concern, not counseling. He had a fear of approaching people of higher strata of society. Yet he soon found that appearance was little indication of former affluence or poverty. One of the most carelessly dressed women he ever met had once been a dress designer for Mary Pickford!

But slowly, as the months and years brought experience and wisdom, he acquired ease and relaxation and with them the practice of certain techniques which he found effective in nursing homes. Some were very simple, merely the tested and proved deductions of common sense, like the following:

If a person is paralyzed on his right side, use your left hand to shake his left hand.

In dealing with a blind person, use the sense of touch. ("Oh, now I know who you are!")

Remember all previous contacts.

If a person has a hand crippled by arthritis, give it barely a touch.

In talking with the deaf and hard of hearing, look straight at them and enunciate distinctly. Sometimes use a pad and pencil.

Don't discuss *your* problems unless they ask, and if they do, reply as briefly as possible. ("You're always cheerful," people often marveled. There was a good reason. "When I'm not," he would reply, "I stay at home and take it out on my wife.")

Emphasize personal interests and give specific praise: a plant, a bit of handwork, a picture.

Visit the residents when they go to a hospital.

Give prayer when needed, but do not force it. You will come to know when and where it is appreciated.

Greet the help and be friendly with the nurses.

Listen to the specific needs of each individual, and if a promise is made to help, always *follow up*.

If a person is asleep, wake him. (At first Roger was reluctant to do this, but after some scoldings on his next visit, he learned his lesson. Sleeping was not usually because of illness or tiredness but from sheer boredom.)

If at all possible, leave when there is a smile on the person's face.

If someone tells you a story, don't try to top it. This is his moment. Let him have it.

Sometimes if a person is very ill or lost to the world, the touch of a hand on the brow will bring a response.

The touch of a hand . . .

Roger never realized how much it might mean until one day when he was calling in the county hospital. There were four beds in one room, a curtain drawn around the one in the far corner. This could mean one of several things. Some people in their loneliness seek more solitude which makes them more lonely until they prefer isolation, a vicious cycle. Roger pushed aside the curtain. He would never forget the moments that followed.

John was about sixteen years old. From his movements Roger judged him to be a cerebral palsy victim, probably from birth. Apparently he had been abandoned to the care of the County Social Welfare Department and was temporarily in this section of the hospital for medical treatment.

"Hello, Johnny," he said. "How are you?"

"Hello," he replied. "Who are you?"

"I'm Roger. I've come to see you."

The boy's voice was pleading. "Will you please come and shake my hand? Please?" When Roger extended his hand, he grasped it, raised it to his lips, and said, "Thank you, thank you very much. Please come back and see me, Roger. Please!"

Some of the techniques were derived from the mistakes of his own visitors—friends, ministers—on his numerous trips to the hospital. There was the hit-and-run caller, who kept glancing surreptitiously at his watch; the one who stayed too long; the one who spent all the time discussing his church problems; the sanctimonious, the joker, the too doleful, the too cheerful ("You're looking fine, Roger, never saw you look better!" when you knew you resembled a cadaver. Roger preferred Dr. Berry's favorite expression, stark but candid: "I swear, Roger, when you came in this time you looked like warmed-over death!")

But the worst mistake ministers had made when calling on him, Roger reflected, was in trying to give him good advice.

"When I started ten years ago," he wrote in his diary on January 30, 1963, "I made the same awful mistake. Gradually I found myself giving less and less advice, finding my ministry more and more effective. Now I listen.

"The greatest help is in quiet silence, an active silence that has a healing effect on a troubled soul. Here is a form of giving that requires great self-restraint and openmindedness. It is a sensitive act: a gentle squeeze of the hand, an arm around the shoulder, knowing meeting of the eyes, one in sorrow, the other in sympathy, so that one cannot tell which belongs to whom. The feeling then passes from sorrow to peace. This is the language of the heart, older than speech itself. How often I have heard after such a session, 'I feel better now.'

235

" 'But surely you offer sympathy?' some people ask me.

"No, I can't say that I really do. Sympathy is not sincere enough. It sounds like a Job's comforter, a person who sympathizes with others and then blames them for their mistakes. These persons I visit are the victims of tragedies for which there are no final and complete answers. I can only allow them to express their feelings and give them enough confidence to work out their own solutions. I have learned not to seek credit for myself. Indeed, most of the folks I call on do not even know my name. Many do not know what denomination I represent. All they know is that I accept them as separate individuals and that somehow I can see their world as they see it.

"I believe with Albert Schweitzer, 'All of us must participate in bearing the burden of grief that rests upon the world.' I try to do this quietly and tenderly."

Roger had plenty of opportunity to observe others' bedside techniques, for his hospital episodes became more and more frequent. In September, 1961, he went in for a series of operations. "Osteo," pronounced Dr. Berry. "We've got to get that bad bone out."

After his first operation Roger overheard the surgeon say to one of his assistants, "And this isn't the last we'll see of him."

He was right. Less than three weeks later he was back again, to remain in the hospital from the last of October to the middle of February. More operations to remove more dead bone. More long weeks of waiting for the tissues to heal. It was while he was there that Ronnie came home from his naval station in Norfolk, Virginia, to marry Bertha Graham, who lived four houses down the street from their home in Belleville. He wanted his father to perform the ceremony. There was a beautiful chapel in the hospital. On the last day of the year Roger got up and dressed, for the first time in two months, wheeled himself to the chapel, and in a beautiful little ceremony pronounced his son Ronald and Bertha Graham man and wife.

As usual, Roger was in a ward by preference. A poor place to spend both Christmas and New Year's, but far better in company than in a private room! Perhaps it was the wedding that made him feel in a holiday mood. At least he was one of the ringleaders in planning some excitement in the eighteen-bed ward for New Year's Eve. Of course they all wanted to be awake until midnight. The first part of the night they slept in relays. Just before twelve all were awakened and alerted, one . . . two . . . three . . .

"NURSE!!!" they all yelled in concert, exactly on the stroke of midnight.

Terrified, sure that dire calamity was in the offing, the nurse came running.

"Happy New Year!" shouted eighteen patients with broad grins.

She looked as though she could have murdered the whole gang.

But the gaiety was thin ice over dark and restless currents. At first Roger had been too weak and sick to care what happened to his ministry. Now as the weeks lengthened into months he lay helplessly fuming. For three months he was unable to sit up or to lie on his back. It took four operations to clear up the difficulty. Patience was not one of his major attributes, and he did not cultivate it now. If he derived benefit from the interminable discipline, it was through a sense of vicarious identity with many of his 2,500 parishioners.

"Noah has to lie like this," he reminded himself, "fourteen hours a day in a rocking bed," or, "John has to stay in bed not for a few months but for the rest of his life!" Yet the reminders brought a feeling of guilt as often as one of increased understanding. "They'll think I've forgotten them, stopped caring, let them down. Lord, how much longer! Let me get out of here!"

One grim comfort was the numerous cards of well-wishing in shaky and spidery handwriting, the messages relayed by Doris Ritter from anxious residents in home after home after home. At least he was furnishing some with the opportunity momentarily to forget their own troubles!

The desertion of his ministry was not his only worry. He knew that he was needed, now as never before, at home. LaVerna was facing severe problems with Faye. He fretted constantly because she must solve them alone. He would have been still more worried if he had known the full extent of her problems.

Two weeks after Ronnie's wedding he was slated to leave with his ship for Cuba on a Thursday afternoon. That night Bertha called her mother, who lived near the Arnetts, and told her that after the ship had left some MP's had come to her house and said that Ronnie was not on the ship. He had gone AWOL. Bertha could not believe it. Appraised of the news, LaVerna was frantic with worry. Saturday she had heard nothing. Finding that Roger was dissatisfied with his progress, she decided it was no time to add to his worries. Sunday, when she went to spend the day with him, he was feeling better and wanted to go to church, so they wheeled his bed into the chapel. And there on the altar were the white mums, still left from the wedding! Wilted, but cloying in fragrance, they seemed to turn the little chapel into a funeral parlor.

Still she bore the burden alone. That night she lost hope. Surely if he had been on the ship Bertha would know by now and would have called her mother. She went to bed, certain that Ronnie was gone forever. But not AWOL! She would never believe that. Ronnie had told about rough elements in the seaport city. She was sure he had been the victim of foul play.

At seven the next morning the telephone rang. It was Bertha's mother. "Bert called last night," she said, "and it's all right. It was just a mistake, maybe a practical joke. Ronnie was on the ship."

"And you didn't call me!" wailed LaVerna.

"Well—after all, it was ten o'clock at night—"

For LaVerna it had been no joke. The incident marked the beginning of nervous headaches which were to recur for many years.

"You should have told me!" scolded Roger. "What's a husband for? Don't you ever dare to spare me bad news again, even if I'm on my deathbed!"

It was not surprising that the headaches continued, for LaVerna was subjected to pressures of worry which could easily have broken a person of less courage and faith. The "deathbed" was no figure of speech, but stark reality, always just around the corner. Every time Roger went to the hospital and she bade him a smiling good-by, the words pounded in her ears, "He may not be back."

This time, as usual, he returned, but weaker than usual. After taking only a brief rest, he was back calling by the middle of March, and again she saw him drive himself relentlessly, following a regimen that would have broken the health of many able-bodied men, answer calls at all hours of the night; spend nine-tenths of his leisure time in an avocation far more demanding than the eight hours he spent at the Research Center five days a week; cheerfully respond to every need that presented itself. Sometimes she tried to protect him, as one day when Al Hartoog called and asked if Roger could preach in his church about forty miles away while he and his sick wife took a much-needed holiday.

"He shouldn't," she temporized, knowing Roger would instantly have said "Yes." "He really isn't strong enough." Then, with determination, "No. I'm afraid he can't do it." And of course Al had understood.

Not Roger. He was vexed when she told him about it some weeks later, but she did not care.

And there was Faye. Uninterested in college, she was studying beauty culture, a choice dictated by long distrust of her own physical attributes. Even the plastic surgery with its resulting restoration of happiness and confidence had not erased the deep scars of insecurity. Perhaps that was why she had broken with the faithful Ken during her last year in high school.

Now she rebelled against all control. If she wanted to stay out half the night, or all of it, she felt it her privilege. In spite of the girl's scornful protests, LaVerna would wait up for her, adding lack of sleep to her other anxieties. There were many arguments. And then, suddenly, after months of tension, the problem was solved. Faye and Ken became friendly again. Then they were engaged. And in June, 1963, in the Belleville Methodist Church Roger united them in holy matrimony. Jim Alward played the organ. Her brother Dick led her to the altar. And in the magic of Chantilly lace, seed pearls, sequins, white roses, a silk illusion veil, and the love in a man's eyes, the child who had never quite escaped from the locked room of rejection, the little girl who had wept at the sight of her twisted face in the mirror, the adolescent who had tried to hide from life behind a concealing hand, were all transformed into an attractive and confident woman.

After seeing them off for California where Ken was stationed with the Marine Corps, Roger and LaVerna felt strangely alone. It seemed even stranger to plan their annual vacation for only two people. But Roger's idea of a holiday was not resting quietly at home. That summer they took a week's trip around the north edge of Lake Superior, then later went to Norfolk to visit Ronnie and Bertha, returning home by way of Nashville, where Roger visited the Methodist headquarters and planted seeds of interest in a film depicting the possibilities of a ministry to the handicapped.

It was not his first attempt to create such an interest. The preceding year he had attended a seminar held in Fayetteville, Arkansas, on the subject, "Handicapped in the Church." He had taken the film made by Bud Mente, and it had been enthusiastically received by the church leaders at the seminar. TRAFCO (The Television, Radio, and Film Commission) had shown an interest in it and made a tape to accompany its use. It had been used successfully by the church Board of Missions as a resource for the seminar. Unfortunately, however, the film had been taken at sixteen frames per second instead of twenty-four, which made it unsuitable for widespread use. But already Roger had plans for a new film, and his conversations in Nashville were encouraging.

The trip was accomplished with such little difficulty that they began planning for a longer one. When the news came that Faye was to have a baby in March, its destination was obvious.

"That's it!" said Roger. "We'll go to California."

"Oh!" LaVerna gasped. "Should we—so far—?" But she knew that already the matter was settled. Roger's eyes were asparkle with the predatory gleam of the prospective grandfather. His new grandson Roger was born on March 27, 1964, the day of the big earthquake in Alaska.

"What a baby!" he exulted. "He shook the world."

They left for California on Saturday the 28th, the day before Easter, and arrived at Faye's on Tuesday, traveling as much as 750 miles a day. Unlike the motels they had found in the East, those in the West had wide doors. Since reading in grade school about them, Roger had always wanted to see the Carlsbad Caverns. Writing ahead, he learned that a wheel chair would present no problem. A personal guide was provided. At the entrance an elevator took them down, wheel chair and all, for a half mile. Although he could not explore all the caverns, he saw enough to fulfill all his boyhood expectations.

They spent ten days with Faye and Ken, who was located at Camp Pendleton. Not that Roger remained in the apartment much of the time! He traveled all over the surrounding area alone, seeing everything possible, patronizing all the tourist attractions. Hearing of some of his activities, Ken marveled, "Even I have never done that, and I've been here three years!" One of their side trips was to Los Angeles, where they visited former friends as well as relatives of some of his nursing-home residents.

But his greatest ambition was to go deep-sea fishing. At first it looked impossible. All the places at which he inquired had no facilities for getting a wheel chair into the boats. Entrance was by means of ladders. But he persisted, traveling about a hundred miles up and down the coast, searching. Finally he found a place called "Davey's Locker" where it was possible to manage transfer from wharf to boat. He and Ken had to drive twenty miles before leaving the dock at six in the morning, embarking in a boat which held about fifty people. There were few fish caught, only about a half dozen, but Roger was thrilled to catch one of them. At least he had satisfied a lifelong ambition.

Another was to see the redwoods, so when they left on Friday of the following week they visited the Sequoia National Forest. The trip home took them by way of Hoover Dam and the Grand Canyon. Here another problem confronted Roger. He wanted to take one of the airplane rides down into the canyon, but when he came to enter the small four-seater plane, he could not be lifted in the door. But again he persisted, and was finally dragged in over the wing, an operation which, in spite of the pad they tried to keep under him, raised havoc with his tender skin. But the thrill of cleaving the magnificent chasm was worth it. They arrived home after a trip of three weeks and 8,000 miles.

Achievements such as these seemed modest compared with the adventures of some of Roger's handicapped friends. Take, for instance, Stefan Florescu, the quadriplegic son of the Romanian immigrant, for whom Roger and Ronnie had built the ramp.

Soon after Roger's visits inspired Stef to get out, the local social agencies decided that he was worth rehabilitating. He helped Roger and Faye Sloan to organize the Downriver Handicapped League and was one of its most active members. In 1956 he met an attractive young woman, Carolyn, at an ice-cream party. Although not disabled herself, she was keenly interested in the league and in social problems relating to the handicapped. Presently he was talking to Roger about the possibility of getting married.

"Sure," encouraged Roger. "Why not? It worked with me. Carolyn's a wonderful girl. Just be sure she understands ALL your problems and knows what she's up against."

The couple encountered the same objections as had Roger and LaVerna. Stef consulted a priest, who referred him to an assistant for counseling, and the latter tried to discourage him. His doctors objected. Carolyn's mother was opposed. But Roger continued to encourage. Carolyn was a teacher. Stefan worked for the Detroit Board of Education reading high school English theme papers.

Carolyn had hand controls put on her car and taught Stef to drive. They were married in 1958 and were extremely happy. After her marriage Carolyn spent three years studying full time in law school and became an attorney specializing in criminal practice and legal aid claims.

"We have more fun than most people," she remarked after eight years of married life, which had included, among others, a trip to England. "It was Stef who gave me the idea of helping people through group action. And if he wants to do anything, nothing can stop him. 'It can be done, and I can do it.' That's Stef."

In the *Paraplegic News* Stefan read articles about the Paralympics, the international athletic contests held for wheel chair competitors every year in England and every four years at the time and site of the Olympics. Having been a star athlete, he determined to promote the idea. Soon he organized the Michigan chapter of the Paralyzed Veterans of America and Michigan's first wheel chair sports team. He began swimming again, largely for muscle and body building. But soon he was involved in competitions local, national, and international, and taking members of his team all over the United States and to other countries. The Florescu living room, already the depository of vast supplies of promotional literature for league activities, became lined with plaques, medals, certificates, and statuettes, won in Stef's numerous competitions. In 1962 he competed in the Stoke-Mandeville annuals in England, in 1964 went to Tokyo, where he won four medals in swimming and table tennis, one a gold medal for placing first in singles. In 1965 he was in France, Spain, and England, placing first in two of the swimming events in the Stoke-Mandeville contests, competing with handicapped swimmers from ten other countries.

Perhaps his most distinctive triumph was the completion of the fifty-mile swim which won him a certificate from the American Red Cross and a plaque from the Paralyzed Veterans of America. It took him two years to complete it, in laps of 440 yards for each swim period. As he churned slowly and tirelessly back and forth across Patton Pool, paralyzed legs dragging through the water, half-paralyzed arms alternating an awkward backstroke and breast stroke, there was a loyal group of friends to urge him on, and he finished to the accompaniment of loud cheers and a flashing of cameras. Then he was lifted back into the wheel chair where he had spent most of his waking hours for thirteen years.

But Stefan was less concerned with making swimming records for himself than with getting other handicapped people "into the swim." Perhaps fifty or sixty handicapped people in the area had started swimming through his efforts. But there were a thousand who needed his program of physical fitness. The Annual Michigan Wheelchair Games which the club organized in cooperation with the Detroit Department of Parks and Recreation and the National Association of the Physically Handicapped provided competition in bowling, swimming, table tennis, softball throw, javelin, shotput, discus, archery, and racing. So keen was his interest that he finally gave up all other work and devoted full time to his organizing, reporting, editing, and promoting, as well as coaching for athletic events, all in the service of the handicapped.

"Roger built a bridge to me," he explained his simple credo, "and it's up to me to build bridges to others."

15

During the first five years of his district ministry Roger's work with the handicapped expanded to almost incredible proportions. The homes open to his services multiplied until he was regularly visiting fifteen, plus several wards in Wayne County General Hospital. In three of the homes church services were conducted. Many individuals were frequently visited in their homes. The work carried on week after week, year after year, by this wheel-chair invalid would have taxed the energies of many full-time, able-bodied ministers. For brief periods during the five years he kept a diary. Glimpses into these fragmentary jottings, often mere scraps of penciled notes, are intimately revealing.

April 30, 1961. A heavy day with visitation in Allen Park and Eastlawn, besides hearing the troubles of some Glenwood members. Over fifty calls.

May 1. A fine day, climaxed when Victor Hopeman took me to the Boy Scout Troop of Handicapped Boys in Redford. I have been working for a year to make the Judson Collins (Methodist Summer Camp) available to disabled children on an integrated basis. The subject was discussed with the parents of this troop.

These parents are so burdened with the mechanics of living that they have little opportunity to take on the wings of eagles in fancy flights of joy that other families take for granted. These boys still know this wonderful world of imagination. I long for the parents to know it, too. But this is hard because they have been hurt deeply through no fault of their own, but where it hurts most, in their children.

May 2. One of those days. I usually go to Ann Arbor on Monday or Tuesday evening to visit persons in St. Joseph's and the University of Michigan hospitals. I got clear to Ann Arbor when my bowels cut loose. I had to return home. LaVerna has always been so wonderful and helpful in such situations.

I regret not making the calls, especially because of Charles, sixteen years old and with leukemia. I'm afraid he won't be with us long. I have followed him since he entered the hospital last August and have been with his parents. Each week I wonder if I will ever see him again.

It is estimated that it will cost 6 billion dollars to place a man on the moon. I am sure Charles and his family are much more interested in a cure for leukemia than having an astronaut riding through space.

May 3. Wednesday, and as usual I went to Woody's Rest Home near Romulus to give the people there a midweek worship service. This time I made it communion, which means a great deal to the older Christians. . . .

May 4. This evening was spent in the Sumpter Convalescent Home. I take time to visit each room on the ground floor. Each person is interesting and leads to new channels of thought and experience.

May 5. Friday, and usually I take a pianist and conduct hymn sings at Eloise; but I couldn't get the piano player so instead I went to the hospitals in Ann Arbor. Visited only ten persons, half the usual number. Charles is still alive, but the sign on his door reads "Reverse Precaution," meaning that I like all visitors had to wear a mask and gown in order not to carry infection to the patient.

May 6. This morning I visited the Bancroft Home in Detroit, all 300 residents. I could not sleep tonight because of deep concern for these folks. The Council of Churches is responsible for the Sunday-evening services. They have no hymnbooks, each Sunday a different minister. Sometimes he cannot get there. This is a tragic situation for these older persons. Many of them have been faithful servants of the church for many years. Now in their final hour of need their church fails them.

May 7. Directly after church I spent two hours visiting about forty out of the sixty-five residents of Allen Park Convalescent Home. This is a new "home," clean, good service, a fine staff. But Elsie R—— is unhappy. She is a gracious lady who lost her husband three years ago after a long, expensive illness. They used to have fine cars, diamonds, furs, a good home. All she has now is social security and a heart condition. She shows no bitterness, only resignation, and a terrible loneliness.

Sunday winds up the week for me. As I look back over the past 168 hours my heart is saddened. There has been so much that should have been done that wasn't. Above all, buildings A and D should have been visited at Eloise.

May 11. At the University of Michigan Medical Center I have gotten acquainted with Bob, twenty-five, in the hospital as the result of a thirty-five-foot fall in prison which may leave him permanently disabled. He has had tough breaks in life and feels very much alone. He was deeply concerned about his ill mother in a distant city. So today I went to see her, 85 miles away, a thin, frail woman with the strong odor of alcohol. A tragic family, so eager to learn about Bob.

A happy day also, for my son Dick, grandson Jimmie, and I traveled to Owosso to attend a Father and Son Banquet with my father. I have many fond memories of the church, where forty years ago I started playing in the orchestra. And I am so proud of my mother and father, who in their seventies are still carrying on a gladiolus business.

May 12–15. Four days spent largely in bed. Caught a cold with intestinal complications, making much work for my dear wife. This sickness has upset my time schedule for pastoral visitations by a week. I do hope my people will understand and forgive me.

May 18. Went to the hospital in Ann Arbor. Charles died of leukemia. Bob cried when I had to leave him. He needs warm human companionship so desperately.

May 19. Took Jim Alward to play for a hymn sing in two of the psychopathic wards at Wayne County General. Used about sixty *Upper Room* hymnals. In the first ward from ten to twenty persons participated, in the second up to fifty. These persons are under lock and key, and we also must be confined when there. A strange feeling the first time, but now we think nothing of it.

In just about every instance these persons have been deeply hurt by society. They vary in age from the teens to the very elderly. Society looks on them as failures, so there is even more need for them to succeed. Hymn singing is often a form of succeeding for them. I go around both before and after the sing and greet each one. Often the only time I see them smile is during the greeting. These persons are *not* subhuman beings. They are God's children and persons in their own right.

May 30. A holiday, in which I do not have to work. So what did I do? Spent it in visitation. Visited forty-two persons in the Arnold Home, and there are forty-two stories that could be told. Just one: Harold Anderson, a stroke victim on the second floor, was looking out the door of the inner courtyard, which is beautiful. He cannot talk. I asked him if he would like to get out on the balcony. He nodded yes, so you should have seen a paraplegic in a wheel chair assist a hemiplegic in a wheel chair out a narrow door over a threshold with a half-inch rise. But we did it.

June 1. I did something today that I very rarely do, spent the whole evening with one person. She had polio when six years old.

In terms of physical disability she is not severely handicapped in comparison with many others I visit. However, when I think of the era in which she was stricken and the way society viewed such persons, she has made a remarkable success in life. She is one of the best adjusted persons I know, and perhaps that is why I enjoy what time I can with her.

She and her husband could not have children by birth, so they adopted three, two boys and one girl. It hasn't been easy to raise three children, but she has never complained. There have been many lean years in her life.

There are two ever-present problems with her: 1. Holding her weight down. She is forever dieting. She isn't heavy at all, but to get around as easily as possible, she must stay light. She is a wonderful cook and likes to eat the goodies she shouldn't have. Luckily her husband is on the same kind of diet. 2. Sloppiness of her children and husband. She must have neatness, and the litters left by other members of the family are the bane of her existence. It is a good thing she is like this, for goodness knows what the place would be otherwise.

Considering all the problems this family has had to face, it has done well. Much credit goes to the wife-mother. Her husband is a minister and spends much time visiting hospitals and nursing homes. One time she remarked that she would have to enter one of these places in order to see her husband.

How did I spend the evening with her? Taking her shopping, two games of pinochle, taking it easy. Wish I could spend more time with her. You see, I must confess I am completely in love with her. She is LaVerna, my wife.

He kept a diary only spasmodically. Many evenings he was too tired to chronicle the day's events. But one month was a pattern for every other. The names of the homes visited might change, usually by addition rather than subtraction. The individuals mentioned would vary, although month after month the same names would recur, objects of prolonged concern: Lloyd Hughes, paralyzed from the waist down, father of two children and separated from his wife. . . . Noah, paralyzed from the neck, practicing his frog breathing and balancing on his rocking bed. . . . Jessie, the piano player in Ward K. . . . Bob, the paraplegic at Eloise who had to have both legs amputated at the hips because of osteo of the bone. . . .

> Lately Bob has been showing a new interest in living. Today he ask me about the sex life of a paraplegic and this relation to the sex life of a woman. I could answer him. This may seem to be no concern of a minister. To me it is a great concern, for one's conception of the Kingdom is built on earthly things and earthly feelings. This assurance to Bob on this concern may well lead to a fuller, useful life.

Only occasionally did the diary make reference to personal problems and frustrations.

> August 3. Not much to report. Pace must be slowed up. My body can take just so much. The pressure sore on the left hip needs more hours of bed rest if it is to heal. But how can I rest when there is so much to do, so many people in need of a minister, and no other minister to call on them? No one can know how much it takes out of me to get in and out of the car, lifting the wheel chair in and out, sometimes twenty and more times a day. It would be easy to say "nuts" to the whole thing. So few really appreciate the effort. Certainly not the church leaders. They won't support the work financially as much as I think they should. But I have to continue to serve as long as God gives me strength.

If there was discouragement or pessimism, it was largely for others, not himself.

> August 7. This morning I awoke at four-thirty with a deep concern for the hundreds (perhaps more than a thousand) poor souls in Building N at Eloise. I shudder at the plight of them. In places they are decked one over another. They go through the motions of living, and still have no opportunity to live. There are rows on rows on rows of them with no chance of privacy. There is no TLC (tender loving care). There isn't time.
>
> Why are they there? Persons like you and me. Each one with a story: one the story of once great or near-great; another the story of failure or near-failure. Like Charlotte. She is the daughter of a Baptist minister, his pride and joy and hope. She grew up in the church. Life was full of meaning. Now here she is near the end of life. She did nothing to deserve this. Once in a while a single, solitary, new-found friend calls on her. . . . Or like Erich. Society

called him "bad." He had gotten in trouble with the law. The last time he met a policeman's bullet, so that now he is paralyzed from the waist. Nowadays there are rehabilitation centers for paraplegics like Erich. But Erich couldn't go to the Detroit Rehabilitation Institute. He went to N Building. There are Gus, and John, and Robert, Mrs. B., Mrs. M., etc., etc., etc. They are there chiefly because they are deaf and blind—and no one wants them.

People say, "It must be such a satisfaction to you to do this work." No. I have a feeling of failure. A failure for society and a personal failure for myself. I shudder at the inhumanity of man to man.

But there were flashes of gaiety and triumph.

August 20. Once in a while I see a flicker of a smile come across a face dark with pain and grief. It's like golden sunshine filtering down in a dark forest. If a person wants drama and adventure he can find them very close at hand. I have found them in full measure.

August 21. My good friend Ted Lupher is an enthusiastic gardener and raises wonderful tomatoes and melons. So today I bought a bushel of each and took them to the wards on the first floor of Building A at Eloise, where there are close to 100 patients who rarely get fresh fruits and vegetables. The nurses took time to fix and serve them. I have visited these folks for two and a half years, and today saw them the nearest to enjoying themselves. The Kingdom is not one great place, in some distant time. It is made up of little things in the "now." Today these people had a little bit of the Kingdom. For a moment they found joy. I left them with many smiles on their faces.

It was soon after this that Roger started his apple project. Disturbed by the lack of any Christmas observance in many of the places he visited, especially in Wayne County General Hospital (once the county poorhouse) with its 7,000 patients, he conceived the idea of giving an apple, together with a Christmas letter, to each one he was in the habit of visiting. He found an orchard nearby where he could purchase twenty-five bushels wholesale. One year he used Jonathans, another Delicious. It was a rewarding project. For some people the apple and Christmas letter were the only presents received. The comments that first year were both gratifying and disheartening, for they revealed the limitations of his work.

"It's been so long since I saw you! Please don't stay away so long next time."

"Just today I was thinking about you, hoping you would come."

"Please come back—I am so lonely."

"Have you got a stick of gum?"

"Thank you, thank you. This is all the Christmas I will have."

Another would not accept the apple when offered because she thought she had to pay for it, and she had no money. Another was so grateful that she kissed his cheek.

The work would have been impossible without his many enthusiastic helpers. There were the Hopemans and the Mentes who contributed generously to the trust fund, now administered by the district, which bought supplies and equipment. There was Jim Alward with his music. There was Mrs. Chilson of Belleville Church, a former teacher, who often visited in homes where Roger was unable to go because of stairs, and who made many of the 200 laprobes which he had distributed. There were Art Shepherd and his son Jim, who often made the circuit with Roger and helped deliver apples at Christmas. There were the Roy Miles and the Touses, who regularly attended some of the three services Roger conducted. And of course there was Doris Ritter.

As his nursing-home ministry expanded, she became more and more involved. When he left Glenwood Church, she continued to be his personal secretary, typing reports, preparing bulletins, handling his official correspondence, making ready his 2,500 Christmas letters. Her services extended far beyond the call of duty. She spent Sundays delivering *Upper Rooms*. She attended many of the religious services. And always she was a stout and loyal defender of both Roger and his ministry.

Sometimes, as on one stormy Saturday evening, she went with Roger to one of the homes to help deliver apples. The residents were still in the dining room when they arrived.

"Do you have an orchard?" asked an old lady curiously.

"No," he replied.

"Then where do you get these beautiful apples?"

"I bought them."

"Out of your own money?"

As Roger nodded, the woman turned to Doris. "He must be a wonderful man. And just think, you've got him. He's your husband."

"Oh, no," disclaimed Doris hastily. "I'm just his secretary. He has a lovely wife."

The woman gave her a long look. "Young woman," she said severely, "you'd better resign. No one should be a secretary who thinks as much of her boss as you do."

But few of her experiences in the homes were so spiced with humor. A sensitive person, with the supply of handkerchiefs she always took along for use by rheumy or tearful residents, she had to include one for herself, for when one started to cry, she cried with him.

One Christmas her church circle donated money to buy candy for the residents in one home, most of them on relief. She bought twenty-five-cent boxes, with eight diet bars for the diabetic patients. She took them to the home on Christmas Eve. There were no visitors, no signs of the holiday except a small tree in the lobby. She wished them all a "Merry Christmas," then drove home, terribly depressed, remembering Al Hartoog's words, "It's hell to be old and sick." Feeling devoid of the Christmas spirit, she could not bring herself to attend the Christmas Eve service. Her own hard life and loneliness were sharpened in poignant memory: the sudden death of her husband, the loss of her only little girl, the struggle to bring up three small boys. Then suddenly, it was as if she heard a voice speaking, "You have the real Christmas spirit. You're not expected to be happy. It's doing for others which makes Christmas."

It was through Doris that Barbara Hass, of the Bethel Baptist Church in Southgate, heard of Roger's work. Barbara had long been looking for a service project in which her fifteen or twenty junior high students could become involved. She wrote to Roger asking if there was anything they could do. He replied promptly.

"Could they come next Saturday afternoon to the Bancroft and sing?"

They came. They kept coming, not merely to sing, but to perform all sorts of services for the residents: wheel them from their rooms and back, guide the ones who were unsteady, find their places in the hymnbooks, restore dropped articles, serve as eyes, hands, limbs, and youthful energy. The residents were enchanted, both distressed and perturbed if the young people failed to show up. Often they would pretend to be unable to find their places merely to get attention. One old lady proudly introduced a boy as her grandson. "I could have died," he confessed later. But he had gone along with the fantasy because he couldn't hurt her feelings.

251

In fact, the experience wrought amazing changes in most of the young people. "I've never been treated like this before," said one seventh-grader. "They really *want* us." One youth who had long been a misfit in school blossomed into a well-adjusted person. Younger children in the church could not wait to be old enough to join the group.

Some, of course, overdid in their enthusiasm. One overactive junior high participant was discovered pushing an elderly lady at breakneck pace down the hall, shouting "Whee!" in great glee. The lady was as disappointed as the boy when he had to be toned down.

"He's a cool guy," the same boy said of Roger.

The sermon which most touched their youthful emotions was one dealing with his own experience, when he told about Alice and the first dark Christmas after his accident.

"But just think," he ended with one of his most beaming smiles, "if this hadn't happened, I wouldn't have met any of you!"

Perhaps the group's reaction was best epitomized in a remark contributed by one of the boys in a junior high discussion group. They were discussing courage.

"What's the difference," asked Mrs. Hass, "between foolhardiness and courage?"

"Well," volunteered one boy thoughtfully. "Take Mr. Arnett. He's got courage. Because he could have just sat and let somebody take care of him. But he didn't. He got out and helped other people."

Other youth groups were soon finding similar projects. Under the influence of their leader, Rachel Wilson, the Girl Scouts in Belleville went to Whitehall for services. Some of them made valentines, 106 of them, for all the residents in a home. They polished apples. While attending a Christmas service, they visited James Barker's room and admired his framed letter from the Queen Mother. It was his eighty-fourth birthday, and they sang "Happy Birthday" to him. He died the following week.

Except for the begrudged interludes in the hospital, the months rolled by with the incessant jerking motion of the wheel chair.

> January 5, 1963. Today I saw, felt, and shared grief of deepest depths, deeper than death itself. It happened in a nursing home in Inkster, integrated, a nice clean place, my third visit. On entering

a room of two ladies, one on the far side struggled to get to her feet. Her right arm dangled at her side, her left leg dragged a heavy brace. Where I see this situation I suspect the patient may have difficulty speaking.

As she came to me, she dropped her head on my shoulder, grabbed my hand, and wrung it, tears streaming down her cheeks, sobbing bitterly. Although the syllables came out at the rate of one every six seconds, she could convey her message. "Through—illness—lost—speech—sister—took—all. Only—this—room. I—don't—want—see—anyone—only—you." She remembered me as the minister who had been there before. All the grief and anguish were stored up within her, and no release valve to let them out. When she couldn't talk, she had been declared incompetent, and she realized it. It is one thing to be declared incompetent and not know it, different when you know it. Loss of speech is not a valid reason.

Nothing I could say would help her. All I could do was weep, which I did unashamedly. And for that moment I felt a sense of oneness with our Lord. I shared the Master with this woman when we wept together. This was true prayer without words. The whole scene lasted no more than five minutes. When I left she kissed my hand and said between sobs, "I—feel—bet—ter—now. Thank—you—for—coming."

February 23. Big day. Our anniversary, the twenty-eighth. All morning spent in the Arnold Home, visiting about 300 residents. Some hard. Jewish man just lost wife. Couple fled Germany, been through so much together.

About four LaVerna, Faye, and I left for the Bancroft. Forty at the worship service. But the important thing is that we celebrated our anniversary with these folks. About seventy-five attended. I furnished the ice cream, spoons, and paper plates. Bancroft provided coffee. Glenwood church members brought cake. Wonderful way to celebrate!

April 27. Left house at seven-thirty, arrived Woody's Rest Home a little before eight. Visited everyone. Among residents are a man and wife, he ninety-three, she in late eighties. A week ago he was taken to the hospital, critically ill, ten miles away. Tearfully she asked if I would visit him. "How about you going with me?" I asked. She got ready. Spent more than an hour with him. Her tenderness and love were something to behold. It was doubtful if he knew her, but he quieted down each time she touched him. Mrs. Harvey was in heaven. She talked about her "Frankie" all the way home. On the way had to stop to pick up a leg brace for a handicapped man.

After lunch got together all the equipment for a worship service:

tape recorder, extension speaker, connecting cord, tape of hymns, pre-service tape, hymnbooks, bulletins, Bible, sermon, *Upper Room* booklets, six lap quilts, my date book, book showing names of people in the home, pen, and writing pad.

Took lady with polio to Ypsilanti to pick up a pair of shoes. It took an hour. Arrived at Bancroft in Detroit about three-thirty. Visited as many as possible before six (about 225). Then held service.

August 8. Visited Carl and Betty Bennett in Ypsilanti, both blind. They have two darling little girls, three and six. Carl and Betty live in an old rundown apartment building on the meager amount given by government in "Aid to the Blind." Due to many steps could not get in. Carl came out to talk. The littlest girl wanted to know where Daddy was going. I realized a ride would be a real treat. All piled in, Carl, Betty, and Carla in front, LaVerna in the back seat with the wheel chair, Jackie in the rear of the station wagon, where LaVerna could hold onto her dress. Drove out toward Ann Arbor about five miles, where there is a little water pond by the roadside. The children were thrilled by ducks, geese, swans, peahens, and little chicks. Carl and Betty enjoyed it through their children's emotions. Afterward LaVerna said we could never realize how much a little ride to a family in this day and age meant.

August 31. This month gave out almost 600 *Upper Rooms*. Visited some 1,300 persons, most of them at least twice. Five deaths among my parishioners.

At Arnold Home is Mr. Wilbur, age eighty-nine, a healthy fellow who goes to the dining room for his meals. I missed him when I arrived in time for breakfast. When I went to his room he explained: "Well, I was teaching an *old* man to play shuffleboard. He lost his balance, and I tried to catch him. Well, he fell down with me under him, and he hurt my back." But he is small and wiry, not hurt badly. He'll soon be back teaching some other *old* man how to play shuffleboard.

Frequently the people Roger became interested in would transfer from one home to another, and whenever possible he would follow them. Often, too, he would run across old acquaintances when making routine visits in a home. "How did you ever find me here?" the delighted new resident would exclaim, not realizing what a wide area his visitation covered.

Vivian Wakeford was one whose life wove like a bright thread through year after year, home after home, the spirit in her tiny, half-paralyzed body as vivid and light-winged as her parakeets.

After her friends, Roger among them, succeeded in moving her from the psychopathic ward of Wayne County General to Woody's, life for Vivian became increasingly adventurous. Tommy, another resident, introduced her to ham radio. A new world was opened to her, as high and wide as the air waves. Limbs were not necessary for traveling. A flick of the wrist, and she could be in California, hear the soft, slurred speech of Louisiana, shiver in the winds and snow of the North Atlantic. She received her novice ticket as a ham radio operator in 1962 after training for two months. Then she started working for her "general" license.

The training for this was much more difficult. While the novice examination could be taken by mail, the general must be given personally by a general class licensee. A knowledge of theory was required, with a code speed of at least thirteen words a minute. It took money also, ten dollars out of her twelve-dollars-a-month allowance, to buy equipment.

In late 1962 she moved to the Dorvin Home, and Roger called on her there. She had become a new person, intensely absorbed in her new interest. Proudly she exhibited all her equipment, demonstrated her increasing skill. By February of the following year, with the help of other fans in the area, she had received her "general" license. Now the whole world was at her fingertips.

Soon she heard about a club for hams, called the "Ragchewers' Club," which contained many handicapped members. One of her friends, Evelyn, wanted to take her to it. "Ride in a car!" she gasped. But the nurses urged her, and she went. At the meeting she was intrigued by the sight of a slight, wiry little man with bright dark eyes and salt-and-pepper hair. "Isn't he cute!" she thought as he darted up from his chair to give his treasurer's report. Gabe Wellett was not only the organization's treasurer, he was a member of one of its antenna crews which later came to the Dorvin at her request to put up an aerial for the club's special frequency. The crew had a difficult time. "A ham radio doesn't belong in a convalescent home," objected the manager. But Gabe was persistent. The aerial was installed. Later the crew tried to put up a bigger one.

"No," said the manager with greater firmness, and tried to throw the seventy-dollar apparatus off the roof. Discouraged, the crew all left except Gabe, who refused to be intimidated. Persistence failing, he remained to comfort the disappointed Vivian.

"You come home with me," he said jokingly, "and I'll let you put up any aerial you want!"

"You're tempting me," retorted Vivian with her sunburst of a smile.

Words spoken as a joke soon acquired sober significance. He started visiting her. He brought her flowers. When she needed another operation (she has had sixty-seven in all!) he drove her to the hospital. He took her to his home for dinner. In November they became engaged. Immediately Gabe's son, thinking his father had lost his mind, flew up from Texas to talk him out of such folly. Apparently failing, he went to the home to visit Vivian and, like his father, succumbed to her charms and gave his blessing to the couple.

They were married in December in the Dorvin Home. It was a big event for both residents and nurses. One of the latter loaned the bride her daughter's wedding gown (a little too tight), and they set her on a table so she would be nearer the groom's height. For many of the guests present, to whom call numbers were more important than names, the ceremony signified the union, not of Vivian Wakeford and Gabriel Wellett, but of WA8EMN and K8OJI.

"It won't last," was the frequently heard comment.

But the couple were ideally happy. Gabe's small, neat house was paradise to Vivian, and her husband the "Angel Gabriel." He narrowed her wheel chair so it would go through all the doors and adjusted shelves, tables, counters, sink, so they were on her level. ("Gabe is marvelous, he can do anything!") She developed both skill and relish for cooking and liked to sit in her wheel chair and watch her cakes rise through the glass oven door. ("I'm a biscuit watcher now instead of a bird watcher!") The four hours a day that she was allowed to sit up in her wheel chair she filled brim full of activity. Then, when Gabe left for his factory job in the afternoon, she was back in bed, self-sufficient and entertained by their mutual hobby, until his return. One whole wall of their bedroom was filled with their ham radio equipment.

But her adventures were not all vicarious. Gabe bought a Greenbriar bus and an air mattress, put her on it, and drove her to California. They were gone for twenty-one days, traveling 6,000 miles and visiting hams all along the way.

For Vivian ham radio and the Ragchewers' Club were not only pleasant hobbies. They were channels for service. "The club does wonders for disabled persons," she explains proudly. "It takes them out of confinement and into the world." Fulfilling Roger's ambition for her to write, she became editor of the *Ragchewers' Club Newsletter*, the monthly publication of this organization "Dedicated to the Handicapped—so They May Live Again Through Ham Radio," devoting all the pith and sparkle of her keen wit and gay courage to her prime purpose of helping other handicapped people.

Vivian was one of the pure satisfactions of Roger's ministry. When the dead ends of loneliness and frustration became too depressing, he would bundle LaVerna into the car and they would pay a visit to Gabe's small house in East Detroit for strong doses of optimism. Like Chico, Vivian had managed to escape her prison cage on gay, bright wings.

Another of Roger's dreams was started toward fulfillment in 1963. One day early in the year Ralph Ridenour, an employee in the same building, stopped at Roger's desk.

"I'm lay leader of the Methodist Church here in Ann Arbor District," he introduced himself. "You and I ought to get together on some plans."

Roger needed no second invitation. When he discovered that Ralph did all the photography work for his Radar and Optics Department and that he had previously shot an eighteen-minute film for the Army, his excitement knew no bounds.

"Ralph," he said one day, "I wish you'd go sometime and see what I'm trying to do. Maybe we could make a film out of it."

Ridenour agreed, and one Saturday in the first part of November he went with Roger to the Bancroft Nursing Home. His perfunctory interest became charged with excitement. The following Saturday he went again and took some shots. During the next week he made plans for the shooting and direction of a film taken at twenty-four frames a second, with sound. The approval of the Bancroft Home authorities was secured. Jim Alward, of course, with his musical equipment and recordings, was an essential member of the producing team. The purpose and plan of the project were to give a pictorial demonstration of the great need for clergy and laymen to minister to residents in nursing homes and hospitals. Jim Alward recorded the sound. Ralph Ridenour wrote the shooting script. Roger did both narration and acting as he played his usual role of visitor and conductor of the regular Saturday-evening church service.

It happened that the evening chosen was the one following the day President Kennedy was shot, and the need for spiritual strength and reassurance was heightened for all concerned. The nurses were more thoughtful and concerned than usual as they wheeled in the chairs and the beds, the residents more appreciative. Guests from Belleville Church added to the atmosphere of fellowship. But the meeting proceeded just as it was habitually conducted: the popular recordings as the people were coming in, the informal preliminaries with greetings, the recognition of birthdays, singing from song sheets; then the formal religious service, with congregational singing, taped selections by a choir, a brief sermon, a benediction.

In spite of Roger's efforts to maintain dignity there were the usual interruptions: some elderly person breaking in with a plaintive, "I want to sit over there"; the few who, like children in a public gathering, had to be taken to the bathroom and brought back again; the murmurings of clouded minds; a few gentle snores. They were part of the picture. It would not have been true to the special needs of his people without them. Plenty of time was given for each person to find the page, or helped to find it, for many who had suffered strokes were one-handed. As usual, Barbara, the Hungarian lady, blind and very hard of hearing, wanted to sit close to Roger, and at some time during the singing of a hymn he wheeled to her side and held her hand for a moment, just to let her know that he was there.

Roger's short, simple sermon that night was on "Courage," a theme double significant because of the recent tragedy. As always, he tried to make his message one of assurance rather than admonition.

"Courage," he said in part, "is one of those qualities of life that can't be measured. It seems to have its root in faith, and faith can be measured only by adversity. When you have to revise your whole scale of values, as many of you have had to do recently, and can still keep your belief in God and keep cheerful about it, you have courage. . . .

"Most of us come to realize as we reach our mature years the fragileness of everything that once filled our life: work, money, affections, pleasure, even home and health. Everyone who has striven only for these things and made them his god is indeed faced with problems. The chief problem is himself. He thought he was strong, but now finds that he is weak. When illness strikes, all these things vanish in thin air. He will find himself facing God for the first time. . . .

258

"Now, dear friends, you still have God. How do I know? God shows through you. Some will tell me that I bring them something, a smile perhaps. It isn't important what I take to you, but what I find in you; *that* is really important. Or, rather, what you find in yourself. Yes, you still have God and you wait upon Him for new blessings. You know that there is nothing in the Bible that authorizes the Christian to seek and desire suffering. But when it comes, it can bring you nearer to Christ, who also suffered."

The film followed Roger on his round of visits. It pictured him admiring a patchwork quilt proudly exhibited by its craftsman, an old lady of ninety-two, and examining a piece of metal hammered into a work of art by a double amputee. It showed him wheeling from room to room, greeting, listening, encouraging, smiling, just being his usual self. It was a complete success, thrilling not only its three producers but all the participants. When it was shown in the therapy room at the Bancroft, Miss Thomas, one of the residents who delightedly recognized herself, exclaimed, "Oh, I've got to have a dozen copies!"

But for Roger the project had barely begun. The next step was to interest leaders of his denomination in accepting the film for widespread educational use. Only so could its primary purpose be realized.

His two henchmen, Jim Alward and Ralph Ridenour, continued to be ardent supporters of the work. Jim purchased a stereo machine with special mikes for the recordings and, with the aid of various local choirs and soloists, notably Bill Brown, another employee at Willow Run, prepared twenty-eight separate services, enough to provide music for the three meetings over a period of two and a half years. Ralph Ridenour and his wife became increasingly good friends of Roger and LaVerna.

A reporter once asked Mrs. Ridenour, "Does Mr. Arnett have both his legs amputated?"

She replied, "I couldn't possibly tell you. His personality shows through so much that I never noticed whether he has one or two."

16

Roger had an allergy to steps, steps in all public places, but especially in churches. They affected him as for generations the sign FOR WHITE ONLY must have affected Negroes, arousing feelings of inferiority, of resentment, and, inevitably, of rebellion. They were a mark of segregation.

"If worshipers should come to church some Sunday morning," he once expressed himself in writing, "and find a wall eight feet high all around it with no opening anywhere, they would raise a howl to high heaven. This wall would be no more insurmountable than is a step of five inches to thousands of would-be worshipers in wheel chairs."

He then quoted Charles E. Caniff, the paraplegic who was the "Handicapped American of the Year" for 1960, who had written:

"For those of us with limited mobility, architectural barriers prevent free access to those buildings which we must enter to work, to vote, to *worship* [Roger's italics], to learn, to play, or even to buy a stamp.

"To fulfill our responsibilities as citizens, we often must circumvent these barriers by entering through the rear door, where freight is hauled in, and make our way through coal bins, storerooms, and boiler rooms, to reach a freight elevator which can accommodate our wheel chairs.

"Architectural barriers have made us back-door citizens."

This was not a problem merely for a few, or even a few hundred. It affected millions. For, according to the findings of the President's

Committee on Employment of the Handicapped, working with the National Society for Crippled Children and Adults, there were 5 million people in the country with heart conditions, 250,000 in wheel chairs, 200,000 with heavy leg braces, 139,000 with artificial limbs, and 16,500,000 men and women over sixty-five who could benefit by easier access to buildings.

To Roger a flight of steps in front of a church or other public building was equivalent to a bold sign: "Handicapped Keep Out."

He encountered the problem personally in many public buildings: post offices, courthouses, municipal buildings, as well as churches. On one occasion it was strikingly demonstrated, and in a building primarily designed for certain types of disability! He had been asked by his friend, Addie Chilson, to call on a patient in the Ypsilanti State Hospital. Calling the hospital, he was told by the social worker that he could see Ruth at any time since he was a minister.

"I'm in a wheel chair," Roger explained, "and if there are steps I would be unable to get to her room."

That would be quite all right, assured the social worker. "You have to come to the Administration Building, anyway, in the evening. You come down the hall past the telephone office to the Nursing Station. Tell them who you are and that you have an appointment to see Ruth. She will be brought here, and you can visit in the hallway."

About six that evening Roger drove up to the Administration Building. At least eight steps! Expecting a ramp or an elevator in the rear, he drove to the back. No ramp, no elevator, no ground entrance. He drove back to the front and parked. Presently a distinguished-looking gentleman came along, perhaps the superintendent. Arrangements were made. Roger drove around to a side entrance, and presently two husky men came out and carried him up the ten steps.

"A good joke," they decided, "telling you to just go down the hall!"

To implement his concern, especially as it related to churches, Roger sent two memorials to the General Conference of the Methodist Church meeting in Pittsburgh in 1964. One proposed that every church with a membership of 300 or more consider the feasibility of installing a ramp and/or elevator; the other recommending that every Methodist Church built after January, 1966, be planned to provide at least one entrance at ground level without steps. Neither memorial was ever brought to the floor of the conference.

But there was one heartening incident, blossoming from a seed long ago planted.

In September, 1964, the *Commercial Appeal* of Memphis, Tennessee, published a news story entitled: "Thought Rooted By Friendship to Bloom Soon." The article continued: "An idea that grew out of a friendship between a Roman Catholic priest and a Protestant minister will soon take shape at St. Peter's Catholic Church. It will be a carefully designed entrance for the handicapped. The Rev. Bernard Schneider, pastor of St. Peter's, first met Rev. Roger Arnett almost twenty years ago . . . and over the years they continued their friendship. During this time the Protestant minister's statement that 'every building should have an entrance for the handicapped' stayed with Father Schneider."

Construction of the $5,000 entrance was expected to start soon in the enclosed garden between the church and the parish house, and would be carefully planned to blend with the architecture of the hundred-year-old-building.

"Merry Christmas!" wrote the priest, enclosing the illustrated clipping with his annual card to Roger and LaVerna. "The enclosed picture tells a story we both understand. It took me a long time. But the incline is fine. Ice cannot form on it, and the door is automatic. Pray for me. Father Bernard."

It was the best Christmas present Roger could have received. Not even the highest honor paid him that year brought him as much satisfaction.

Nominated by the local chapter 76 of the National Association of the Physically Handicapped for the "Handicapped American of the Year" award, given annually, he was selected by the President's Committee on Employment of the Handicapped as Michigan's "outstanding example of a handicapped American" and was presented a certificate.

In fact honors were becoming of less and less importance. After one busy day which included much visiting and a nursing-home service he wrote in his diary: "Today I had to give the invocation at Ypsilanti for the Alumni Luncheon for Eastern Michigan University, my alma mater. I appreciated meeting many of my old friends again. At one time I might have gained much satisfaction from being accorded the honor of taking a bit part. Today, however, it fell flat as far as I was concerned. Superfluous frosting on life when there is so much hard core of suffering and burdens of just living for so many people. That is where I should have been instead of at a frivolous luncheon."

Empathy was a costly business. Mere sympathy and concern would have been much easier, cheaper. For empathy meant personal involvement with every one of the hundreds of people to whom he ministered.

It was partly because of his handicap that he was able to identify so completely with them. Isolation in a wheel chair and ostracism from many of life's normal functions had made him a partner even in their loneliness. And loneliness, he had long since discovered, was the major ailment among the residents in all the homes he visited, whether the poorer ones or the finest and best regulated, where constant activities were being promoted. It far surpassed physical ailments in its power to create unhappiness. "A disease," Dr. Leslie Weatherhead called it, "something that ought not to be there, an evil thing." Another writer termed it "one of the major social evils of our day."

Roger saw it, heard it on every hand. "Oh, yes, I'm happy here, but, oh, so lonely!" . . . "Please—will you come again soon?" . . . "It's the first time for years that I've had an arm around my shoulders." . . . "I have an ache—here," with a vague motion toward the head. But it was not a physical ache, as Roger well knew. It was simply loneliness.

Why? They were well cared for, surrounded by many people, people of their own status, with much the same former interests. Society had outdone itself in its concern for the sick, the aged, the handicapped. It had provided mass security, mass medical treatment, mass nourishment, mass rehabilitation—everything, in fact, except the things needed most, *love and concern as individuals.* Well versed in psychology, society considered the separation of a child from its parents, unworthy though they might be, a traumatic experience, yet it looked with favor on an equally traumatic uprooting, segregation of the aged, the helpless, from home, family, community, church, friends—all the normal relationships which had made life full and satisfying. No wonder loneliness was the result!

And loneliness—loss of relationship—was a spiritual, not a physical sickness. It could not be cured by social agencies, however efficient or highly organized, only by individuals with a spiritual concern. And if the Christian church and other religious groups did not try to meet the need, who would?

It was astonishing how much difference even a bit of concern could make. In 1963 some of the groups of the Belleville church invited about twenty-five ladies from Building A in Wayne County General Hospital to a dinner. Many of the guests had been residents for a good many years and were there only because they had no other place to go. For some it was the only time they had emerged from behind the locked doors in years, the only social event they could remember. Their joy and gratitude were pitiable to watch. Like many church dinners, it was a potluck meal.

"If only we could have had chicken!" one guest was overheard to murmur wistfully.

The next year, on a Sunday in September, an even larger group was served chicken. But Roger, although the instigator of the project, was not present. That very afternoon he received notice that the bed for which he had been waiting was available in the Flint hospital where Dr. Berry was surgeon and he had to leave before the dinner. Reluctantly but creditably LaVerna assumed the role of hostess, her mechanical smile and polite greetings a cover for the nagging fear, "This time he really may not be back."

It was always there each time he went into the hospital, the possibility—probability?—of final separation. She had long since grown used to a confrontation with death, had even ceased to feel bitterness at the prospect. Seeing him grow weaker and weaker, as during the last weeks of this summer of 1964, the effort to fulfill each day's tasks more and more taxing, she sometimes coveted for him a cessation of the suffering and struggle. Yet, knowing how much he wanted to live, to continue the work which he felt no one else would be willing to do, she coveted life for him far more. And because she had been told so many times by doctors that this was it, this time he could not possibly make it, the polite words and mechanical but warm smile covered as much hope as fear.

The trouble was a pressure sore of increasing magnitude on his right hip. In early September he had gone up to Flint to see Dr. Berry, who had moved there from Ann Arbor. "Thank goodness he didn't go to Timbuctoo!" was Roger's fervent expression of gratitude.

"Guess you'll find it a little hard to operate this time, won't you,

Doctor?" he asked half jokingly. "After that last session there isn't much flesh left."

"You'd be surprised," returned Dr. Berry, his face unusually grim. "There's still a lot of flesh on that amputated leg. We can always take out the bone and use the flesh to bring back over the hip. But, as you know, it will be no picnic."

Roger did know. He went into the hospital that Sunday afternoon with no illusions. He was fully aware that he had been living on borrowed time for years. As he lay in the hospital bed, it seemed that he had come at last to the end. The last few weeks of struggle to keep going had drained his energy to the dregs. Never had he felt so bereft of the will to live. Suppose he did survive this present crisis—and he knew Dr. Berry was dubious—what lay ahead? More days, months, years, of dogged, endless struggle merely to keep up the business of living. More misunderstanding and criticism from his fellow ministers and a church bureaucracy which could not understand the importance of the work he was trying to do. And what to show for it? A few people made a little happier. A few more hundreds of bushels of apples handed out, prayers said, communion cups doled, sermons preached, hymns sung . . . but the whole vast problem of the loneliness and frustration of the handicapped still barely touched! He closed his eyes and sank back against the pillow, his half body that possessed feeling yielding to a relinquishment he had not known for years. Blessed rest, blessed lethargy, yes, even blessed oblivion!

But oblivion was impossible—yet. And even in rest and lethargy there was no escape. Faces and voices kept pursuing him. Lloyd . . . Stef . . . Vivian . . . Jessie . . . Bob . . . Betty . . .

"Please—won't you come again soon?" . . .

"I—feel—better—now. Thank—you—for—coming—"

"I do so miss my church—friends—everything—"

"How did you find me here?" . . .

"How am I? Terribly lonely." . . .

Roger struggled up out of the comfortable semi-lethargy. He couldn't die yet! His work would die with him. Certainly it would not be continued on the district. And so far all his attempts to have a study made or similar ministries established on other districts had ended in failure. But he had made a beginning. And there was the film. If he could only get it used, church wide! Just a few more years, even months. . . . God, just let him live long enough to stir

265

concerned Christians into caring enough about the needs of the handicapped to *do something about it!*

The surgeon stood looking down at one of his most amazing and baffling patients, lying with his eyes closed, gaunt, grim, down-and-out straight. This time he looked like death itself, not even warmed over. According to all medical odds he should have been dead long ago. The surgeon could not even remember how many operations he had performed on him, most of them potential killers. Yet always he had come bouncing back, like a battered rubber ball; no, more like a kicked puppy, fairly asking to be kicked again.

What kept him going? That generator inside of him, what sort of mechanism was it, super ego or super *alter?* Probably a little of both. No man, the doctor had discovered, was all good or all bad, about fifty-fifty. The do-gooders, like this one, were seldom pure *alter* any more than doctors. How separate the yen for service from the desire for success, for the esteem of one's colleagues, or for pure self-achievement?

And that consummate, everlasting cheerfulness! Was it an act or was it genuine? Which was the real Roger, the one who was smiling, confident, hopeful, positive 90 per cent of the time, or the one he was looking at now, drained to the dregs of energy and courage? What was his source of supply? Would it finally run out, and was this the time? With all his heart the surgeon hoped not. Whatever his source of supply—ego, faith, or just sheer human spunk—heaven knew he was going to need it!

As he watched, he saw a change take place in the inert figure. The sagging muscles tightened. Color crept into the cheeks. The long, slender fingers clenched into fists. With a feeling almost of awe the surgeon knew that he was seeing the dynamo recharging.

Roger opened his eyes. His face broke into a broad smile. "Hello, Dr. Bob. Well, what do you know? Here I am back again!"

Days passed, and LaVerna heard nothing. Then on Thursday a friend was riding up through Flint. "Want to go along?" he asked. Of course she did.

"I can't help thinking he's been operated on," she worried aloud.

"But surely they would have let you know!"

"Not if Roger told them not to."

The minute she saw him her fears were confirmed. He had been operated on that morning. Her heart lurched. Never had she seen him look so hopeless. And with good reason. The operation had been five times as severe as the surgeon had expected. He had found the hip joint and socket completely decayed, the tibia almost ready to puncture the hip. Thanks to the fact that Dr. Arnold had removed the right leg just above the knee rather than higher, there had been flesh available to form a flap covering for the deep cavity. The doctors gave LaVerna no assurance of the operation's success. She expected none. And what they said made little difference. She had been told plenty of times before that he could not live. She was not likely to give up hope now.

It was the most trying hospital experience Roger had ever encountered. At first the operation seemed to have been a success. Then, suddenly, it looked like failure. Severe infection developed. His temperature soared. One day, finding the area of the surgery fiery red and hard as a rock, Dr. Berry shook his head.

"You've got to keep off of this, Roger," he said tersely.

Roger had been lying part of the time on his back, part on both sides. Now there was only his left side or his face to lie on. Within twenty-four hours he developed a severe pressure sore on the joint of his left side. Because of the colostomy and cystostomy, lying face down was complicated by the necessity of four or five pillows under his chest. After three or four hours his chest would become excruciatingly sore. Then he would turn on his left side, but could remain there only a half hour. He developed pressure sores on shin and foot. The agony was unbearable. He asked for an alternating pressure air mattress, but none could be found in the hospital.

"I'll buy one," he said in desperation to the nurse. "I'll do anything."

Finally a brand-new one appeared. It gave some help, but he had reached a stage of such intense exhaustion that he was scarcely aware of relief. How he managed to live through the agonizing days and weeks he would never know. But finally, when the swelling started to go down in the region of the operation, both he and the doctors knew that an end of the torture was in sight. Still the area stubbornly refused to heal. Roger well knew that with this type of operation, even one far less serious, the patient was never permitted to put weight on the area until the healing process was complete. He might easily be here three or four months! About four weeks after the operation he was impatient as a caged lion.

"Now," he broached hopefully to the doctor, "how about my sitting up on it?"

The doctor eyed him severely. "After telling my classes all these years that under no conditions—!" But he did not say no. Presently he agreed rather reluctantly. "All right. I'm coming in tomorrow. You may sit up then for ten minutes."

When the ten minutes were over he examined the area. "Well, it doesn't look as if there is any damage. Tomorrow we'll do the same thing." A look almost of awe came into his eyes. "You know, Roger, for the first time I think we're going to make it."

This was Saturday. On Monday Roger sat up twice for a half hour.

"I say, this is looking a lot better!" The doctor scratched his head. Then, after thoughtful consideration, "But who knows? Maybe use *is* more beneficial even to a major open wound than rest. Who am I to be so sure we doctors are always right? Some of you folks manage to live in spite of us!"

On Tuesday Roger called LaVerna and asked her to make arrangements for Dick to come after him on the following day. He waited for her happy response. None came. There was a good reason. She had been sick the previous Sunday when she had come to visit him, almost fainting under the weight of a huge box of fruit and candy from the NAPH chapter in Ypsilanti; had hardly been able to drive home. Yesterday the sickness had been diagnosed as a severe case of flu. Now she sat by the telephone speechless and trembling.

"My, you sound awfully glad to hear I'm coming home!"

She gasped. "Oh, I am, I am! It's—wonderful. Only—I was so surprised. I hadn't expected you for weeks, maybe months."

He did not suspect the truth. She sent Dick to get him, and somehow they managed to live through the next few weeks, with both of them confined to bed. Women from the church came in at noon and served them a meal; then Val would come at night. It was Roger who recuperated more rapidly. At the end of a week he was up getting their meals, and he was back at work before Thanksgiving.

But he was even more dependent on LaVerna, and he hated it. There was constant drainage from the area of the last operation, from which it was impossible to give full protection. She had to wash every day, and even the boon of wash pants that kept their press and no-iron shirts only partially relieved the burden. The cloths used for bandages, changed several times during each twenty-four hours, all had to be ironed because the dryer left curled edges hazardous for the skin. His endurance was so lessened that bed rest was imperative as soon as he came home from work, which meant extra waiting on him and the serving of their evening meal in his bedroom. His hatred of dependence was compounded of a variety of elements: concern for LaVerna, guilt for causing her so much extra work, the old nagging doubt as to whether he should have let her marry him, humiliation, a smattering of self-pity, and, yes, fear.

The latter swelled to giant proportions one Sunday in January. Although still weak, he was making his usual calls and had held his evening service at the Eastlawn. LaVerna was invariably waiting when he returned home after the twenty-mile drive. But tonight the house was dark. He tooted the horn. No response. Immediately anxiety ballooned into unreasoning panic. If he went into the house, what would he find? He drove the three miles to Dick's. Val explained that she had gone over to the house earlier in the afternoon, found LaVerna gone, a cake in the oven, and a note to "Virginia" on the table. She took her car and followed Roger home, helping him out and into the house. Roger knew a Virginia. He called her. Yes, her mother had asked LaVerna to go to Ann Arbor to visit Clara Kelley. The note to "Virginia" had left directions concerning the cake. The balloon of panic deflated into a hard core of equally unreasoning resentment. When LaVerna returned nonchalantly sometime later he had difficulty controlling his anger.

"If you go away like that again," he admonished with asperity, "please put a note on the garage door!"

The incident was sobering, a little frightening. Was he actually that dependent on another person? And if so, what would he do in case of a genuine crisis?

A few months later he found out. LaVerna went into the hospital for eleven days of tests and rest. The prospect of staying alone was staggering. Val was profuse in her offers of help. Faye was now back in Michigan and living a few miles away, but she had her hands full with two babies, and Roger would not think of asking her for help. Both girls were busy enough with their own problems.

"The best way to acquire confidence," he had read, "is to do the thing you are afraid to do."

He insisted on staying alone. It was a harrowing but liberating experience. The first day Val helped him out of the car, got supper, and saw to it that he got in bed. After that Roger came home, got out of the car without assistance, prepared his own supper, went to bed, then called Val to assure her that all was well. He visited LaVerna almost every day at the hospital, carried on his nursing-home visitations, as usual, and managed all necessary details of housekeeping. Not that he or any other handicapped person could ever be free from dependence on others! But the sense of fear was gone.

The experience yielded another unexpected dividend, a new father-daughter relationship. For Faye's deep concern, her sense of guilt that she was unable to come more substantially to his aid, her growing understanding of the problems they had faced with her through her experience with her own children, were all given expression in her daily telephone calls. A short time later the new relationship was even more tangibly confirmed when she went with him one day to the Allen Park Nursing Home to help him give communion to about twenty-five of the residents. As she assisted with the simple service, gracious, sweetly reverent, sensitive, and poised in her new womanly dignity, Roger felt a genuine fellowship with his daughter.

It was an even more simple encounter which wrought the miracle for LaVerna. Sometime later she was having trouble with her hair. The day after a visit to her hairdresser it was in hopeless condition, and the girl would do nothing about it. In desperation LaVerna called Faye.

"Of course, Mother. Do come right over this evening." When LaVerna arrived, Faye scolded her soundly. "I've never seen a head of hair in such a mess! I'm surprised it hasn't broken right off at your scalp!"

As she expertly tackled the problem on this and subsequent visits, LaVerna felt the unfolding of that close mother-daughter understanding for which she had always yearned. But when Faye insisted on her coming back each week, she protested. "We shouldn't take a whole evening from you and Ken so often."

"Mother," said Faye earnestly, "I want you to keep coming. We have never been so close as since I have been doing your hair. I don't want to lose it."

Strange, thought LaVerna, for a simple shampoo and wave to accomplish what years of care and devotion had failed to achieve! And yet perhaps not so strange. For to develop true understanding in any human relationship one had to receive as well as give.

It was a lesson which Roger was learning increasingly as he pursued his ministry. For every gift, he had discovered, there were two givers and two receivers. For the giver was also the receiver. The resident in a home who returned sincere appreciation for his gift of cheerfulness was just as much a giver as he was, and the gift was of equal importance. For well did he know the satisfaction derived from appreciation. That was why he felt it so important that every person giving should give unselfishly and every person receiving should receive graciously. It was a principle of human relationship as pertinent to nations as to individuals.

The movie made by Roger and Ralph Ridenour and James Alward was accepted by TRAFCO. Roger took it to Nashville in the summer of 1964 and showed it to the executives of the Television, Radio, and Film Commission of the Methodist Church.

"We'd like to have it," they said immediately.

When edited, the film called *The Visit* ran for eight minutes, and it became available for purchase or rental early in 1966. It was entirely nondenominational in its impact, and it was hoped that it would receive wide use by theological schools, churches, and religious groups of all faiths as a means of alerting both ministers and laymen to the spiritual needs of the handicapped in nursing homes and hospitals.

There were other encouraging developments. Under the dynamic leadership of the Rev. Allen Rice II the Belleville church had contributed more than a thousand dollars to the handicapped ministry fund with the promise of continuing support. In addition two lay persons were manifesting a degree of interest which might well result in their full-time commitment to this specialized ministry.

Mrs. Patricia Speaks, who had been assisting in calling since January, 1965, at the Eastlawn Nursing Home, took the first step by being approved as a local preacher of the Methodist Church and started the conference course of study. She was soon able to ease some of Roger's load by assuming calling responsibility for six of the homes in his parish and by assisting in others.

Ray Edwards from Riverview, disabled by polio at an early age but able to walk with the aid of crutches, also manifested a desire to participate in the same type of ministry. After assisting with calling and communion services in several of the homes, he was even more enthusiastic.

Roger welcomed their services not because they made his own load easier—the extra help had made it possible for him to increase the number of homes visited from fifteen to eighteen!—but because they gave some promise of continuing support and widening interest in the work.

17

It was a Saturday morning, and Roger rose earlier than usual. Since he was going to a certain nursing home before the day was over, he put on the shirt which Josephine, one of the residents, had made for him. It was less convenient than others because she had made it to button like a woman's blouse rather than a man's shirt, but he always wore it when he expected to see her. By seven-thirty he was on his way to a home about twenty miles away and arrived a little before eight. After visiting in the dining room with some of the residents who were having breakfast, he made his round of the rooms.

There was a reason for his coming so early. He had long since discovered that this was the time of day when many needed a little extra help. For instance, in one room there was Joe Brown, suffering from paralysis. He had just turned over, and his legs were misplaced. Roger straightened his feet against the pillow. George, another paraplegic, was irrigating his bladder and needed two more experienced hands. Going down the hall, Roger heard a peculiar noise in one of the rooms. Mr. Silvers, who had had a paralytic stroke which had affected his right side and speech, wanted help. Trying to dress himself in his wheel chair, he was unable to get on his trousers. Roger helped get them up and zipped. But most of all Mr. Silvers wanted someone to talk to, someone who understood his frustrating speech problem and could wait patiently for him to express himself.

During his visits on the women residents Roger gave out three of the lap quilts made and donated by a group of women in Belleville Church. The ladies had made more than two hundred of the little quilts, appropriate for lap coverings, for shawls, for bed throws, or just for room decorations. It was a joy to see the pleasure brought by these simple gifts. And, since it was near the end of April, he had brought with him a hundred copies of the devotional booklet, *The Upper Room*, prepared to give them out during the day to those who he had learned from long experience would welcome them.

After spending some two and a half hours here and visiting perhaps a hundred people, he drove to a smaller home five miles away, where he made longer calls on a few residents whom he had come to know well. There was Lloyd, a young quadriplegic about nineteen, disabled for four years and desperately eager for company. His moody face lighted.

"Chess?" he begged. "Just one game?"

Roger could not refuse. He spent twenty minutes or more with the boy, simulating great chagrin when he was triumphantly checkmated.

There was Eddie, gray head bent intently as usual over his worktable, arthritic fingers slowed but still skillful as they labored over one of the small electrical jobs at which they had once been so adept. Roger stopped to watch him.

"Good work, Eddie! I sure do admire anybody who has such a knack with those delicate tools!"

The intently frowning features broke into a smile.

In one room Roger found four women, all cheerful and smiling. He knew them all well. One was a Baptist, one a Presbyterian, one a Lutheran, one a Catholic. When he offered a short prayer, knowing that in this room it would be appreciated, all heads were bowed, all hands folded, even the ones which held the rosary. Georgie, one of the women, sang a hymn.

It was early afternoon when he left this home. After eating his usual lunch in the car—a sandwich, an apple, and milk—he drove fifteen miles to an integrated home, where about 40 per cent of the residents were Negroes.

Wheeling into the long, narrow lounge, he found a row of men ranged side by side against one wall, some watching television, some nodding, a few mumbling to each other, most of them just sitting. They looked like bits of flotsam cast up by a wave which had long since receded.

"Hi ya, fellers!" called Roger with a wave of his hand.

The row stirred into life. Dulled faces brightened. Hands waved. One man wheeled to meet him and began eagerly pouring out his troubles. Another, Jack, greeted him with his usual firm handshake, his gleaming smile as startling a contrast to his black skin as was his white artificial leg.

Here also Roger found long-time friends as he whisked through the corridors, wheeled into one room after another.

"Got a story for me today, Mrs. Fraulein?"

"Yah, that I have. "I've been saving it. Have you heard the one about . . ."

Josephine, as usual, was busy at her sewing machine.

"Well, bless your pea-pickin' heart, Josephine, and what are you making today?"

"A blouse, Mr. Roger, for my granddaughter." The eyes in the dark face kindled. "I see you're wearing that shirt I made you."

"I sure am. And do I appreciate it! You're a good seamstress, Josephine."

John was deeply disturbed. He beckoned Roger into his room and glanced warily about at the other occupants before confiding his troubles in a lowered voice. He was sure things were missing from his belongings. And he should have got his check from welfare two days ago. And it was so noisy here, he really couldn't sleep, and he just wasn't happy. He wished he could move to another home. If his sister only knew how he felt and could come to see him . . .

Knowing the proneness of idle loneliness to brood, to worry, to imagine, Roger listened with sympathy and understanding.

"Yes, John, I'll try to do something. I'll call your sister this very day. I promise."

He took the pittance of a contribution that Mrs. Jones, a former missionary, always insisted on giving him "for your work" and carefully earmarked it for the district fund. He listened to Mrs. Oliver's eager story of how she had had a visitor only two days before, one of Roger's friends from Glenwood, a Mary Thompson.

"Of course—Mary! How wonderful that she could visit you!"

By the time he had visited the home's ninety residents, the afternoon was far advanced and he was tired. But there was still one more to go, less than three miles away.

Hans was looking out a window and saw him coming. Big, friendly, eager, he ran out to the car, helped him out, and insisted on pushing his wheel chair up the ramp and into the hall. Hans was about thirty-five, his problem a nervous breakdown.

"Thanks, Hans. I'm alone today. Don't know how I'd have managed without you."

"Yah. Dat's goot. I be here ven you go."

Here it was Mr. Pember who needed the extra time and attention. As usual he was eager to talk about his beloved Mrs. Johnson.

"Such a wonderful woman! But I needn't tell you, Roger. You knew her."

Roger did indeed. He had known them both when they had been in the Dorvin Home, where they had met. Mrs. Johnson had been blind, and Mr. Pember, kind, lonely, missing his wife who had died ten years before, had taken her under his wing from the day she arrived.

"Come and meet my mother," Mrs. Johnson's son had begged him.

Mr. Pember had visited her four times that afternoon and become her companion, admirer, protector, for the next four and a half years. They had eaten together, gone for rides in his car, later moved to the same home. Visiting him at the hospital after he had had a heart attack, Roger had found Mr. Pember more worried about Mrs. Johnson than about himself. There had been talk of their getting married before she had died a year ago.

It was of Mrs. Johnson now that Mr. Pember wanted to talk, not of his thirty-seven years of loyal service to the Ford Motor Company.

"Let's see, did I show you her picture, Roger, the one her folks gave me? Her son was in to see me just last week."

Roger looked at the picture for perhaps the dozenth time, agreed that Mrs. Johnson had indeed been a wonderful person.

"Come again, Roger, soon. Every time you come, I hear your name spoken all over the place, not just for a day but for many days. And there aren't many people I can talk to about *her*."

"I'll come again, Mr. Pember. I promise. In another month, if possible."

Roger delivered the book of postage stamps which he had promised to Franz. He spent some time with Richard, forty-five, tall, spare, slow of motion, dangerously prone to accidents because of *grand-mal* seizures and brought here to be under protection while his mother was in the hospital. It took long and unhurried assurance to banish the lost uncertainty from Richard's eyes.

He admired Mrs. Gray's begonia; bought a large perfumed artificial daisy from Mrs. Carsons ("to hang in your closet"); gratefully accepted from Mrs. Maddocks the gift of two flamboyant silk roses which must have taken her loving, painstaking fingers many hours to fashion. ("For your wife, dearie. The idea! As if I'd take any money from you!") From the bulletin board in the dining room he copied the list of residents who were having birthdays that month, so that Addie Chilson could send each one a personal card.

Hans was waiting at the door when he left, and he appreciated the help, even the usually unwelcome push, for he was tired. It was good, too, to see LaVerna come out to meet him when he rolled into the yard some ten hours after leaving it.

"Any telephone calls?" he inquired before leaving the car.

"Addie Chilson called. Mr. Jackson has passed away."

"Oh—oh! And I didn't get to call on him again!"

"And Virginia. She wants to see you. She sounded terribly disturbed."

"O.K. I'll call her. She can come tonight."

LaVerna had dinner ready, but before doing anything else Roger called John's sister as he had promised. She agreed to go to see her brother the next day. Then he called Virginia, making an appointment for that evening at seven.

He went to bed immediately, less for rest than to relieve the pressures attendant on long hours of sitting. He and LaVerna ate their dinner in his bedroom, and it was here that he received Virginia.

She was very much distraught. Her small son, three years old, had a clubfoot, so badly deformed that it could not be corrected. She had just learned that the doctors wanted to amputate it just above the ankle. What, oh, *what* should she do!

Roger did not advise her. It must be her decision. But he did tell her of some people he knew who had adjusted well to amputation, who had participated in sports, even played football. She went away still troubled, but with the bewildered panic replaced by calmer reasoning.

His workday was by no means over. There was a telephone by his bed, and there were sure to be several calls before the evening ended. Doris Ritter wanted advice about typing the bulletins for use in next Saturday's service. Pat Speaks had a report on her afternoon of calling. Mrs. Touse cheerily reported that the women had made three more quilts. And there were others.

The day had drained him of energy. He felt deathly tired. But the sensation was not new. It was becoming more and more frequent. His body was a machine which had long since outworn its potential, which was slowly but surely running down. How long before a day like this would be impossible, when the number of homes visited must shrink to three . . . two . . . one? And what then? Who would play chess with the Lloyds, reassure the Richards, listen to the Mr. Pembers, try to make the Johns a little more contented? Not that he considered himself at all indispensable. Hardly! But there were so few people who seemed to *care!*

It was time for the sportscast. From force of habit he flicked on the radio above his bed. But the quick, staccato voice barely penetrated his consciousness. College baseball scores, winner of the latest golf tournament, the next heavyweight championship bout . . . all seemed of little import beside the questions plaguing him. *How long? . . . What then? . . .*

But suddenly the clipped voice penetrated.

"In the state intercollegiate track meet today at Ann Arbor competition was keen. Records were broken. In the mile race . . ."

Race! Roger listened with avid interest to the end of the broadcast. How times had changed! In his day of running, a four-minute mile had been unheard of. Now college men, even high-school boys, were breaking the old records right and left.

Race! The word aroused memories long dead. "This is where I came in," he thought, remembering that first contest in Olympia Stadium, reliving it, actually feeling the aches in his joints and muscles, the screaming pain in his lungs, everything but the agony in his legs and feet. What was it they had called it? A *handicap race!* He laughed aloud. He was still running it . . . with time, with death, with human need, with his own self-preoccupation, with the lack of concern and the indifference of other people. How long could he keep going? And then what? He did not have to know. It had not mattered then. It did not matter now.

A burst of fresh vigor pounded through his tired fragment of a body. A handicap race . . . where you just ran and ran until you couldn't possibly go any farther, and then you kept running some more!

About Dorothy Clarke Wilson

DOROTHY CLARKE WILSON has acquired a large following through the years with her inspirational
fiction and nonfiction, her recent books, *Dr. Ida,*
Take My Hands, and *Ten Fingers for God* still
reaching a wide readership. A native of Maine, Mrs.
Wilson has traveled extensively in India and the
Bible lands researching her work. However, she and
her husband, a retired Methodist minister, still enjoy
the beauty of the Maine coastlands where they
make their home.